高校英语选修课系列教材

COMMUNICATIVE ENGLISH WRITING

交际英语写作

U0362206

主　编　罗　莎

副主编　闻　燕　孙静波
　　　　[美] 布莱德利·菲利普斯（Bradley Phillips）

编　者　胡亦杰　李　明　姚　辉
　　　　蓝一洲　傅竹夏　韩　晔

清华大学出版社
北京

内 容 简 介

本书分为"交际性写作入门""不同文体的交际性写作"和"英语考试中的交际性写作"三个部分，共九章，以提高英语写作的交际性为主要教学目标，对交际英语写作进行深入讲解。本书以"交际性""以读促写""自主评价"和"策略学习"为主要特色，写作讲解和文本分析相辅相成，练习部分根据学习重点布置写作任务，辅以自评和互评检查清单，并提供扩展阅读材料。每章的重点内容配有英语微视频，供学习者扫码观看。本书还设有两个附录，对写作学习进行语言知识的补充。

本书既可用于高校英语专业教学，也可作为高校英语通识选修课教材，还可供有一定学习基础的广大英语爱好者阅读参考。

图书在版编目（CIP）数据

交际英语写作 / 罗莎主编. —北京：清华大学出版社，2022.8
高校英语选修课系列教材
ISBN 978-7-302-61074-8

Ⅰ. ①交…　Ⅱ. ①罗…　Ⅲ. ①英语—写作—高等学校—教材　Ⅳ. ① H319.36

中国版本图书馆 CIP 数据核字（2022）第 098188 号

责任编辑：方燕贝　刘　艳
封面设计：子　一
责任校对：王凤芝
责任印制：沈　露

出版发行：清华大学出版社
　　　　网　　　址：http://www.tup.com.cn, http://www.wqbook.com
　　　　地　　　址：北京清华大学学研大厦 A 座　邮　编：100084
　　　　社 总 机：010-83470000　　　　邮　购：010-62786544
　　　　投稿与读者服务：010-62776969, c-service@tup.tsinghua.edu.cn
　　　　质量反馈：010-62772015, zhiliang@tup.tsinghua.edu.cn
印 装 者：三河市国英印务有限公司
经　　销：全国新华书店
开　　本：185mm×260mm　　　印　张：16.75　　　字　数：337 千字
版　　次：2022 年 9 月第 1 版　　　　印　次：2022 年 9 月第 1 次印刷
定　　价：69.00 元

产品编号：093727-01

本教材获深圳大学教材出版资助

前　言

英语写作是用英语传递信息的一种交际方式，可是很多英语学习者缺乏英语写作的理念、策略和训练，在写作时常常言不由衷，甚至无言以对。

针对中高级英语学习者亟待提高书面表达和沟通能力的需求，《交际英语写作》一书以"交际性""以读促写""自主评价"和"策略学习"为主要特色，采用以写作交际性为主线、以写作模块为框架、以多媒体互动为载体的创新型英语写作教学体系，为学习者铺垫英语写作之路，引导其进入言之有物、言之有理的写作佳境。

根据教育部颁布的《大学英语教学指南（2020版）》，并参考教育部和国家语言文字工作委员会发布的《中国英语能力等级量表》之写作标准，本书作为通用英语和跨文化交际课程的写作教材，旨在帮助中高级英语学习者提高书面互动、书面叙述、书面描述、书面说明、书面论述等多方面的能力，掌握构思、撰写、修改等书面表达策略，通过有效使用英语和跨文化交际实现自我提升与发展。

一、本书特色

"**交际性**"强调"写作即交流"的理念，关注为什么写、写什么和如何写等问题，重点教授如何根据写作交流的目的和对象来选择材料、内容、体裁和语言。

"**以读促写**"结合英语阅读和写作任务，以写作产出为导向，引导学习者阅读范文、分析语言、诠释信息，使其获得语言形式和内容两方面的辅助，进而提高相应体裁和题材的写作水平。

"**自主评价**"鼓励学习者在过程性写作中进行自我评价和同伴互评，通过评价和修改帮助其掌握英语写作评价标准，提高英语写作的认知能力，并提升自主合作写作的动力。

"**策略学习**"贯穿全书，帮助学习者获得有效的写作策略，并在写作实践中加以运用，让其能够有意识、有计划地调控自己的写作过程，逐步提高英语写作能力。

二、内容编排

本书以写作模块为框架，共分三个部分，含九章，另有两个附录。

第一部分"**交际性写作入门**"有两个单元，分别讲解交际性写作的基本原理和写作过程，从写作理念和基本方法着手，为学习者系统性的写作学习奠定基础。

第二部分"**不同文体的交际性写作**"有五个单元，分别对应五种文体：应用文、记叙文、描写文、说明文和议论文，详解各种文体的特点和交际性写作的策略。

第三部分"**英语考试中的交际性写作**"有国内考试和国际考试两个单元，分别聚焦于大学英语四、六级考试和雅思、托福考试，用交际性写作的理念为学习者分析考试任务，并结合文体知识讨论应对策略。

各单元的写作讲解和文本分析相辅相成，体现"以读促写"特色，为写作产出作铺垫；第二至第八章另设练习部分，根据学习重点布置写作任务，辅以自评和互评检查清单，并提供扩展阅读材料。

两个附录为写作学习进行语言知识的补充，分别总结了中国学习者在英语写作中的常见错误和常用英语标点符号及其用法，帮助其掌握相关语言知识，提升识别错误、自主修改的能力。

三、多模态学习资源

《交际英语写作》包含纸质书、微视频和慕课等多模态学习资源。学习者可以充分利用纸质书和新媒体的优点，既有教材在手，又能与网络相连接，在多模态学习方式中实现交流互动和深度学习。

纸质书基于先进的写作教学理念而编写，强调写作是一种交际方式，以有一定英语基础的高校学生和社会人士为读者对象，采用与读者对话的方式进行写作指导，并提供大量优质范文和文本解读。

本书每个单元都包含微视频，在相应小节标题处印有二维码，学习者通过手机扫码即可观看。其中，中、美、澳三国教师用英语授课，创设语言使用的场景，激发学习者的学习兴趣，这与教材的中文讲解相辅相成，使学习者在学习英语写作的同时提升语言理解和运用能力。

"优课联盟"平台的"交际英语写作"慕课课程与本书内容基本一致，学习者可以在注册后免费观看在线视频、下载资料、参加测试等。优课联盟高校的学生若按要求完成课程，还可获得相应学分。

参与本书编写的主要成员有 10 人，具体分工如下：罗莎主编，编写第一章、第六章和第九章雅思考试部分；闻燕副主编，编写第四章、第五章和第八章；孙静波副主编，编写附录一、附录二，并对全书中文部分进行校对；[美] Bradley Phillips 副主编，负责全书英语校对；蓝一洲编写第二章；姚辉、李明编写第三章；傅竹夏编写第七章；韩晔编写第九章托福考试部分；胡亦杰、李明为第三章和第七章提供慕课授课原稿。此外，[澳] Ilia Leikin 和罗宇佳为第九章的编译作出贡献。

本书所用视频材料均来自"交际英语写作"慕课，出镜教师有罗莎、[美] Benjamin Brown、李明、闻燕、Bradley Phillips 和 [澳] Henry Mogulsky，拍课脚本由罗莎、胡亦杰、李明、闻燕和 Ilia Leikin 编写。

《交际英语写作》能够与读者见面，离不开多方的支持和鼓励。恳请使用本书的师生多提宝贵意见，使之有机会不断发展与完善。

编者
2022 年 1 月于广东深圳

目　录

第二部分 不同文体的交际性写作
Communicative Writing in Different Genres

第三部分　英语考试中的交际性写作
Communicative Writing in English Tests

第一部分

交际性写作入门

INTRODUCTION TO COMMUNICATIVE WRITING

第一章

交际性写作的基本原理
The Basics of Communicative Writing

学习要点

- 交际性写作的概念
- 交际性写作的要素
- 交际性写作的策略
- 以读促写示例

 第一节 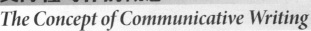 交际性写作的概念
The Concept of Communicative Writing

写作通常有三种含义（Johnson, K. & Johnson, H., 2001）：

（1）写作作为产品（writing as product）：写作即写出来的文章；

（2）写作作为过程（writing as process）：写作是一种心理活动或行文过程；

（3）写作作为社会活动（writing as social activity）：写作是与人交流的方式和手段。

这三种含义代表了三种写作类型：以文本为中心的写作、以作者为中心的写作和以读者为中心的写作；也分别对应了写作教学理论发展过程中的三种范式，即传统以关注写作结果为主的"文章中心"写作、20 世纪 60 年代以来以关注写作过程为重心的"作者中心"写作，以及当代以关注写作目的和社会功能为中心的"读者中心"写作（荣维东，2016）。

交际性写作是指以交流为目的的写作，这意味着无论写作主题是什么，作者都必须为自己的文章找到一个特定的目的：或是提供信息，或是说服议论，或是娱乐读者，同时必须知道谁会读自己的文章：同学、老师，还是一般性读者。

在交际性写作中，作者需要考虑文章的写作目的：我为什么要写这个主题？我希望我的写作能达到什么目的？同时需要考虑读者是谁并问自己：谁会读我的文章？他们为什么读我的文章？还需要根据写作交流的目的和对象来选择材料、内容、体裁和语言。这种以交流为目的的写作才是有动力、有意义的写作，因为它不仅最大限度地实现了写作的社会功能，而且还原了写作的真实状态。

如果说"文章中心"写作关注的是写作结果，即文章本身，"作者中心"写作关注的是写作过程，即文章怎么写，那么交际性写作重点关注的是为什么写、写什么和如何写等问题。在交际性写作中，写作不仅仅是遣词造句、谋篇布局的技能，也不仅仅是作者的心理认知过程，更多的是作者与直接的或潜在的读者在社会环境下的交流活动，是作者和读者基于知识、信息和情境的意义建构。这种"写作即交流"的理念是本书的重要指导思想。

第二节　交际性写作的要素
Major Elements of Communicative Writing

交际性写作从本质上看是以"读者为中心"的写作，涉及六个重要因素，分别是读者、作者、目的、话题、体裁和表达，每个要素对作品交际性的实现都起着重要作用，缺一不可。

一、读者：文章的合作建构者
Reader: Cooperative Constructor of an Essay

缺乏读者意识是传统写作中常见的一个问题，而现代写作赋予了读者重要的意义——文章的合作建构者。任何文章都要靠读者的阅读才能产生意义，而且读者事实上常常以潜在的方式进入作者的写作意念，和作者一起塑造作品。

根据写作心理发生机制，在写作过程中想写什么、想怎样写，不仅受作者主观意愿的制约，还受制于其心目中的读者对象，因而有经验的作者通常比新手作者更具备读者意识、更重视读者，比如他们常花较长的时间思考这些问题：我需要给读者提供什么样的背景知识？怎样能更好地把自己的想法呈现给读者？我的文章对读者能产生什么影响？（Flower & Hayes, 1981）

在交际英语写作中，读者是作者的合作伙伴，也是作者写作中主要关注的对象。写作不再是作者以自我为中心来表达想法、呈现材料的过程，而是与读者进行对话交流和意义建构的过程。作者只有设想读者的信息需求、考虑读者的知识状况，才能提出吸引读者的观点和给出相应的材料，并依据读者的需要来展开主题，引领他们共同进行思考、参与对话，这样的写作才具有社会性，才是积极有效的。

二、作者：对话的设计者和参与者
Writer: Designer and Participant of a Dialogue

交际性写作是一场作者与不在场的读者之间的对话。作者是这场书面对话的设计者，会根据自己的想象来设计读者，再根据读者的需要来确定话题和交流方式，并参与对话，在与读者的互动中一点点实现自己的意图，实现交流的目的。

在以交流为目的的写作中，作者不再是传统写作中那个具有绝对权威、以自我为中心的写作者，而是以读者为中心，考虑读者的感受、信息需求和知识背景，并根据这些信息来设计和建构自己的作品。作为话题的发起者，作者有责任选择读者感兴趣的话题，或是通过激发读者的兴趣来引导他们参与对话，让读者有动机进一步展开交流。

作者不仅要召集读者加入对话，还要以平等友好的态度组织、开展对话。在这场作者预设的书面对话中，作者需要使用一些方法，根据读者的需要确定写作内容、写作技巧以及语言风格，并不断思考：我想说什么？我说出来了吗？读者能理解吗？进而通过对自己的写作行为进行反思来掌控和调整对话过程，实现有意义的交流。

三、目的：写作的交际意图
Purpose: Communicative Intention in Writing

写作目的是指作者通过内容想要达到的交际目的和意图。作为一种有意识、有目的的交际行为，交际性写作具有明确的交际意图：或是分享经验，或是传达信息，或是说服他人。写作目的不同，作品的内容、结构和表达也会各不相同。

写作目的决定了写作话题。作者对写作话题、内容和材料的选择受写作目的的制约，在"以读者为中心"的写作中，作者应该优先选择读者感兴趣的话题以及能对读者产生重要影响的内容。

写作目的也决定了写作文体。如果作者想分享人生经验，可以选择记叙性文体；如果想传递信息，可以选择说明性文体；如果想说服他人，可以选择议论性文体。总之，文体的选择与写作目的的紧密相关。

写作目的还决定了语言表达的方式。如果是文学作品，语言风格以记叙、描写为主，可以采用生活语言，也可以尝试其他语言风格；如果是说明文，多运用概念、说明等具有客观性的表达方式；如果是议论文，则需要诉诸推理、分析等逻辑性强的表达方式。

四、话题：话语的信息范围
Subject: Information Range of an Intercourse

话题是指话语交流的信息范围。交际性写作要求作者根据交流目的来选择话题和内容，同时，作者在思考、交流的过程中逐渐形成并确定话题。

成功的写作往往从发现好的话题开始。交际性写作的话题一般是作者和读者已知的且共同感兴趣的话题。如果交流的话题超出了读者的认知范围，他们会产生认知和理解障碍，有可能会终止阅读，因而达不到交流的目的。有经验的作者会有意选择读者感兴趣的或相对熟悉的话题，在读者可以接受的信息范围之内，采用循序渐进的策略来展开话题，一步步地引导其参与到自己发起的话题讨论中。

五、体裁：书面交流的类型
Genre: Types of Literary Communication

体裁是指写作文本或文章的类型或样式，是人们在语言实践中逐渐形成的言语模式或框架。交际性写作的文体是以交际任务为取向的，不仅受写作的外在形式（如文辞）和内在形式（如结构）的影响，还受写作的交际语境，即读者、目的和话题的制约。

在交际性写作中，体裁具有鲜明的交际特色，并与写作时的交际语境要素（如交际目的和对象）有着紧密联系。根据交际功能，体裁主要分为四大类，即记叙文写作（narrative writing）、说明文写作（expository writing）、描写文写作（descriptive writing）和议论文写作（argumentative writing）。作者应根据情景需要驾驭各种体裁，以达到准确、得体、有效地表情达意的目的。

不同于强调规范的传统写作，交际性写作强调写作的功能目的，不同功能目的的语篇对应不同的表达方式，如记叙文是为了叙述事情，使人知道；说明文是为了解释事情，使人明白；描写文是为了描绘场景，使人感知；议论文是为了阐明道理，使人接受（刘锡庆，1992）。

交际性写作还强调读者意识，要求作者能够针对不同的读者采用不同的体裁，并结合写作目的，运用多种策略和恰当的方式进行书面交流。

六、表达：合乎语境的语言
Expressions: Language That Fits the Context

传统写作讲究语言的准确、简明、连贯、具体、生动和形象，这些表达特征都很重要，在此基础之上，交际性写作还强调语言的交际性，即语言表达要符合语境，并有助于实现交际目的。

不同的写作目的赋予了作品不同的功能，而目的和功能又决定着语言使用的风格特征。交际性写作要求作者根据不同的交际对象来选择表达方式，比如根据读者的身份、年龄、知识背景等特征来选择语言风格，同时根据不同的交际目的来选择符合具体语境的言语表达，比如在叙述的交际语境中，可以采用讲故事的方式，并运用环境、细节等要素使故事情节和人物形象更加生动。

在交际英语写作中，只有合乎语境和表达意图的语言表达才被认为是有效的，语言不仅要使用规范，还要具有流畅性，能清晰地传递信息，并符合写作目的、满足读者需求。

第三节　交际性写作的策略
Strategies for Communicative Writing

写作策略是作者采用的有效方法、技巧，以及对写作活动的整体性把控。与传统意义上的写作知识、写作方法和写作技能相比，它居于更高层面，是写作主体有意识、有计划的认知活动，更具灵活性。

除学习语言知识和写作知识以外，学习英语写作更重要的是掌握有效的写作策略，并在写作实践中加以运用。国内外英语写作研究发现，有经验的作者和写作新手在写作能力上的差别主要表现在写作策略的认知和运用上，也就是说写作策略的掌握在很大程度上决定了作者的写作能力（Lam, 2015; Zimmerman, 1997）。

为了帮助学习者培养交际写作能力，本书主要介绍三种交际性写作策略，分别是：（1）分析写作目的和读者需求；（2）以读促写并建立读写联系；（3）写作互评以掌握评价标准。

在后面的章节里，本书将通过范文讲解、自主阅读、写作和同伴互评等学习活动，帮助学习者理解、运用和巩固这些策略。

一、分析目的和读者策略
The Strategy of Analyzing Purpose and Audience

交际性写作最重要的一条原则是写作目的清晰并体现读者意识，因此，学会分析写作目的和读者需求是培养交际写作能力的关键，也是本书论述的重点。对这一写作策略的讲解将贯穿于全书所有章节中。

当你学写英语信件时，确定写作目的和读者似乎不难，因为写信的对象通常也是读者，你也很清楚为什么要写这封信——或是介绍自己，或是感谢别人，或是申请一份工作。当你需要写一篇文章时（它可能是记叙文、描述文、说明文、议论文等体裁的一种或几种的组合），你可能会迷失在展开主题的过程中而忽略了读者的需要。

其实，不论写哪种体裁的文章，你都需要知道谁会阅读你的文章，也需要了解他们关心什么，只有这样才能写出读者能够理解并接受的作品。即使是在英语考试中写作文，你也应该清楚这篇文章的写作对象和写作目的。只有当它达到了预期的沟通目标，你才能取得较好的成绩。

培养分析目的和读者的能力可以从以下三个方面着手：

第一，明确写作目的（find a purpose）。开始每次写作之前，你都得为这次写作找到一个特定的目的，并问问自己：我为什么要写这个话题？我将如何影响我的读者？我希望这次写作能实现什么目标？回答这些问题有助于你决定这篇文章的写作目的。最常见的写作目的是说服读者、提供信息和娱乐读者。在论证性或说服性的写作中，你会提出一个观点或主旨，并以各种方式支持它；在说明文中，你以提供信息为主要目的，来告知读者有关特定话题的知识；你有时也会在写作中提供生动幽默的细节，以吸引读者。

第二，建立读者意识（discover your audience）。一旦确定了写作目的，你就需要认真考虑读者对象了。在决定把什么信息放进文章之前，你必须知道谁将阅读你的文章以及他们为什么会读，只有这样，你才能选择合适的信息。同时，了解你的读者也有助于确定在文章中采用什么样的语气。在写作过程中，当决定哪些观点需要强调、哪些观点可以省略、哪些观点需要额外的解释以及需要采用何种表达形式时，你都需要充分考虑读者的背景，比如年龄、教育程度、职业和兴趣等。

第三，分析读者（identify your audience）。分析读者时可以遵循以下步骤：

第1步：明确写作任务是否指明了读者。如果写作任务没有指明读者，则需要想象读者是哪一类人，这将有助于你进行清晰、有效的沟通。

第2步：在确定读者后，试想他们出于什么动机或理由而阅读你的文章：

- 这些读者想了解什么?

- 他们希望获得什么?

- 他们需要你的信息来作出决策或设计新项目吗?

- 你希望他们采取什么行动?

回答这些问题将帮助你明确写作的目的和内容。例如,如果你正在写一封求职信,试图说服未来雇主录用你,则需要强调这家公司看重的个人技能、教育经历等相关信息。至于你的业余爱好或家庭成员等个人信息,则不需要提及。

第3步:仔细思考读者对你所选话题的了解程度:

- 你认为你的读者对这个话题有多少了解?

- 他们需要哪些背景信息才能理解这个话题?

- 哪些事实、解释或例子最能说明你的观点?

- 哪些术语需要被定义?

这些问题将指引你为这篇文章收集、挑选信息。当你站在读者的位置来思考问题时,才能决定哪些信息对他们来说是必要的。

第4步:更深入地了解读者的身份和态度:

- 你的读者是支持还是反对你的观点?

- 他们与你的话题有正面或负面的联系吗?

- 他们有不同的期望或兴趣吗?

在开始写作之前,你只有越了解读者的态度,你的文章才越有说服力,你才能在内容和结构方面作出最好的选择。具体来说,在讨论某个问题时,你有可能写给同意你观点的人,也可能写给反对你观点的人。读者不同,写法肯定不一样。

第5步:思考任何可能会使你的读者区别于其他人的特点:

- 他们是你的同龄人吗?

- 他们有类似的教育经历或培训吗?

- 他们处于权威地位吗?

充分了解你的读者能帮助你确定文章的选词和语气。比如,你给朋友写信时的选词和语气肯定不会像写一封求职信那样正式。

综上所述,在写作时,你需要认真考虑写作目的和读者需求,只有这样才能有效地选择观点和组织信息,并选择恰当的词语和语气进行表述。

二、以读促写策略
The Strategy of Reading for Writing

　　与分析写作目的和读者需求的策略一样，"以读促写"策略也是培养交际写作能力的重要途径。在语言学习中，阅读和写作能力之间存在着一定的联系，写作能力强的人通常爱好阅读，并经常进行广泛而深入的阅读。

　　优秀的读者有潜力成为出色的作者，因为他们会留意其他人的写作效果，并把这些观察结果放在自己的写作中。通过仔细阅读，他们能用更好的想法来阐明自己的观点，能更明智地选择文章的组织方式和风格。这如同运动员会经常观看比赛一样，他们能从观察比赛中学习如何提高自己的技术。

　　本书每单元都设置了"以读促写"章节，旨在引导学习者分析性地阅读专业作家的文章，以取长补短，提高自己的写作水平。通过这种仔细阅读，你能学到很多对写作有帮助的经验：首先，如果你能很好地理解这些文章所表达的观点，就能为自己的文章找到有意义的观点；其次，从阅读中学习其他作者组织和解释文章的各种方式，你能更明智地选择写作策略和支持证据；再次，当你学习了其他作者行之有效的修辞手法和选词方式后，你会更有勇气地创新使用各种表达；最后，非常重要的是，在分析他人的文章时，你能深入了解作者在写作过程中如何做决策，从而更好地策划、写作并修改自己的文章。

　　总而言之，作为分析性读者（analytical reader）所实践的技能也是作为一个好作者所需的各种技能。那么如何通过"以读促写"策略成为分析型读者呢？这需要通过"以读促写"学习活动进行大量的分析性阅读，也就是通过 10 个阅读步骤来研读不同体裁的专业文章，并以此为基础发展相应的写作能力（Wyrick，2008）。如果在之前的阅读中，你只是扫视一下页面上的单词，那么分析性阅读需要你投入更多：你不仅要了解作者的观点，还要考虑这些观点是如何呈现的、作者为什么会这样呈现观点，以及这种呈现方式是否有效。

　　分析性阅读要求阅读指定文章两遍，第一遍用于记笔记，第二遍用于作注释。这个过程一开始比较有挑战性，但你作为读者和作者最终会受益匪浅，会发现所有付出的时间都是值得的。分析性阅读有 10 个步骤：

　　第 1 步：在开始阅读文章之前，注意每篇文章开头提供的出版信息和关于作者的生平介绍。试问自己这样的问题：文章最初发表于何时何处？是针对特定受众还是面向普通受众？它是为回应某一事件或争议而写的吗？这篇文章是否有现实意义，还是已经过时？你认为作者有权威写这个话题吗？

第2步：注意文章的标题。它能吸引你读这篇文章吗？它是否暗示了特定的语气？

第3步：第一遍读正文。有些读者喜欢不停顿地通读文章，有些读者会不时停下来在主要观点处作标记或在遇到生词时查词典。读完这一遍后，你需要写一两句话来总结自己对文章内容或观点的整体印象，并认真思考作者想通过这篇文章实现什么写作目的以及是否实现了这个目的。

第4步：仔细读第二遍。读完之后，请再次查看标题和介绍性段落，思考它们是否介绍了文章的主题、是否符合你的期望。

第5步：找到文章的主要观点或主旨。这个观点可能被明确地提出，也可能暗含在字里行间，请标记这个观点以便回看。

第6步：找到支持或说明主旨的重要语句。这些支持性语句通常是正文段落里接近开头或结尾的主题句。请为这些句子编号，并在空白处写下相应的关键词。

第7步：问问自己作者是如何发展、解释或论证主旨的。你可以写下简短的评论来评价作者做得如何，比如 convincing example、good comparison、generalization without support 等；也可使用符号进行评价，比如星号表示语句有效、问号表示语句混乱等。

第8步：回顾文章的整体组织。作者使用了什么策略来发展观点，是说明性、描述性、叙述性或论证性策略，还是这几个策略的组合？这种方法有效吗？有没有其他方法能更清楚地阐明要点？

第9步：关注文章的过渡词句。问问自己：文章的推进是否具有逻辑性和连贯性？遇到能表现作者如何实现统一和流动感的过渡词或短语时，给它们打上括号。

第10步：考虑作者的风格和行文的语气。你可以问自己：作者是否使用了各种修辞手法使文章生动而令人难忘？作者是否出于特定目的而选用了特殊的词汇？作者的语气是否得以清晰地传达？这篇文章的语气是怎样的？是严肃的、幽默的、愤怒的、快乐的、悲伤的、讽刺的，还是其他？这种语气是否适合本文的目的和受众？

完成这10个步骤后，请浏览自己的笔记，并思考以下问题：这是一篇有效的文章吗？在完成分析性阅读后，我发现这篇文章有哪些优点和缺点？我能把哪些新想法、新策略或新技巧融入自己的写作中？

三、同伴互评策略
The Strategy of Doing Peer Review

同伴互评是指评价写作同伴的文章，这一策略有助于提高写作者的批判性思维和读者意识，并促进交际性写作能力。

在同伴互评活动中，你需要仔细阅读同伴的英语文章，并对它们作出评价。与此同时，你需要从读者的角度来反思自己的文章，考虑如何更有效地呈现自己的观点，如何在写作时具有更强的目标感，以及如何把自己的想法更好地传递给读者。

由于不同的写作任务对应不同的写作功能、目的和情景，写作评价并没有绝对统一的评分标准。评价同伴的英语文章时，可以重点从以下六个方面考察作品质量，如表1.1所示：

表 1.1　同伴互评的通用标准

评价维度	评价细则
写作目的性 （purpose & audience）	作者综合考虑了写作目的、读者对象、交际情景等各种要素。（The author demonstrates a good awareness of writing purpose, audience, and context.）
文章一致性（unity）	作者在文章开头明确提出主旨，主体部分各段有中心句，全文论点一致，并贯穿在所有细节当中。（The author clearly states the thesis in the introductory paragraph and presents a topic sentence in each of the body paragraphs, and all the details in the essay are related to the thesis and to the supporting topic sentences.）
论据充分性（support）	为解释或说明论点，作者提供了大量具体的细节作为例证。（There are separate supporting points for the thesis, and there is plenty of specific evidence for each supporting point.）
行文连贯性（coherence）	文章的组织清晰、有条理，主体部分段落的推进有逻辑性，段落之间有连接词或连接句衔接，段落内部行文连贯。（All the supporting ideas and sentences are organized so that they cohere, or flow together smoothly. The method of organization is clear and logical, and there are transitions between and within paragraphs.）
词汇（vocabulary）	用词准确丰富，表意清晰。（Writing demonstrates adequate range of vocabulary. Meaning is clear.）
语言使用（language use）	语言表达符合规范，恰当运用复杂句式。（There are few errors in grammar. Writing demonstrates effective complex constructions.）

为了能给予同伴有意义的评价并使之有更多的学习收获，在评价同伴文章时需要做到以下六点：

第一，培养建设性态度（develop a constructive attitude）。当你认为自己可能会伤害别人时，你会感到不自在，因此有时很难给予诚实的批评。但请记住，作者需要真诚的反馈，所以在提供建议时应尽量诚实。

第二，尽量明确具体（be clear and specific）。模糊的回答很难帮助作者知道需要修改什么或作何修改，你可以用这样的形式来表达评论：首先，你对这篇文章的看法；

其次，产生这种看法的原因；再次，要求作者作出修改；最后，具体的修改建议。例如，在评价同伴的求职信时可以这么说："I'm confused when you say you'll be qualified in the position of assistant manager of foreign trade operations, because you didn't mention your familiarity with foreign trade operations or your foreign language skills. Would it be more convincing to include your courses or working experience in this field and your foreign language abilities?"。

第三，指出重要问题（address important issues）。在读完同伴的文章后，你可以先对以下主要问题发表评论：文章是否达到了总体目的，主旨是否清晰而有说服力，主要观点和证据是否能被理解，以及文章是否有序并合乎逻辑。在作品刚成形时，对标点、词法、语法等细节的关注可能不如对文章思想、组织和发展等方面的反馈更有价值。

第四，鼓励作者（encourage the writer）。你需要尽可能具体地对同伴的文章给予肯定，在同伴做得不够好的地方，应该告诉他/她如何发挥现有优势以做得更好，比如"Could you add more 'showing' details here so that your description of your language abilities is as vivid as the depiction of your management skills?"。尽量少用一个词的标签，如 awkward 或 unclear，而是代之以具体评价和建议。

第五，做批判性读者（understand your role as a critical reader）。评价同伴文章时，你可以从读者角度提出问题，比如"Will all your readers know the meaning of this technical term?"；如果不太确定某个表述是否准确，可以要求作者讲清楚，比如"Could you recheck this quotation? Its wording here is confusing me because…"。

第六，检查自己的文章（look over your own draft）。一开始，你可能会觉得分析别人的文章比分析自己的要简单。在参加了同伴互评活动后，你可以把这些批判性阅读技巧转移到对自己作品的审阅中，训练自己成为一流的作者。

以读促写示例
A Sample of Reading for Writing
第四节

如本章第三节所述，以读促写学习策略是培养交际写作能力的一条重要途径。本书各章的以读促写示例，旨在引导你通过分析性地阅读专业作家的文章，从不同方面改进自己的写作能力，能更准确地评价自己文章的优缺点，从而成为一名更好的作者。

下文是选自《成功写作入门》（*Steps to Writing Well*）（Wyrick, 2008）的一篇专业作家文章，并根据第三节提到的以读促写策略的 10 个步骤加了注释。

范文

USA Today: High Schools, Wake Up!

The following essay on school schedules was first published in USA Today *in a "Today's Debate" Column (January 23, 2006). This essay represents the views of the newspaper's editorial board.*

1   For a typical U.S. high school student, the morning alarm goes off no later than 6:30 a.m. Breakfast (aka "the most important meal of the day") is either scarfed down or skipped altogether. The school bus arrives by 7 a.m., and the first class starts by 7:30 a.m.

2   This schedule works well for sports coaches: With school out by 2:30 p.m., they have plenty of time to whip their teams into shape. It works well for employers and employees. And many work-bound parents like the idea that their kids leave the house before they do.

3   The schedule doesn't work well, however, for the students themselves, who by second period can be seen nodding off at their desks. Sleep researchers side with the teens, whose brains appear wired to stay up later and who require more sleep than kids of other age groups do. Sleep-deprived teens are grouchier, poorer learners, more prone to attention deficit disorders and more likely to cut classes, say sleep researchers from Brown University and the University of Minnesota.

4   So why does nearly every school district in the U.S.A. start high school so early? Bus schedules and money.

5   School buses need to make three full cycles to bring elementary, middle and high school students to school. Starting high school later would mean buying more buses and hiring more drivers—or sending younger students to school earlier. Sending the younger students sooner isn't as bad as it sounds. Many are up early anyway. And there's unlikely to be a shortage of parents willing to stand with them at bus stops on dark mornings.

6   School leaders in Edina, Minnesota flipped bus schedules nearly a decade ago. For teens and educators there, high school starts at 8:30 a.m. And they're happily sticking with it.

7   Few school districts have followed Edina's lead, however. That's shortsighted. Pushing back high schools' start times can produce:

- Better school attendance. A study of seven Minneapolis high schools that pushed back start times showed higher school attendance in all grades, especially ninth. The same study showed a small improvement in academic performance.

- Happier students and parents. Parents in Edina reported that improved sleep far outweighs concerns over busing, sports and jobs. After one year on the new schedule, 92% of those surveyed approved the change.

- Safer teens. Dumping unsupervised teens onto streets at 2:30 p.m. never made a lot of sense to parents or police. Not only would more teens have less time to get into trouble before adults arrive home, but teens who drive would also be less vulnerable to fatigue-related accidents, sleep experts say.

8   School superintendents defending the status quo cite sports, after-school jobs and school bus schedules. But schedules are the only reason to hesitate. Even advocates of pushing back high school start times acknowledge that bus schedules are nightmarishly complicated.

9   But if Edina managed to figure it out, so can other districts. The payoff—more alert, less grumpy teens—is worth the effort, even if the school board needs to pull a few all-nighters to work out the details.

分析性阅读讲解

第1步： 留意出版信息和作者介绍。*USA Today* 表明本文的对象是大众读者，而 the newspaper's editorial board 表明作者是该报的编辑委员会成员，即新闻工作者。

第2步： 注意文章标题是如何引出主题的。好标题如诱饵，能迅速地把读者带入文章。"High Schools, Wake Up!"这个题目有两个信息点："中学"和"醒来"，不仅引出关于中学生上学时间的主题，也暗指某些中学规定的上学时间不合理，需要公众更多关注。

第3步： 第一遍阅读文章，并写下你对文章的大致印象。例如，"General impression: The writer proposes to push back high schools' start times. There are many benefits for schools, students, and parents."。

第4步： 再次查看标题和介绍性段落。标题和介绍性段落介绍了文章的主题，也暗示了作者的态度，并提出问题：十几岁的孩子们不得不迅速吃早餐，而且早上睡眠不足可能会导致一些学习问题。

第5步： 找到作者的要点或主旨。这篇文章的主旨是："It's shortsighted that few school districts have followed Edina's lead. Pushing back high schools' start times can produce lots of benefits."。

第6步： 查找支持或说明主旨的重要语句。第七段有三个主要的支撑点：better school attendance（更高的入学率）、happier students and parents（更快乐的学生和家长）以及 safer teens（更安全的青少年）。

第 7 步： 分析作者是如何推进主题的，又是如何发展、解释或论证支持性观点的。第七段中，作者通过提供示例、证词和统计数据来支持这些观点，如"A study of seven Minneapolis high schools that pushed back start times showed…""Parents in Edina reported that…""92% of those surveyed approved the change."。

第 8 步： 查看文章的布局和组织形式。作者有效使用了论证策略来组织文章，并通过举例明确要点。

第 9 步： 分析文章的推进是否有逻辑性和连贯性。作者使用了一些过渡性短语和句子来实现文章的逻辑严密和行文流畅，如第二段中的"This schedule works well for sports coaches."，第三段中的"The schedule doesn't work well, however, for the students themselves."。此外，第四段是将原因与效果连接起来的过渡段。

第 10 步： 思考作者的风格和文章的语气。作者采用新闻风格，文章虽然包括了不同方面的意见，但作者的立场很明确：目前中学的上课时间表需要改革。这篇文章略有讽刺性的语气迎合了写作目的，即主张推迟中学的上课时间。

第二章

交际性写作的过程
The Process of Communicative Writing

学习要点

- 交际性写作的步骤
- 写前准备的概念和五个技巧
- 第一稿写作的要点
- 如何修改文章

 ### 交际性写作的步骤
The Steps of Communicative Writing

 ### 一、作为过程的交际性写作
Communicative Writing as a Process

在完成交际性写作任务时，许多英语学习者会觉得困难，这种困难通常贯穿于写作的每个阶段。例如，在选择主题时，面对空白的文稿毫无头绪；写初稿时，既没有列好提纲，也没有安排好修改初稿的时间，结果临近交稿时才发现错漏重重。这些情况通常是因为写作者缺乏对写作步骤的规划。本章将对交际性英语写作步骤作细致的说明，帮助你避免上述情况。

写作不是一次动笔就能完成的任务，你的作品也不是一蹴而就的"流水线产品"。写作是一个思维过程（thinking process），也是一项解决问题的认知活动（problem-solving cognitive activity），它和解决一个复杂的数学问题差不多。写作包含了很多步骤，包括写作之前的准备工作、列提纲、写初稿、修改和校对等。写作并不是线性的：为了完成一篇出色的文章，有时候你需要重复这些步骤。假设一篇完美的文章具有一个令读者有所收获的"意义"，有经验的作者会保持思维的活跃，不断试用各种语言技巧，逼近自己想要到达的"意义"。这个思维过程就被称作"写作步骤"（writing steps）。

正如第一章所述，写作需要以读者的获得感为先。所以在写作之前，你需要问自己：我打算通过写作传达的观点是否有价值？我的读者是否希望了解这一观点？由于文章需要根据特定的读者和特定的目的来选择材料、内容、句式和语言风格，你应该优先选择读者感兴趣的主题以及能对读者产生重要影响的内容。同时，你需要考虑如何为读者呈现出最满意的作品。因此，完成写作任务需要具备两个基本条件：第一，拥有一个新颖的观点（或主题）；第二，具有准确传达观点（或描述主题）的意图，即"有话要说"和"好好说话"。一篇文章是否成功很大程度上取决于作者是否愿意与读者进行交流，是否将观点清晰、有说服力地传达给读者。作者其实只是观点的"搬运工"，需要想方设法地以最佳方式让读者准确领会文章的意图。

在本章中，你将学习使用写前准备——一种逐步形成观点和篇章结构的重要方法；你会了解初稿写作中要实现的四个目标，包括整体性高、支撑有效、逻辑完整和句法无误（unity, support, organization, and error-free sentences）；你还会学习一些修改和校对技巧，通过对文章的内容、句子结构、选词、语法甚至标点符号等进行修改，使作品更为通顺。

二、交际性写作的步骤
The Steps of Communicative Writing

那么，写作过程包括哪几个步骤呢？你可能会疑惑：我不是拿起笔就能开始写作吗？我为什么要特意学习写作步骤呢？实际上，学习写作步骤是非常重要的，了解写作的一般认知模式会让你不再焦虑，会带给你更多的信心。

写作是一个集构思、分析、组织、写作和修改等步骤于一体的过程，真正的动笔仅是其中的一小步。写作过程始于构思和提纲，你可以运用多种写前准备技巧来形成不同想法，并从中选择合适的想法形成文章结构。在写完初稿之后，你还需要打磨文稿，并对其进行多次修改和校对。当进入初稿修订阶段时，你可以设想自己是读者，以全新的视角来审视文章。你可以这样揣度读者的阅读心理：如果没有任何背景知识，我能够理解这篇文章想要传达的信息吗？在这种换位思考中，你可以尝试着去了解读者对文章可能产生的反应和看法。

具体来说，有效撰写文章的步骤可以分成以下四步（见图 2.1）：

（1）通过写前准备方法找到合适的主题；

（2）列出写作提纲，通过使用更多写前准备技巧为选取的题目找到有效的细节支撑；

（3）有效组织主旨句和细节，撰写初稿；

（4）对初稿进行修改和校对，确保文章内容、逻辑、语言等方面正确且得体，没有低级错漏。

图 2.1　写作过程的四个步骤

写前准备
Pre-writing

写前准备指的是作者在动笔之前的多种思维活动，其中确定主题便是写作交际的起点。写前准备可以是一个单独的步骤，也可以贯穿于每个写作步骤当中。本节将首先解决写前准备的核心问题，即如何选择主题及选择时应该遵守哪些原则；其次介绍五种写前准备技巧，以帮助你找到合适的题目，并形成自己的观点。

 如何选择主题
Choosing a Topic

凡写文章，必有主题。选主题是写作思维活动中最关键的一步。本节将介绍选择主题的四种方法。

第一，选择你感兴趣的主题（choose a topic of your own interest）。如果允许自定主题，那么你可以问自己内心深处想写什么，对写什么最有热情。如果你对初步选定的主题没有太多倾诉的欲望，那就需要重新选择。只有无聊的作者才会写连自己都感到无聊的文章。你应该选择那些会引起强烈共鸣的主题，比如尝试仔细观察自己的环境：你的生活——过去、现在和未来，你的校园，你的家乡，你的国家，甚至更广阔的世界，从中发现满足写作要求的主题。如果你不确定自己感兴趣的内容是什么，可以思考自己对什么主题的信息最感兴趣。比如你在翻看报纸杂志时，是更喜欢停留在有关科学新发现的故事上，还是会先浏览旅行、体育或娱乐版？又比如在看电视或浏览互联网时，你的兴趣点在哪里？思考这些问题都有助于你尽快找到合适的写作主题。

第二，收窄你的主题（narrow down your topic）。如果你想要就环境这一主题写一篇文章，首先需要将主题的范围缩小，例如环境污染。但是，环境污染仍然是一个宽泛的主题，你必须将主题进一步缩小到某一特定的环境污染类型，例如海洋污染。同样，海洋污染这一主题仍然太大，因为海洋污染包括石油、化学药品、污水和垃圾的污染等。因此，你需要进一步缩小主题范围，例如将石油视为海洋污染源，确定主题为"具体分析石油泄漏对海洋生物的影响"。至此，你终于将主题收窄至足够精练而不肤浅。这样一来，你和读者都能不太费力地传达和获取具体的信息。对于一篇几百字的学生习作，这个主题的内容范围比较合适；对于篇幅更长的学术论文写作，你需要将主题进一步缩小，也许只限于某种海洋生物，比如海鸟或贝类。

第三，明确写作目的（identify your purpose）。当你将一个较为宽泛的主题收窄后，你仍然需要为文章确立一个特定的写作目的。你为什么要写这个主题？是想为读者提供新的信息、说服读者相信某个观点，还是引起某种情感的共鸣？你希望通过自己的写作完成什么任务？回答这些问题将帮助你明确写作目的和选择体裁，并为段落和层级的规划提供帮助。本书的第三章至第七章将对不同体裁的写作作出具体指引。

第四，囊括控制性要点（include controlling ideas）。为了将一个较为宽泛的主题收窄，你还必须为文章找到明确的重点或方向。例如，你无法将体育运动的所有好处告知读者，因此需要选择一项特定的运动（如游泳），并确定观点中最新颖、最有力的部分，也就是所谓的"控制性要点"（controlling ideas），比如"游泳可以增强心肺功能"。为了更好地理解控制性要点，你可以想象正在使用一台相机：肉眼能看到的景色很广阔，但取景框只能聚焦于某一处景色上，你可以选择场景中特别有趣的部分，也就是将"控制性要点"作为照片的焦点。控制性要点可以体现在题目中，也可以放在文章的主旨句里（主旨句的写法将在后面的章节中详述），但无论何种形式，你都必须在动笔之前考虑清楚。

 ## 二、写前准备技巧
Pre-writing Skills

在初步了解如何选择主题之后，本节将介绍五种写前准备技巧，在写作实践中你可以通过运用这些技巧为撰写初稿做足准备。

1. 自由写作
Free writing

自由写作是针对某一宽泛写作主题的探索性活动，尤其适合不知如何下笔的新手作者。开始自由写作很简单：用短语或句子粗略记录下当前你能想到的关于已定主题的所有内容。在自由写作中，你需要天马行空的遐想。这一过程仅是写作过程的萌芽阶段，重要的是弄清楚你想说什么，并记录下来形成原始材料。在此阶段，无须考虑拼写、标点、材料组织或单词选用等问题，你只需让思绪流动起来，探索任意一个冒出来的想法。

下面的例 1 至例 5 摘自《美国大学英语写作》（*College Writing Skills with Readings*）（Langan, 2014）一书。假设你的同学 Diane Woods[1] 需要完成一篇英语文章，题目是"Everyday Annoyances"（日常生活中的烦恼）。她决定从自由写作入手确定具体的写作内容，如例 1 所示：

例1 Diane 的自由写作

There are lots of things I get annoyed by. One of them that comes to mind is politicians, in fact I am so annoyed by them that I don't want to say anything about them, the last thing I want is to write about them. Another thing that bothers me are people who keep complaining about everything. If you're having trouble, do something about it just don't keep complaining and just talking. I am really annoyed by traffic. There are too many cars in our block and it's not surprising. Everyone has a car, the parents have cars and the parents are just too indulgent and the kids have cars, and they're all coming and going all the time and often driving too fast. Speeding up and down the street. We need a speed limit sign but here I am back with politics again. I am really bothered when I drive to the movies all the congestion along the way plus there are just so many cars there at the mall.

---

1 为拉近与读者之间的距离，后文用 Diane 指代 Diane Woods。

No space even though the parking lot is huge it just fills up with cars. Movies are a bother anyway because the people can be annoying who are sitting there in the theater with you, talking and dropping popcorn cups and acting like they're at home when they're not.

解读 在完成以上自由写作后，Diane 重读了自己的笔记，并反思道：我意识到我有几个潜在的主题，但我能想出这篇文章的重点吗？在所有这些写下来的烦恼当中，我最了解什么？也许我能将主题缩小到"看电影时遇到的烦恼"，因为关于这个题目我有很多有趣的细节可写。

根据这些反思，Diane 在例 2 中进行了更加集中的自由写作，以深入探讨观看电影时遇到的问题。

例2 Diane 的集中自由写作

I really find it annoying to go see movies anymore. Even though I love films. Traffic to Cinema Six is awful. I hate looking for a parking place, the lot isn't big enough for the theaters and other stores. You just keep driving to find a parking space and hoping someone will pull out and no one else will pull in ahead of you. Then you don't want there to be a long line and to wind up in one of the first rows with this huge screen right in front of you. Then I'm in the theater with the smell of popcorn all around. Sitting there smelling it trying to ignore it and just wanting to pour a whole bucket of popcorn with melted butter down my throat. I can't stop thinking about the chocolate bars either. I love the stuff but I don't need it. The people who are there sometimes drive me nuts. Talking and laughing, kids running around, packs of teens hollering, who can listen to the movie? And I might run into my old boyfriend—the last thing I need. Also sitting thru all the previews and commercials. If I arrive late enough to miss that junk the movie may be sold out.

解读 你是否注意到 Diane 的两篇自由写作中存在一些拼写、语法和标点符号错误？在这个阶段，她只是在记录一些思考，形成一些将来写作中可能会用到的内容，所以这些错误是可以暂时忽略的。在后续阶段，她将会放弃其中很多内容，并把剩下的有用部分整理和修改成更精细的大纲和初稿。因此建议你在自由写作时尽量自由地探索主题，而不用担心用词、语法、标点等是否准确。

2. 提问
Questioning

提问能帮助你打开写作思路。具体来说，通过询问与主题有关的一些基本问题来产出观点和细节。这些问题包括最基本的"5W1H"：who、when、where、what、why 和 how。你可以以这六个疑问词为引导，尝试提出尽可能多的问题并予以回答。因为提问能帮助你从多个角度思考主题，是开拓思路的有效方法。通过自问自答，你可以更快地生成有关主题的具体细节。Diane 在撰写《看电影时遇到的烦恼》一文时，想到了以下几个问题，并给出了答案，如例 3 所示：

例3 Diane 的提问过程（自问自答）

Questions	Answers
Why don't I like to go to a movie?	There are just too many problems involved.
When is going to the movies problematic?	Could be any time—when a movie is popular, when the theater is too crowded, when traffic is bad, or when the trip is a drag.
Where can I find the problem with movie-going?	Problems may occur on the highway, in the parking lot, at the concession stand, or in the theater itself.
Who creates these problems?	I have to deal with wanting to eat too much. The theater owners do by not having enough parking space and showing too many commercials.
How can I deal with the problems?	I can stay home and watch movies on video or cable TV.

解读 Diane 用 why、when、where、who 和 how 这五个问题帮助自己打开了思路。

3. 列清单
Listing

列清单是一种集思广益的方法，它主要指收集与主题相关的想法和细节，并将其罗列在一起。在此阶段，你只需要将这些想法和细节一一记录下来，而不是直接从这些项目中挑选出哪些是主要的，哪些是次要的，或试图用任何顺序来排列它们，你只需要列举出来即可。当 Diane 完成自由写作和自问自答后，她将记录下的内容生成一个详细的清单，如例 4 所示：

例4 Diane 的清单

Traffic is bad between my house and theater.

Noisy patrons.

Don't want to run into Jeremy.

Hard to be on a diet.

Kids running in aisles.

I'm crowded into seats between strangers who push me off armrests.

Not enough parking.

Parking lot needs to be expanded.

Long lines.

High ticket prices.

Too many temptations at snack stand.

Commercials for food on the screen.

Tubs of popcorn with butter.

Huge chocolate bars.

Movie may be sold out.

People who've seen movie before talk along with actors and give away plot twists.

People coughing and sneezing.

Yucky stuff on floor.

Teenagers yelling and showing off.

解读 Diane 列举清单时发现，一个细节往往可以连上另一个细节。慢慢地，她的脑海中涌现出了更多细节，当然并不是所有细节都是有用的。在后续的步骤中，她将仔细审视这些细节，并明确找出哪些是可以在撰写初稿时使用的。

4. 思维导图
Mind-mapping

思维导图，也称为思维图表或映射，是用于生成写作材料的一种方法。与以上三种方法不同的是，思维导图的层级更加明显，有助于理顺文章各部分之间的逻辑关系。这种方法对于喜欢边思考边做笔记的人尤其有帮助。在思维导图中，一般使用连接线、文本框、箭头和圆圈来表现想法和细节之间的关系。例如，你可以先用几个关键词列出主题，再将想法和细节用方框或圆圈形式放在主题周围，并用连接线在细节之间以及细节与主题之间建立联系。图 2.2 是 Diane 为《看电影时遇到的烦恼》一文做的思维导图。

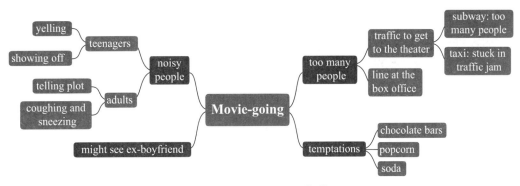

图 2.2　Diane 的思维导图

5. 撰写提纲
Writing an Outline

提纲是一份帮助作者实现文章主题连贯、细节充分、组织良好的蓝图。对于一篇由引言、主体段和结论组成的文章而言，提纲尤其重要。它可能只有几句话，但却是整篇文章的重要基础框架。

撰写提纲是前四种写前准备技巧的自然延伸，通常在最后进行，也可能在这些技巧的运用中逐渐浮现。能否写出一份完整的提纲是检验作者是否需要进行更多写前准备的一种好方法。如果你不能写出一份令人满意的提纲，这意味着你需要做更多的准备工作来阐明要点，例如返回提问和列清单的步骤，以发现更多细节来支持你的想法。在撰写提纲的过程中，你需要仔细考虑提出的要点之间、该要点之下的次级要点（支撑点）之间的逻辑顺序。

当 Diane 完成思维导图后再回看例 4 的清单时，她的写作计划逐渐清晰和立体。她先将这些细节概括成三个分论点：外出时的烦恼、商场诱人的小吃和电影院里的其他观众，再返回列表划掉不合适的项目，并根据这三个分论点对所有相关细节进行分组，在每项前面标上数字 1、2、3，形成删改后的清单，如例 5 所示：

例5 Diane 删改后的清单

1 Traffic is bad between my house and theater.

3 Noisy patrons.

~~Don't want to run into Jeremy.~~

2 Hard to be on a diet.

3 Kids running in aisles.

3 I'm crowded into seats between strangers who push me off armrests.

1 Not enough parking.

1 Parking lot needs to be expanded.

1 Long lines.

1 High ticket prices.

2 Too many temptations at snack stand.

~~Commercials for food on the screen.~~

2 Tubs of popcorn with butter.

2 Huge chocolate bars.

1 Movie may be sold out.

3 People who've seen movie before talk along with actors and give away plot twists.

3 People coughing and sneezing.

1 Yucky stuff on floor.

3 Teenagers yelling and showing off.

在该列表下，她列出了自己的写作提纲：

Going to the movies offers some real problems.
1. Inconvenience of going out.
2. Tempting snacks.
3. Other movie-goers.

解读 经过所有的写前准备步骤，Diane 现在已胸有成竹——这篇作文既有明确的观点作为主题，也有一些有趣的细节作支撑。下一步，她可以以这个提纲为指导来撰写初稿，如传统的三段式结构（引言段、主体段和结论段）。

第三节　写初稿
Writing Your First Draft

撰写初稿过程中，你需要做好准备：处理随时可能冒出的其他想法和细节，并对之前的材料进行修改。在撰写初稿时，一般采用以下步骤：（1）确定提纲；（2）提出中心论点（主旨）；（3）用分论点支持主旨；（4）用具体细节支撑分论点；（5）依照顺序整理细节。

一、确定提纲
Fixing Your Outline

写提纲可以看作是一个过渡的步骤，它既是写前准备的最后一步，也是写初稿的第一步。当你在写前准备阶段做了很多从无到有的工作之后，你需要提炼列在清单上的想法，并形成读者容易理解的结构和层次，这就像平面的建筑图纸被搭成三维的立体结构一样。

二、提出中心论点（主旨）
Raising Your Point or Thesis

与写前准备不同的是，撰写初稿时需要把所有的想法和细节完整地呈现出来，而且首先需要构思文章的要点或主旨，并将其写成主旨句。你必须从一开始就清楚这篇文章是围绕什么而写的，因为清晰的主旨句可以作为后续写作的行文指导。在任何阶段，你都可以暂停写作对自己发问：我写的内容和细节是否支持文章的主旨句？这会大大降低偏题的可能性。

一篇成功的文章，"要点"通常在引言段中以主旨句的形式呈现。一个好的主旨句需要做到两点：首先告诉读者这篇文章的主题；其次表达作者对主题的态度或观点，即前文提到的"控制性要点"。因此，主旨句一般以"主题＋控制性要点"的方式呈现，如例 6 和例 7 所示：

例 6

Owning a pet **has several important benefits**.

解读 这篇文章的主题是"养宠物"，控制性要点是"养宠物有几个重要的好处"。

例 7

The Internet **has led to new kinds of frustration in everyday life**.

解读 这篇文章的主题是"互联网"，控制性要点是"互联网给人们日常生活带来了新的挫败感"。

你也可以通过列表的方式规划主旨句，即先选择一个宽泛、模糊的主题，再通过有效方法逐步收窄它的范围。假设需要撰写一篇关于婚姻的文章，这一主题明显太过宽泛，区区 300 词的文章无法将其论述透彻。所以你需要收窄主题，缩小范围，直到可以用规定字数将其说清楚。在表 2.1 中，从左列至右列分别代表了规划主旨句的三个思维过程：宽泛的主题（general topic）；已收窄的限制性主题（limited topic）；衍生出来的主旨句（thesis）。

表 2.1　主旨句的收窄方法

General Topic	Limited Topic	Thesis
Marriage	Honeymoon	A honeymoon is perhaps the worst way to begin a marriage.
Family	Older sister	My older sister helped me to overcome my shyness.
Children	Disciplining of children	My husband and I have several effective ways of disciplining our children.
Sports	Players' salaries	Players' high salaries are bad for the game, for the fans, and for the values our children are developing.

三、用分论点支持主旨
Supporting the Thesis with Sub-points

在撰写完主旨句之后，你需要想出一些分论点和具体细节来支持它。在这一步，你会发现非正式的提纲对写作非常有帮助，你可以记录一些简短的构想，比如支持主旨句的三点理由。例 8 是 Diane 写下的关于看电影时会遇到烦恼的简短理由：

例 8

主旨句：Movie-going is a problem.

分论点：(1) Inconvenience of going out.

(2) Tempting snacks.

(3) Other movie-goers.

例 8 的提纲看起来很简单，但实际创作通常需要花费很多时间，因为通过使用五个写前准备技巧提炼出一份富有逻辑性的提纲需要大量的思考。不过，一旦有了逻辑清晰的提纲，你就可以大胆地继续撰写了。例 9 是另一个具有三个平行分论点的提纲草稿：

例 9

主旨句：College is stressful for many people.

分论点：(1) Worry about grades.

(2) Worry about being accepted.

(3) Worry about future jobs.

四、用具体细节支撑分论点
Supporting the Sub-points with Specific Evidence

正如主旨句必须有分论点作为支撑一样，每个分论点也必须有生动的细节作为支持。千万不要忽视具体细节的写作，它的关键性体现在两个方面：首先，细节能够激发读者的兴趣，因为细节的可读性更高——一般情况下，人们更喜欢阅读有关人物、场所和事物的详细信息，而不喜欢读一些大道理；其次，细节有助于解释作者的观点，证明其主要观点的正确性，以帮助读者准确地理解主旨。

如果文章的正文段落仅包含模糊的概括性内容，而缺少吸引和说服读者所需的具体支持性细节，那么这是不妥当的。继续以 Diane《看电影时遇到的烦恼》为例，例 10 作为主体段缺少生动详细的支持性证据，读着缺乏说服力：

例 10

Some of the other patrons are even more of a problem than the theater itself. Many people in the theater often show themselves to be inconsiderate. They make noises and create disturbances at their seats. Included are people in every age group, from the young to the old. Some act as if they were at home in their own living room watching the TV set. And people are often messy, so that you're constantly aware of all the food they're eating. People are also always moving around near you, creating a disturbance and interrupting your enjoyment of the movie.

表 2.2 将例 10 列举的一些较模糊的细节（vague support）与定稿中的清晰细节（specific support）进行了对比。

表 2.2　模糊细节和清晰细节的对比

Vague Support	Specific Support
Many people in the theater show themselves to be inconsiderate. They make noises and create disturbances at their seats. Included are people in every age group, from the young to the old. Some act as if they were at home in their own living room watching the TV set.	Little kids race up and down the aisles, usually in giggling packs. Teenagers try to impress their friends by talking back to the screen, whistling, and making what they consider to be hilarious noises. Adults act as if they were at home in their own living room and comment loudly on the ages of the stars or why movies aren't as good anymore.
And people are often messy, so that you're constantly aware of all the food they're eating.	And people of all ages crinkle candy wrappers, stick gum on their seats, and drop popcorn tubs or cups of crushed ice and soda on the floor.
People are also always moving around near you, creating a disturbance and interrupting your enjoyment of the movie.	They also cough and burp, squirm endlessly in their seats, file out for repeated trips to the rest rooms, and elbow you out of the armrest on either side of your seat.

　　如表 2.2 所示，定稿中的段落提供了非常生动具体的细节，清楚地表明了观众的不当行为给人们观影时造成的不便。Diane 先是划分了确切的年龄段（小孩子、青少年和成年人）以及详述了每个年龄段的不当行为（如咯咯笑、交谈、吹口哨、大声评论等）；再是详细介绍了电影院中各种令人感到不适的垃圾（如座位上的口香糖、掉落的爆米花和汽水瓶等）；最后绘声绘色地描述了其他干扰行为（如咳嗽、打嗝、移动座位、频繁去洗手间等）。

　　总之，表格左列中缺失了许多细节，读者只能靠猜测去想象究竟发生了什么；右列中的清晰细节则能唤起读者的兴趣，使其能够分享作者的经验并与之共情，从而理解作者的观点。由此可见，提供详细、清晰的细节能使分论点更具有说服力。

五、依照顺序整理细节
Arranging Details in Order

　　在完成前期的分论点和具体细节的准备工作之后，你需要有效组织并联结这些支持信息。在这一阶段，你需要设法保证文章中所有细节的连贯性。换句话说，就是把所有细节按照一定的逻辑顺序联结在一起，以便读者能够自然地从一个段落过渡到下一个段落。常用的整理细节的方法有：时间顺序、强调顺序和过渡性文字。

1.　时间顺序
Chronological/Time Order

　　时间顺序是指按时间发生的先后顺序列出详细信息，既可以使用 first、next、

then、after that 等来指示时间顺序，也可以使用表示时间的连接词（since、while、until、when 等）。例 11 是一个使用时间顺序的提纲：

例 11

主旨句：To exercise successfully, you should follow a simple plan consisting of arranging the time, making preparations, and warming up properly.

分论点：(1) To begin with, set aside a regular hour for exercise.

(2) Next, prepare for your exercise session.

(3) Finally, do a series of warm-up activities.

例 12 对上述提纲中的第二个分论点进行了扩写：

例 12 使用时间顺序的主体段

Next, prepare for your exercise session. You do this, first, by not eating or drinking anything for an hour before the session. Why would you risk your stomach? Then, dress comfortably in something that allows you to move freely. Because you'll be in your own home, there's no need to invest in a high-fashion dance costume. A loose T-shirt and shorts are good. A bathing suit is great in summer, and in winter long underwear is warm and comfortable. If your hair tends to flop in your eyes, pin it back or wear a headband or scarf. After dressing, prepare the exercise area. Turn off the phone and lock the door to prevent interruptions. Shove the coffee table out of the way so that you won't bruise yourself on it. Finally, get out the simple materials you'll need to exercise on.

2. 强调顺序
Emphatic Order

强调顺序有时被描述为"将最好的保存到最后"（saving the best till last），这与英语短语 last but not the least 有异曲同工之妙：通过把强调内容放在文章的最后一部分或最后的支持性段落中，读者可以注意到文章中最有趣或最重要的细节。因为从认知偏好上讲，人们一般最有可能记住最近阅读的内容。finally、last of all、most important 等都是显示"最后且最重要"的分论点的典型标志。例 13 是一个使用强调顺序的提纲：

例 13

主旨句：Celebrities lead very stressful lives.

分论点：(1) For one thing, celebrities don't have the privacy an ordinary person has.

(2) In addition, celebrities are under constant pressure.

(3) Most importantly, celebrities must deal with the stress of being in constant danger.

例 14 对上述提纲中的最后一个分论点进行了扩写：

例 14 使用强调顺序的主体段

Most importantly, celebrities must deal with the stress of being in constant danger. The friendly grabs, hugs, and kisses of enthusiastic fans can quickly turn into uncontrolled assaults on a celebrity's hair, clothes, and car. Celebrities often get strange letters from people who become obsessed with their idols or from people who threaten to harm them. Worst of all, threats can turn into deeds. The attempt to kill Ronald Reagan and the murder of John Lennon came about because two unbalanced people tried to transfer the celebrity's fame to themselves. Famous people must live with the fact that they are always fair game—and never out of season.

3. 过渡性文字
Transitions

过渡性文字包括过渡词、过渡性短语、过渡性从句（transitional clauses）和句子（transition sentences）以及过渡段。就像引导旅行者的路标一样，过渡性文字标志着作者思考的方向（或者说作者想让读者循着自己的思考方向）。表 2.3 中列举了一些按功能分类的常见过渡性文字，请注意某些过渡性文字具有不止一种功能。

表 2.3 常见过渡性文字的功能分类

功能分类	示例
表递进	one, first of all, second, the third reason, also, next, another, and, in addition, moreover, furthermore, finally, last of all...
表时间先后	first, then, next, after, as, before, while, meanwhile, soon, now, during, finally...
表空间顺序	next to, across, on the opposite side, to the left, to the right, above, below, near, nearby...

（续表）

功能分类	示例
表转折	but, however, yet, in contrast, although, otherwise, still, on the contrary, on the other hand...
表举例	for example, for instance, specifically, as an illustration, once, such as...
表总结	therefore, consequently, thus, then, as a result, in summary, to conclude, last of all, finally...

观察例 15 中阴影部分的词语，你能指出这些过渡性文字具有哪些功能吗？

例 15 过渡性文字

Genetic research has produced both exciting and frightening possibilities. Scientists are now able to create new forms of life in the laboratory because of the development of gene splicing. On the one hand, the ability to create life in the laboratory could greatly benefit humankind. One beneficial application of gene splicing is in agriculture. For example, researchers have engineered a more nutritious type of rice that could help alleviate the serious problem of vitamin A deficiency. It is estimated that 124 million children worldwide lack vitamin A, putting them at risk of permanent blindness and other health issues. In addition, genetic engineers have created larger fish, frost-resistant strawberries, and cows that produce more milk. Indeed, agriculture has already benefited from the promise of genetic engineering.

On the other hand, not everyone is positive about gene-splicing technology. Some people feel that it could have terrible consequences. In fact, a type of corn engineered to kill a certain insect pest also threatened to annihilate desirable monarch butterflies. In another accident, a genetically engineered type of corn that was approved only for animal consumption because it was toxic to humans accidentally cross-pollinated with corn grown for humans. As a result, many countries banned imports of genetically modified corn for several years. Furthermore, the ability to clone human beings is a possibility that frightens many people. In 2004, two South Korean scientists reported that they had successfully cloned a human embryo. The embryo did not develop into a baby; however, it is possible that one could do so in the future, a possibility that not everyone is comfortable with.

—cited from *Writing Academic English* (4th ed.)

在段落之间使用过渡性文字，可以帮助作者将文章中的支持性段落联结在一起，并带领读者平稳地从一个段落过渡到下一个段落。例 16 是 Diane《看电影时遇到的烦恼》这篇文章中的一个过渡句，请留意加粗的过渡性短语：

例 16

Many of the other patrons are even more of a problem than **the concession stand.**

> **解读** 本句中的 the concession stand 提醒读者前一个主体段中的分论点主题是什么，而 Many of the other patrons 则预告了本段的分论点主题。

第四节 习作修改
Revising Your Essay

"行家作文，三易其稿。"这句话说的是，即使最优秀的作者也需要不断修改自己的文章。好的作品从来都不是一蹴而就的，而是千锤百炼的成果。修改和校对文章是继写前准备和初稿写作之后的一个重要写作阶段。修改文章有时仅是小修小补，有时则意味着重写（rewrite）一整段，甚至一整篇文章。在这一阶段，你需要将已完成的文章修改得更清晰、更通顺、更易懂。写完初稿后，你可能认为文章可以提交了，但实际上将初稿修改两到四次（二稿到四稿），也是写作的一部分。除必不可少的自主修改以外，在交际英语写作中，你还可以发动潜在读者（包括老师、同学、朋友等）提出修改意见。

 一、修改过程
The Revising Process

文章的修改过程一般分为四个阶段：修改文章内容、修改句子句法、编辑和校对，以及同伴互评。下面将依次进行简要介绍，并且在本章末尾设有具体练习。

1. 修改文章内容
Revising the Content

关于初稿，并非所有内容都能完美地支持你想要表达的主要观点。为了更好地查找内容方面的错漏，你可以通过询问自己以下三个问题来自查：

（1）文章是否自成整体？

- 引言段是否明确陈述或暗含了主旨？

- 所有主体段的主题句是否真正支持主旨？
- 结论段是否重复或深化了主旨？

（2）文章有丰富的细节作为支撑吗？

- 文章是否有三个独立的分论点？
- 每个分论点是否都有对应的支撑细节？
- 这些细节都是必要的吗？是否足以证明分论点？

（3）文章的逻辑性强吗？

- 引言段是否主题鲜明？结论段是否可靠？标题是否准确？
- 文章的组织结构清晰吗？
- 是否使用了合适的过渡性文字或其他逻辑连接词？

2. 修改句子句法
Revising the Sentences

句子的连贯性和词汇的恰当使用有助于作者准确地传达信息和表达观点。为了更好地修改文章中的句子，你可以通过询问自己以下五个问题来自查：

（1）文章是否使用了平行结构用于平衡观点？

英语中的"平行结构"（parallel structure）是一种把相似的句子结构同质化的用法。例如，若在并列的句子中使用不定式或动名词，需要将前后句子改为相同的形式；当相邻句子的动词相同时，可以将第二个句子的动词省略。例如：

例 17

- The people pass through the mountains and into the dessert.（后半句省略了动词 pass）
- Alan Turing **is not only** a genius in mathematics **but also** a musician.（后半句省略了系动词 is）

（2）文章的词汇是否准确且不宽泛？

在实际写作中，需要注意避免语意宽泛的动词和名词，如 make、do、thing 等，同时避免中式英语和逐字翻译。例如：

例 18

- We should **make** many **things** to be happy.
- The poor writing **let** us know the **poverty of words**.

以上两句均不符合词汇准确性的要求，可以改为：

例 19

- We should **strive to ensure** happiness.
- The poor writing **reflects** the **lack of vocabulary**.

（3）句子之间的逻辑关系是否清晰？

请注意下列两例都是短句，句子与句子之间缺乏逻辑连接词：

例 20

- My father never attended the festival parades. He hated gatherings.
- All these participants claim to be experts of aliens. None of them has ever seen an alien.

为了使句子之间的逻辑关系更清晰，可以改为：

例 21

- My father never attended the festival parades, **for/because** he hated gatherings.
- All these participants claim to be experts of aliens, **but/yet** none has ever seen one.

（4）文章用词是否得体并符合英语书面写作的要求？

在英语书面写作中，需要避免使用俚语、陈词滥调、自夸或啰唆重复的语言等。例如：

例 22

- Before then we'd taken lessons on DIY in BJ.
- I **ain't got** a **damn** thing left in my pocket.

以上两句均不适合出现在英语书面写作中，可以改为：

例 23

- Before then we had taken "Do it yourself" (DIY) lessons in Beijing.
- There **was nothing left** in my pocket. / I **am penniless**.

（5）文章是否使用了多种句型结构？

简单句的滥用叠加会导致句法缺乏多样性。常见的不规范句型结构有粘连句（run-on sentence）、断章句（choppy sentence）和连珠句（stringy sentence）等。

首先，一句话中不可以出现两个谓语动词，否则就是粘连句（详解请见附录一）；其次，文中尽量不连续出现多个短句，否则就是断章句过多，导致句式过于单一；同时，尽量不用 and、but 等词联结多个类似的短句，否则就是连珠句，导致句式十分单调。例如：

例 24

- John left his homeland Russia. Then he attended a boarding school in America. Then he got his work permit. Then he traveled to China. And he works and lives there now.
- John left his homeland Russia, and he went to a boarding school in America; then he got his work permit, and he traveled to China, and he works and lives there now.

针对以上两种情况，可以使用从句、逻辑连接词等将原句改为复杂句，长短结合，使句型变得更加多样。例如：

例 25

- **After** John left his homeland Russia, he attended an American boarding school for a few years. **As soon as** he got his work permit, he traveled to China, **where** he works and lives now.

3. 编辑和校对
Editing and Proofreading Your Essay

在仔细修改内容和句子结构之后，你就可以进行编辑和校对了。校对是指检查并纠正语法、标点符号和拼写等细节方面的错误。你可能会发现，对文章进行仔细的编辑和校对是一件难事，因为回过头来反复阅读自己的文章不是一件轻松的事情。但你仍然要做好这一步骤，只有这样文章才算真正完成。虽然语法错误不是最致命的错误，但一篇好的文章一定不能有太多的语言错误。

附录一总结了中国学习者在英语写作中的常见错误，可以帮助你提高对错误的认知水平，并供你在编辑和校对文章时参考使用。

4. 同伴互评（可选）
Peer Review (Optional)

不同的作者对于好文章的理解是不同的。你可以借助同伴的力量，通过邀请一位或多位同伴阅读初稿或修改稿，听取他 / 她的建议以提高写作质量。这个过程可以面对面地进行，也可以直接在稿件上做批注（手写或电子批注）。

当进行同伴互评时，你可以提供以下四条意见，这些意见是逐条深化的，对作者来说有很强的借鉴意义：

（1）阐明写作意图。要求作者解释清楚文章中某些难以理解的内容（包括词组、搭配、观点等），如："What do you mean by 'the poverty of vocabulary'?"。

（2）找到问题所在。提醒作者文章中存在一些有问题的单词、词组、句子、段落、想法等，或缺乏某些衔接内容，如："I think this example cannot effectively support your argument."。

（3）解释问题性质。对于你认为文章中存在的问题，你需要给出具体理由，做到有理有据，如："You should put some phrases before you make this quotation because the last paragraph is unrelated to the fourth paragraph."。

（4）提出改进建议。你可以直接指出怎样增添、删减、置换才能让文章变得浅显易懂，如："If you're trying to say many people have more than one cell phone, maybe you can say 'the majority of the people have a cell phone with them, some even with more than one'."。

在收到同伴给出的修改意见后，你就可以根据这些意见进行修改了。你需要去伪存真，找到真正有价值的意见。请注意，处理同伴互评中的修改意见时存在先后顺序：先找到高层次的修改内容，比如文章主旨、主体段和主题句、连贯性等方面的问题；再进行低层次内容的修改，包括语法、例子、句子结构、词汇选取、拼写和标点符号等细节。例如：

例26 同伴评价

School Shouldn't Just Be a Place of Education

There is no doubt that schools are places to educate students. Although most people has no objection that the primary responsibility of education is to train students' minds, quick thinking and developed minds are not all we pursue. At the same time, a strong and healthy body is also essential. Therefore, I believe that schools should require students to excise at least one hour each day.

> 批注 [T1]: Good thesis statement. But why one hour specifically?

Exercising for one hour a day makes the students physically healthier! Chairman Mao once said: "The body is the capital of the revolution." We should understand that a healthy body and hard work are not an irreconcilable contradiction. Physical health is a prerequisite condition for us to study, live, and work. However, for some college students, irregular work and rest seem to be their norm. A heart-wrenching incident happened not long ago: A college student stayed up late to study and died suddenly. This is news that we don't want to hear, but it did happen. This incident has sounded the alarm for us: Learning is important, but health is more important!

Exercising for one hour a day makes the students mentally healthier! In the atmosphere of high-pressure learning in the school for a long time, some middle school students have become tired of studying. Some students who fail the exams do dare not face their parents and teachers. They are psychologically vulnerable and sensitive. If they cannot get timely psychological counseling, these students may become depressed and prone to excessive behavior. Studies have shown that exercising daily can not only reduce the occurrence of depression (*citation?*), but also cultivate an open mind ~~and eliminate~~ while eliminating gloomy moods.

One hour of exercise every day can help strengthen students' confidence and courage. Exercising for one hour a day is not as easy as it sounds. The existence of individual differences makes some students not interested in sports. In this case, the promotion of the school's requirements and the participation of other

批注 [T2]: Good sub-point. But why exclamation mark?

批注 [T3]: Is it directly related to lack of exercise? Consider using another example.

批注 [T4]: Not relevant to this sub-point.

批注 [T5]: Needs more effective supporting details to establish the link between exercise and psychological well-being.

批注 [T6]: How is it different from the second sub-point?

students will help them improve their resistance and
overcome psychological barriers.

 解读 例 26 中，评价者既做了语法方面的批注（如主旨句的标点修改、倒数第二段的语法修改等），也加入了针对内容方面的批注（如认为例子不当、一些句子与分论点关系不大等），还有格式上的建议（如缺少引用）。整体看着不错，但如果再多一些直接的改进建议就更好了。

二、关于修改文章的其他建议
Other Tips on How to Revise Your Essay

　　在介绍了初稿的修改过程之后，下面有一些小贴士，可以帮助你提升文章修改的效果。

　　第一，写完初稿后不急于立即修改。你可以将初稿搁置一段时间之后再动手修改，比如间隔几个小时，甚至间隔一两天。通过这种方式，你可以以一种全新的、更客观的第三者角度来重新审视初稿。

　　第二，最好使用打印稿进行修改，不推荐使用手写稿。打印稿上最好是雪白的，不带有先前修改的痕迹，并做到每次修改时都能如此。通过这种方式，你可以不带任何先入为主的观念来修改文章。打印稿尽量调节为双倍行距，留有足够的页边距。这样做可以留有足够的空间，供你更改或添加内容，从而使文稿看起来更清晰，也便于撰写下一稿。

　　第三，如有可能，把文章内容大声地朗读出来。这种通读方式有助于你考量文章的用词和风格是否恰当。

Exercises

I. Which of the following topics are too broad for a 300-word essay?

1. The role of modern university
2. My first experience at the university canteen
3. Solar energy
4. How to get along with roommates
5. Computers
6. The best teacher I've ever had
7. Selecting the right course
8. Animal rights
9. Smart cars
10. My favorite song

II. Find out the topic and controlling idea for each of the following thesis statements.

1. There are many reasons why pollution in ABC Town is the worst in the world.
2. To be an effective CEO requires several characteristics.
3. There are many possible contributing factors to global warming.
4. Fortune hunters encounter many difficulties when exploring a shipwreck.
5. Dogs make wonderful pets because they help you to live longer.
6. Crime in poverty-stricken areas occurs as a result of systemic discrimination.

III. Fill in the following blanks with the transition words or phrases in the box. Change the form if necessary.

as soon as the lesson begins	in the next few minutes
when you return	finally
when he or she asks you to speak up	before you sit down
in conclusion	then
first	a third time
second	next

How to Annoy a Teacher

It is quite easy to annoy a teacher—even the most patient, kind-hearted teacher in the world—if you follow these simple steps.

1. _____, always come to class just a little late. 2. _____, make as much noise as possible as you enter the room. 3. _____, greet all your friends with a cheerful wave—or even better, with a shouted greeting. 4. _____, slam your heavy backpack down on the floor next to your desk and do a few stretching exercises. (After all, you will be sitting still for the next 40 minutes or so!)

5. _____, make a big yawn and take your seat. 6. _____, go to the restroom. 7. _____, be sure to slam the door, and again, make as much noise as possible while taking your seat.

8. _____, turn the pages of your book noisily, search in your backpack for a pencil, ask your neighbor if you can borrow an eraser, and announce in a loud voice that you cannot find your homework. 9. _____ raise your hand and ask to be excused to look for it in your locker.

If the teacher should happen to call on you during the class, mumble (含糊不清地小声说) an answer. 10. _____, mumble again—maybe a little louder this time, but still not loudly enough to be heard. If the teacher dares to ask you 11. _____, give a loud and clear answer to the previous question—the one that your classmate answered a minute ago—and smile cunningly as you do so.

12. _____, if these techniques do not achieve the desired results, you can always fold your arms across your desk, put your head down, and take a nap. Just do not forget to snore (打呼噜)!

IV. Proofread the following paragraph. Pay attention to grammatical errors, inappropriate words, and inconsistencies.

Last week Mary get good job at big city. I very happy he got this job. I was thinking like to go to mall to shop and buy her some clothing, but instead go to market to buy three roasted duck for celebrate her congratulations. However, to my surprise, she said: I am on a diet this month. Maybe I go vegetarian. I thought. Mary like to eat meat; he definitely not vegetarian. But I make him green salad anyway.

Answer Keys

I. Topics 1, 3, 5, 8, 9 are too broad for a short essay.

II. 1. Topic: pollution in ABC Town being the worst in the world

Controlling idea: many reasons

2. Topic: an effective CEO

Controlling idea: several characteristics required

3. Topic: global warming

Controlling idea: many possible contributing factors

4. Topic: fortune hunters

Controlling idea: many difficulties when they explore a shipwreck

5. Topic: dogs are wonderful pets

Controlling idea: pets help you to live longer

6. Topic: crime in poverty-stricken areas

Controlling idea: systemic discrimination as a reason

III. 1. First   2. Second

3. Next   4. Before you sit down

5. Finally   6. As soon as the lesson begins

7. When you return   8. In the next few minutes

9. Then   10. When he or she asks you to speak up

11. a third time   12. In conclusion

IV. Last week Mary got a good job in a big city. I was very happy that she got this job. I planned to go to a mall and buy her some clothing, but instead, I went to the market and bought three roasted ducks to congratulate her. However, to my surprise, she said she was on a diet this month. I did not think she would go vegetarian because she likes to eat meat. However, I made her a green salad anyway.

第二部分

不同文体的交际性写作

COMMUNICATIVE WRITING IN DIFFERENT GENRES

第三章

应用文写作
Personal and Business Letters—Practical Writing

学习要点

- 应用文的概念
- 信件的格式
- 信件的交际性写作
- 私人信件和商务信件的写作策略
- 信件的分析性阅读

第一节 应用文写作概述
Introduction to Practical Writing

一、应用文的概念
Concept of Practical Writing

  应用文是人们在工作、学习和日常生活等社会实践活动中，用以处理公私事务、传递交流信息、表达意愿、解决实际问题等具有一定格式的文体。可以说，应用文是人际交往中必不可少的重要文体。

  撰写信件（writing letters）是社会生活中一种基本的沟通方式，也是本章应用文写作学习的重点。你可能会问，如今发送电子邮件或短信已十分方便，为什么还要学习撰写信件？这是因为大多数严肃的沟通仍然以书面信件的形式进行，比如申请信、录取通知、公告等。

二、信件的格式
Letter Format

作为应用文的一种重要形式，信件可分为私人信件与商务信函。本章将以私人信件中的感谢信与商务信函中的求职信为重点进行讲解，首先讨论这两种信件的格式。

一般英文信件由以下五个基本部分组成：信头、问候、书信正文、结束语 / 敬辞和署名。根据需要，还会使用以下四个部分：信内地址、附件（通常缩写为 Enc. 或 Inc.）、附言（通常缩写为 P.S.）和复制抄送（通常缩写为 CC.、cc. 或 xc.）。表 3.1 呈现了英文信件的格式：

表 3.1 英文信件的格式

私人信件（感谢信）		商务信函（求职信）	
基本部分	信头	基本部分	信头
	称呼		称呼
	信件正文		信件正文
	结束语 / 敬辞		结束语 / 敬辞
	署名		署名
其余常用	信内地址	可选	信内地址
	附件		附件
	附言		
	复制抄送		

1. 信头
Heading

信头，包括写信人的地址和写信日期，通常置于信纸的右上角，还可以作为一个整体与左边缘对齐。有的信纸带有部分信头，即地址已打印在信纸上方。例如：

例1 私人信件信头

23 Linping Road

Shanghai, China 200045

September 26, 2020

例2 商务信函信头

Dept. of Civil Engineering

Shenzhen University

Nanshan, Shenzhen 518060

May 6, 2021

> **解读** 如例1和例2所示，信头不可省略日期，即使是带有地址信头的信纸也是如此。同时，日期需要置于地址下方，不可高于地址。

信头可采用美式英语的形式，将月份置于日期之前，也可采用英式英语的形式，将日期置于月份之前。前者不需要在日期后面加上 st、nd、rd 或 th 这样的序数词词尾，后者则需要加上，例如 1st、2nd、3rd 或 5th。例3是信头日期的几个示例：

例3　美式英语和英式英语的信头日期

American Style	British Style
January 1, 2021	1st of January, 2021
March 3, 2021	3rd of March, 2021
December 15, 2021	15th of December, 2021

> **解读** 不论是英式英语还是美式英语的日期形式，务必在月份及日期之后、年份之前加上逗号。

2. 称呼
Salutation

称呼，即对致信对象的问候，放在信笺信头下方的左侧，并且在信头和称呼之间需要留下一或两行空间。比较正式的称呼包括：（1）Dear；（2）收信人的称谓（Mr., Ms., Mrs., Dr. 等）；（3）收信人的姓氏。不太正式的称呼只包括两个部分：（1）Dear；（2）收信人的名字。表3.2左列是私人信件中称呼的示例，按比较正式到不太正式降序排列；右列则为商务信函中称呼的常用形式，相对私人信件而言都较为正式。请注意表中右下方的特例。

表 3.2　英文信件的称呼

正式程度	私人信件	商务信函	
比较正式	Dear Mr. Johnson Dear Ms. Lee Dear Mrs. Johnson Dear Dr. Lopez Dear Professor Wang	比较正式 （同私人信件）	Dear Mr. Johnson Dear Ms. Lee Dear Mrs. Johnson Dear Dr. Lopez Dear Professor Wang
不太正式	Dear Jane Dear Haihua	**商务信函特例**（如果不知道致信对象的名字，可以用该人所担任的职位或泛称来称呼，如 General Manager、Dear Sir、Dear Madam、Dear Sir or Madam）	

在人名后面，可以使用冒号或逗号。在私人信件中（如家庭信件或情书）可以使用非正式的问候，如 My Dearest 或 My Darling。此外，切忌单独使用人名，如 Mr. Donald Johnson，以这样的问候作为书信的开头通常是不恰当的。

3. 信件正文
Body of the Letter

信件正文是书信最重要的部分，可以传达信息、想法等。如果是私人信件，可以不必那么正式，就像对话一样；如果是商务信函，就要相对严肃，并且意思明确、紧扣主题。

在技巧方面，需要注意拼写、语法和选词等细节。如果一封信满是拼写错误，或是好多句子不符合语法习惯，其传递的信息可能会具有误导性，甚至会令收信人感到不安。比如，每个句子需要以大写字母开头，并通常以句号结尾；当进入一个新主题时，则需要另起一段，因为一封不分段的长信读起来不仅无趣，而且层级关系不突出。

4. 结束语 / 敬辞
Complimentary Closing

结束语是一个告别问候，通常写在信件正文下方一两行的位置。表 3.3 列举了一些最常用的结束语，排序从较正式到较亲密。

表 3.3　英文信件的结束语

正式程度	结束语
较正式	Yours truly,
	Very truly yours,
	Sincerely yours,
	Yours very sincerely,
	Cordially yours,
	Faithfully yours,
较亲密	Yours ever,
	Yours affectionately,
	Always affectionately yours,
	Your loving aunt,
	With love,

请注意，第一个单词的首字母必须大写，且短语的末尾必须补上逗号。结束语的 yours 一词可以放在短语的开头或结尾，如 "Yours sincerely," 或 "Sincerely yours,"。这两个短语的含义没有区别。在私人信件和非正式信件中，yours 一词可能会被省

略。在这种情况下，结尾只包括一个词，如"Sincerely,"或"Affectionately,"。此外，"Respectfully yours,"只适用于下级对上级的信件中，例如雇员对雇主；"Gratefully yours,"只适用于真正感谢某人的信件中，例如当你写信给一位对你帮助很大的老师或治愈你重病的医生时可以使用。

5. 署名
Signature

署名写在书信正文结尾的下方。署名应尽量手签，并写出全名。在私人信件中，可以忽略姓氏只签名字部分；在正式的商务信函写作中，则需要补上头衔作为署名的一部分，但不要把它写在署名前面。例如：

例4 署名

- Ming Lee, Ph.D.
  Director
  Human Resources Division
- Robert Mayor
  Principal
  High School of Science

虽然建议署名部分要手写，但在手写署名下键入姓名也是一种常见做法，这样在拼写上也不会出错。例如：

例5 更完整的署名

HANDWRITTEN SIGNATURE of LINDA LEVINE

Linda Levine

General Manager

Shanghai Fashion Department Store

6. 信件的其他四个部分
Four Less Important Parts of a Letter

1）信内地址（Inside Address）

信内地址主要用于正式的社交和商务通信，通常置于纸张左侧的信头下方、称呼上方。它不仅仅是一个地址，还包括收信人的完整姓名、头衔、所在机构或公司。

例如：

例 6

- Mary Carpenter
  Principal
  United Nations School
  1 United Nations Plaza
  New York, NY 10324
- Dr. John Lee Chairman
  Department of Biology
  Shanghai Teachers University
  100 Guilin Road
  Shanghai, China 200234

2）附件（Enclosure）

附件通常缩写为 Enc. 或 Inc.，用于指称除信件本身以外的其他部分，比如支票、照片或文档等。它通常写在署名下方一行或两行的位置。

3）附言（Postscript）

附言缩写为 P.S.，表示在一封信中增加了一个简短的内容。它通常放在署名下方一行或两行的位置。虽然使用 P.S. 很常见，也广为接受，但不建议在正式书信中使用，因为它会给收信人留下一个印象：写信人对这封信的思考似乎不够透彻。

4）复制抄送（CC.）

复制抄送（通常缩写为 CC.、cc. 或 xc.）表示该信已抄送给特定人员外。具体来说，CC. 或 cc. 代表喷墨复印，xc. 代表激光复印。它经常用于办公室间的通信或商务通信。例如：

例 7

cc. Clark James, Dean

Bill Max, Chairman

Jay Wong, Program Director

解读 例 7 用于告诉收信件人，此信已抄送给另外三个人。

例 8 是包含以上九个部分的信件示例:

例 8

(Heading)

23 Linping Road

Shanghai, China 200045

September 26, 2020

(Inside Address)

Dr. Moss Roberts Director

East Asian Studies

New York University

375 Broadway, Suite 364

New York, NY 10003

(Salutation)

Dear Dr. Roberts:

(The Body of the Letter)

(Complimentary Closing)

Yours sincerely,

(Signature)

Li Ping, Ph.D.

P.S. Copies of my recent publications will be sent under separate cover.

Enc. Résumé and photo

cc. Li Feng, Dean

Zhang Linping, Department Chair

 三、 信件的交际性写作
Communicative Writing in Letters

撰写信件时应充分了解致信对象，并明确该信件为交际而写。本章重点讲解的私人信件（感谢信）及商务信函（求职信）都有明确的读者对象和写作目的——信件的读者就是致信对象，而写作目的是感谢某人或申请某个职位。

写信时需要根据致信对象来决定信件的正式程度，即非常正式、不那么正式或非正式，并决定信件的使用语言类型，比如感谢大学教授或工作主管时使用的语言与感谢朋友时使用的语言肯定是不相同的。

在感谢信中，你必须说明感谢的原因。感谢信就是要表达谢意，说明为什么要感谢收信人。写感谢信还应该及时，这会让收信人觉得你更真诚，并更为之感动。

写求职信也是如此。致信对象可能是你未来的雇主，写信目的是为了获得某个职位，这要求你必须在开头明确自己申请的特定职位。求职信就是要"推销"自己，因此需要以最大限度满足雇主需求的方式来介绍自己。

写信时还应表述自然，就像和写信的对象说话一样。建议使用简单明了的语言，宽泛而空洞的词并不合适，因为这些词会让信件显得不自然也不真诚。

另外，信件不能太短或太长。如果过短，可能会给人一种你很着急的感觉，觉得你只是在完成写信这件事情；如果过长，则会让人厌烦。所以需要把握好信件的长度，做到长短适中。

 第二节　私人信件的写作策略
Strategies for Writing Personal Letters

感谢信是人们常写的一种令人愉快的信件，目的是向致信对象表达感谢。及时、自然真诚、长短合宜的感谢信能最大限度地实现信件的交际功能。本节将先介绍常见的感谢信类型，再总结写感谢信的经验法则。

一、感谢信的类型
Types of Thank-you Letters

本部分基于四种常见的交际情境，结合范文讲解如何写好不同情境下的感谢信。

1. 感谢他人记住某事
Thank-you Letters for Remembering

写这一类感谢信是因为他人记住了关于你的某件事，你想向他们表达谢意。这表明你们之间已足够熟悉，或足够亲密，因此语言无须那么正式。表达谢意是你此时的想法，因此时态需要选用一般现在时，但提及已经发生的事情时需要使用过去时。例如：

例 9

Dear Philip,

How can I thank you enough for remembering my graduation? The words you put in your greeting card really sounded special. You really touched me. It made my graduation an even more special occasion than it was.

With great appreciation,

Helen

 解读 这是一封为了感谢朋友记得自己毕业时间而写的私人信件。从称呼 Dear Philip 及结尾的署名 Helen 看出他们关系亲密，信件也没有使用"Sincerely yours,"之类的客套结束语。

2. 感谢他人送礼物
Thank-you Letters for a Gift

你收到的礼物可能来自熟悉的朋友或亲戚，也可能是不那么熟悉的送礼人。为了表达对送礼人的谢意，你需要根据你们关系的亲密程度来决定信件的措辞：是非常正式，还是不那么正式，又或是非正式。收到礼物是已经发生的事情，因此在感谢信中提及此事时需要使用过去时。关于如何使用这件礼物或对礼物的想法，可以选用一般现在时；如果你的想法涉及未来打算，则需要使用将来时。例如：

例 10

Dear Mrs. Jack,

It was very kind of you and Mr. Jack to send us such a pretty gift—and such a useful one! We really love the clock radio. It is just what we needed for our study. We can now chat or read with our favorite classical music on it all the time.

We hope you and Mr. Jack will come and visit us soon, and have coffee with us in the study.

David and Ruby

> **解读** 这封感谢信的称呼为 Dear Mrs. Jack，从中可以看出写信人和收信人是关系不那么亲密的朋友。David 和 Ruby 的写信目的是感谢 Mrs. Jack 和 Mr. Jack 送上的一份特别礼物，并表达非常喜欢这份礼物。虽然信中没有使用结束语，但是通过邀请对方来家里喝咖啡，同样表达了他们的极大谢意。

3. 感谢他人接受拜访
Thank-you Letters for a Visit

你去拜访朋友或亲戚，甚至在那儿小住，这表明你们之间足够熟悉与亲密。为了表达谢意，你需要及时写一封自然且真诚的感谢信。信件所使用的语言可以根据你与收信人的亲密程度来合理选择。拜访一事既已发生，则需要使用过去时来简短叙述；关于现在的想法或相处下来的感受，则可选用一般现在时来表达。例如：

例 11

Dear Allen,

I'm safely home and I want to thank you very much for the wonderful time I had at your home. My visit with you was both relaxing and entertaining. Your home is lovely, and your cooking was terrific.

I hope that I can soon repay your hospitality. Please feel free to visit me whenever you get the opportunity.

Gratefully yours,

Lawrence

> **解读** 这封感谢信与例 9 的相似之处是称呼均较为亲密，略有不同的是它的结束语相对正式一些。正如前文所说，使用"Gratefully yours,"可以表达出写信人对收信人衷心的感谢。

4. 感谢他人提供帮助
Thank-you Letters for a Favor

为了感激他人提供帮助的感谢信，同样需要根据你与收信人的亲密程度来选择适当的语言。如果对方是长者或老师，你所使用的语言与你写给朋友的感谢信肯定是不一样的。在动词时态的选择上，需要特别注意事情发生的时间是指向将来、现在还是过去。例如：

例12

Dear Dr. Schnur,

I am writing to tell you how very kind of you to send me the list of reference books. They are exactly what I need for my thesis.

When I was going through the book list yesterday, I realized how much time you have saved me. As a matter of fact, I had been looking for those books in the library for quite a while, but without any luck. Now here they are in the mail from a mentor as well as a friend.

I feel deeply indebted to you and I really don't know how to thank you enough for your help.

Sincerely yours,

Guoling

解读 这封感谢信的致谢对象是老师，从称呼与结束语可以看出措辞比较正式。正文第一句就表达了感谢原因，即老师提供了写论文所需的参考书目。写信人还在结尾部分再次表达了自己的感激之情。

二、写感谢信的经验法则
Rules of Thumb About Letter Writing

在写感谢信时，你需要记住以下要点：致信对象决定了你该采用非常正式或不那么正式或非正式的语言；写作目的是要真诚地感谢致谢对象；说清楚为何感谢对方；正确使用感谢信的格式。以下是写感谢信时可供参考的一些经验法则：

第一，书写自然（write naturally）。就好像在和致信对象说话一样，写信时可以使用简单明了的语言。记住，你是在对话而不是在写作文，所以应该使用脑海中第一时间浮现的那些词。

第二，简化常用的信头和问候（simplify the usual heading and salutation）。日期，加上 Dear John 或者 Dear Mom 就足够了。

第三，不要害怕语言错误（don't be afraid of making mistakes）。虽然写完信后进行重读是必要的，但不必太在意语言错误，只要不让对方误解就可以。

第四，没有固定的长度（there's no fixed length）。作为私人信件，感谢信应该长短适宜，比如可以跳过不必要的细节、事实和数字等。

第五，写感谢信要及时（give a timely reply）。这更能体现你的礼貌与真诚，还可以省去因写信不及时而做道歉说明。

第三节 商务信函的写作策略
Strategies for Writing Business Letters

与感谢信相比，求职信内容丰富、篇幅较长，致信对象是未来的雇主，写信目的是应聘某一职位，因此采用的语言会正式一些。本节会先介绍求职信写作的三个关键要素，再从过程性写作的角度分析如何结合这些要素撰写求职信。在写作过程中，请牢记你的读者对象与写作目的，考虑未来雇主需要哪些信息，并仔细考量信件的内容和语言风格，以实现既有意义又得体的交流。

一、求职信的写作要素
Essentials in Writing Job Application Letters

求职信的目的是使未来雇主相信你是适合某个岗位的最佳人选，因此在信件开头需要明确说明你申请的职位。

由于致信对象是未来的雇主，你在写信时应该认真考虑他们的需求，了解清楚具体的岗位要求。对此你需要提前做好功课，比如访问公司网站以尽可能多地了解这份工作的具体职责；又比如关注工作内容描述和人员要求细则，做到有效地"推销"自己。

可以说，写求职信就是"推销"自己，以最能满足雇主需求的方式介绍自己，并展示潜力。当你试图在信中"推销"自己时，请记住以下三点：

第一，相关性（be relevant）。通常雇主最关注的是这三件事：你的经验、技能以及个性，你不需要面面俱到、解释一切。求职信需要突出与工作相关的要点，以证明你符合基本要求。

第二，可迁移性（be transferable）。有时你会觉得自己的经历与雇主要求的并不那么匹配。在这种情况下，你需要转换思考，从"技能"的角度为自己找到一些可迁移的技能。可迁移的技能可以在不同岗位上发挥作用，并助你为所求职位作出贡献。找到这些技能，并将它们与所求职位的职责联系起来，这是非常重要的，可以帮助你更有力地证明自己是最佳人选。

第三，诚实可信（be honest）。永远不要撒谎。人们总想以最好的方式展示自己，但记住，绝不能歪曲事实或过分夸大，而应该保持诚实。当然，有时你可以转换叙事角度。假设你还没拿到计算机等级考试合格证书，你不用说"我还没拿到计算机二级证书"，而可以说"我系统学习过 Office 办公软件系统，现仍在继续学习以达到熟练精进"。你仍然诚实，也没有撒谎，不同的是，你突出了消极事件的积极方面。

二、求职信的写作过程
Development of Job Application Letters

求职信正文的写作是信函的核心部分，共分为三个步骤。

1. 写前活动
Pre-writing Activities

当你开始思考求职信的写作目的、致信对象和组成部分，以及如何根据招聘要求来选取相关经历时，你就是在做写作前的准备工作了。

写前活动有两个要点：（1）明确写信目的，即为了申请特定的工作或职位，这必须在开头明确说明，因为你的最终目的是说服未来雇主邀请你去面试，并获得工作；（2）考虑信件的组成部分，一封完整、有说服力的信件需要包含开头、中间和结尾部分。

在开始求职信的写作时，可以按照商务信函的七个组成部分分步骤完成，并在完成后进行重读、修改和订正。

2. 撰写求职信
Writing Activities

下面将重点讨论如何撰写求职信的正文部分。

1）开头部分（Beginning Part）

在开头部分，你需要清楚地说明写信的原因，即申请的是哪个职位，以及何时何地得知这条招聘信息的。例如：

例 13

With reference to / In answer to / In reply to / Referring to your advertisement in *Shenzhen Special Zone Daily* of December 12 for a certified public accountant, I offer myself for the post / I wish to render my services.

例 14

Your advertisement for a certified public accountant in *Shenzhen Special Zone Daily* of December 12 has interested/intrigued me very much. I feel I can fill that vacancy / I feel I am the right person you are seeking.

例 15

Learning from http://www.chinahr.com that you are looking for a certified public accountant, I am sending a letter of application for the position together with my résumé by e-mail.

例 16

I am applying to be the trainee accountant. It was advertised in my college careers office. Please find my résumé attached.

例 17

Having noticed the advertisement in *Shenzhen Special Zone Daily* of November 1, I wish to apply for a part-time job as a salesgirl for your beauty products.

以上示例只是帮你初步了解开头段落的写作方式。你也可以采用与众不同的方式，比如用问句开头以吸引雇主的注意。例如：

例 18

Are you looking for someone who works well with people of all nationalities and backgrounds? Are you looking for a person who enjoys assisting individuals from diverse cultures and who is strongly interested in international relations? I will bring these qualities and more to the position of Assistant Director for International Studies that you posted on July 3, 2021 on the Internet Job Website.

请记住，无论选择以何种方式开头，你都必须在这部分交代清楚申请的职位以及获得招聘信息的途径。

2）中间部分（Middle Part）

中间部分包括两段或两段以上关于自己的详情介绍，包括与职位相关或相匹配的经验、技能和性格特点等优势。你应该清楚地阐述为什么你与这份工作非常匹配，你能为这份工作作出什么贡献。你要强调的是你能如何使公司获利，而不是单从公司获益。以下是关于求职信中间部分的写作建议：

第一，尽量使用招聘信息中出现的术语和短语（try to use the same terms and phrases as those used in a job description），这能清楚地表明你有能力做好这份工作。它们是关键词（key words）或触发词（trigger words），可以帮助你更有机会被注意到。

第二，描述工作经验时要具体而不是泛泛而谈（be specific rather than general when you describe your working experience）。例如，你可以写"我过去三年在工作

中都使用 Excel 表格"，而不是"我有三年的计算经验"。

第三，跟进之前提过的优势（follow up your general claim），即用具体的示例说明你拥有某种技能和经验来胜任这份工作。

第四，始终关心雇主的需求（take the "You" attitude），并根据这些需求来介绍你的技能。例如，相比于"我可以说流利的英语和西班牙语"，"许多客户会说英语或西班牙语，而我精通这些语言，具有良好的沟通技巧，能有效地满足这方面业务的需求"会更有说服力。

第五，如果附件中有简历，记得提及（make a reference to your résumé）。

若你在申请工作时缺乏相关的实习经验或工作技能，请记住你的学校生活或活动也可以是你的亮点，比如兼职经历或志愿者工作也值得一提。更重要的是，若从技能的角度看待你的学校生活或活动，你会发现有些技能是可迁移的，这会让你看起来和富有工作经验的求职者一样值得雇用。例如：

例 19

During my four years at college, I volunteered to work at the university radio station. As a radio news broadcaster using both Chinese and English, I sharpened my language, leadership, and teamwork skills. Please let me put my energy and skills to work for you.

解读 这位学生巧妙地强调他在学校活动中获得的技能（sharpened language, leadership, and teamwork sills），这使他有可能把这些技能从"电台新闻播音员"转移到他想要的新职位上。

3）结尾部分（Ending Part）

你可以在结尾部分用礼貌和愉快的方式总结所有的信息，包括感谢对方付出的时间和精力、提及你希望得到的反馈等。例如，你可以说自己非常期待面试，并提供准确的联系方式，以便雇主能及时联系到你。一个典型的结尾段落如例 20 所示：

例 20

Please give me the opportunity to discuss how my qualifications have prepared me for the position. I can be reached through e-mail at emily@sina.com or at 133-5678-9100 to schedule an interview. Thank you for your time and consideration.

在完成正文这三部分之后，再加上其余六个部分（信头、信内地址、称呼、结束语、署名、附件)，一封完整且正式的求职信就基本完成了。

3. 写后活动
Post-writing Activities

为了确保信件内容准确无误，且令人印象深刻，你还需要进行写后活动，即修改和完善已完成的写作内容，包括呈现形式与语言风格等。简单地说，你需要仔细检查信件内容，让雇主从信中看出你是一个具有良好沟通技巧的候选人。求职信需要尽可能完美，不能有丝毫差错，否则这将影响你的求职结果。检查信件时，请注意以下三个方面：

1) 内容是否得体（Decency in Content）

首先需要检查内容部分，确保所有内容都得体，且是必要的、相关的和有效的，并无多余的信息。下面是一个检查列表：

- 你是否在开头就明确说明了你的目标职位？
- 你是否只提供了必要的、相关的细节？你是否提供了任何不必要的或不相关的信息？
- 你是否遗漏了任何有用的信息？
- 你是否明确表示了你可以作出很多贡献？
- 你是否展示了可迁移的技能？
- 你是否表示愿意来参加面试？
- 你是否表现得自信、准备充分、彬彬有礼和专业？

2) 形式是否得体（Decency in Form）

雇主不仅对内容感兴趣，也对你的信件外观感兴趣。你需要检查信件形式是否得体，确保它布局良好，并对雇主具有吸引力。试问自己以下问题：

- 它是一封商业信函吗？必备的六个部分都包含了吗？
- 它的长度合适吗？（最好不超过一页）
- 字体会不会太花哨或浮夸？（尽量选择 Times New Roman）
- 字号是否大小合适？（可读大小通常为 12 pt.）
- 信件是否用要点或下划线来突出重要元素了？
- 信件的纸张是否质量良好？

3) 语言是否得体（Decency in Language）

信件内容会直接反映你的写作能力。如果雇主遇到写得不好的求职信，他甚至会懒得通读。务必确保你的信件用语得体、准确、无差错，你可以根据以下问题进行自查：

- 有些单词或短语是否会让读者感到困惑，甚至被误导？
- 有没有长篇大论的句子？比如有些表达其实用五个词就可以，而你却用了十个词？
- 有些部分是否需要使用连接词，以帮助读者轻松地跟上你的思路？
- 有些言语或表达方式是否不礼貌或具有负面的含义？
- 是否有单词拼写错误、句子不合语法规范、姓名或地址不准确或标点符号错误等问题？

第四节　以读促写应用文
Reading for Practical Writing

以读促写是一个能帮助提高写作技能的实用策略，尤其在评估和修改信件内容方面。本节将按照分析性阅读的 10 个步骤来分析两篇应用文，包括一封感谢信和一封求职信。

例 21　感谢信

11 Mulberry Road

Islip, New York 11751

July 2, 2019

Dear Aunt Grace,

Thank you for the subscription to *Popular Mechanics*. Someone must have told you that it is my favorite magazine; and, of course, you know my weakness for putting things together.

Every month the arrival of a new copy will mean new projects and seeing the new magazine will remind me of your kindness. You couldn't have chosen a better present for me.

Gratefully yours,

Elena

分析性阅读讲解

第1步： 留意出版信息和作者介绍。这是一封感谢信。

第2步： 注意文章标题是如何引出主题的。感谢信属于私人信件，没有信头，不需要标题。

第3步： 第一遍阅读文章，并写下你对文章的大致印象。通读之后可以得知，Elena 感谢姑姑/姨妈为她征订了一本杂志，说明每个月收到杂志对她的意义，并表示这是姑姑/姨妈送她的最好的礼物（You couldn't have chosen a better present for me.）。

第4步： 再次查看标题和介绍性段落。查看感谢信的开头段落，可以看到 Elena 清楚地说明了主题，即"感谢姑姑/姨妈为她征订杂志"（Thank you for the subscription to *Popular Mechanics*.）。

第5步： 找到作者的要点或主旨。Elena 的主要观点就是要感谢姑姑/姨妈，她在感谢信的第一句就阐明了——"Thank you for the subscription to *Popular Mechanics*."。

第6步： 查找支持或说明主旨的重要语句。Elena 感谢姑姑/姨妈征订杂志，因为那是她最喜欢的杂志（Someone must have told you that it is my favorite magazine.）。

第7步： 分析作者是如何推进主题的，又是如何发展、解释或论证支持性观点的。Elena 先说姑姑/姨妈帮她订的杂志是她最喜欢的杂志，而且说到姑姑/姨妈了解她不太会组装东西（You know my weakness for putting things together.），暗示这本杂志或许会对她有帮助。

第8步： 查看文章的布局和组织形式。这封感谢信里包含私人信件的五个基本部分：信内地址、称呼、正文、结束语和署名。

第9步： 分析文章的推进是否有逻辑性和连贯性。这封感谢信正文有两段：第一段明确说明写信的目的是感谢姑姑/姨妈帮她征订了最喜欢的杂志，也说明姑姑/姨妈了解她的弱点；第二段陈述了每个月收到杂志会让她想到姑姑/姨妈对她的好（remind me of your kindness）。整体逻辑清晰，语意连贯，分段得当。此外，Elena 表示"没有比这更好的礼物"，可见她非常感谢姑姑/姨妈的礼物。

第10步： 思考作者的风格和文章的语气。Elena 的致信对象是她的长辈。为了表达自己的感谢，她在信件的结束语采用了相对比较正式的形式"Gratefully yours,"。这样的表达体现了 Elena 的尊重与诚挚，适合本文的致信对象。

例22 求职信

School of Foreign Languages

Sichuan Normal University

Chengdu, Sichuan 610066

January 6, 2018

Ms. Serena Fang

Personnel Manager

World Trade Corporation

5398 Shangri La Road

Shanghai 200120

Dear Ms. Fang,

1   Your Friday's advertisement in the Business Internet Connection informed me of your entry-level position of Assistant Manager of Foreign Trade Operations. After a self-evaluation with your criteria, I feel confident about being the person you are seeking.

2   Ten years of reading business magazines and newspapers in English, six years of private tutoring by native English speakers, and four years of college classes in business and international trade that were all taught in English have provided me with efficient written and oral English. My knowledge of English and business continues to expand through daily listening to business news broadcasts on the Internet.

3   As a part-time commercial radio broadcaster, I use both Chinese and English and continue to sharpen my communication skills. I financed all four years of my tuition by working part-time. I can also bring to your company a responsible attitude and a deep respect for teamwork.

4   From the enclosed résumé, you can also get detailed information about my excellent grades in college and extensive organizational experiences.

5   Please consider me for this position. I can be reached through e-mail at mary66@hotmail.com or at (028) 8267-0923 from 1 p.m. to 6 p.m. to schedule an interview to discuss how my qualifications can meet the needs of your assistant manager position. Thank you for your time and consideration.

Sincerely,

Wang Hai

Enc.: résumé

分析性阅读讲解

第 1 步： 留意出版信息和作者介绍。这是一封针对招聘广告的求职信。

第 2 步： 注意文章标题是如何引出主题的。求职信不需要标题。

第 3 步： 第一遍阅读文章，并写下你对文章的大致印象。通读之后可以得知，Wang Hai 应聘外贸业务助理经理一职（entry-level position of Assistant Manager of Foreign Trade Operations），并介绍了他的资历和技能。

第 4 步： 再次查看标题和介绍性段落。开头第一段清楚地说明了目标岗位，并体现了以下三点：（1）Wang Hai 仔细研究过这份工作（self-evaluation）；（2）他认真思考过这份工作有哪些要求（your criteria）；（3）他有信心（feel confident）。

第 5 步： 找到作者的要点或主旨。Wang Hai 的观点是他想要这份工作，并相信自己有资格胜任这份工作，比如第一段中提到"I feel confident about being the person you are seeking."，第五段提到"...my qualifications can meet the needs of your assistant manager position."。

第 6 步： 查找支持或说明主旨的重要语句。信中主要有三个支撑性观点：（1）第二段中提到的具备英语和商业知识（knowledge of English and business）；（2）第三段中把做双语主持人的经历和四年的兼职经历迁移到新职位所需的沟通技巧（communication skills）、责任感和团队合作精神 (a responsible attitude and a deep respect for teamwork)，这将有利于其应聘；（3）第四段中提到简历里的"...my excellent grades in college and extensive organizational experiences."。

第 7 步： 分析作者是如何推进主题的，又是如何发展、解释或论证支持性观点的。第二段中，Wang Hai 通过提供示例来支持说明自己如何具备英语和商业知识，如 ten years of reading business magazines and newspapers in English、six years of private tutoring by native English speakers、four years of college classes in business and international trade that were all taught in English、daily listening to business news broadcasts on the Internet。第三段则说明做双语主持等兼职经历培养的技能，比如沟通、责任感和团队合作。第四段则准备了简历，包含成绩与就读期间的活动经历。

第 8 步： 查看文章的布局和组织形式。Wang Hai 用商务信函的形式撰写信件，涵盖了详细的个人基本信息，包括第四段中提及的所附简历。

第 9 步： 分析文章的推进是否有逻辑性和连贯性。这封信合乎逻辑且具有连贯。具体来说，它遵循了重要程度的逻辑顺序，第二段的信息最重要，第三、第四段次之，构成了一个完整有序的整体。第二、第三段主要围绕个人相关能力展开，第四段使用过渡性词语 also 以引出简历中的内容，实现了语言层面的聚焦和逻辑层面的连贯。

第 10 步： 思考作者的风格和文章的语气。这封信是正式信函，语气热情、自信、礼貌，同时具有专业性，契合求职信的目的，即让雇主相信他是这份工作的最佳人选。

Exercises

I.   Write a thank-you note for someone remembering your graduation, your birthday, or when you were ill. In your letter, you will express gratitude for his/her remembering you on a certain occasion and state clearly that you like whatever you have been given as a token of remembrance.

II.   Write a thank-you note for the gift given by someone. In your letter, you will express thanks for the gift and state clearly how much you like it.

III.   Write a thank-you note for the visit you paid to someone's place. In your letter, you will state how pleased you were with the visit and then give thanks for the hospitality showed to you and tell you had a good time there.

IV.   Write a thank-you note for the help given by someone. In your letter, you will express thanks for the help you received and stress your appreciation of the time he/she spent or the trouble he/she had in helping you.

V.   Read the following advertisement and then complete the tasks.

Job Vacancy

    Flute and Saxophone Tutor (Independent Providers)

Your Role

    At DCIS we have an established Instrumental Music Program and are looking to expand our lessons specifically with a flute and saxophone specialist. Your role would be to engage children in individual instrumental lessons and to encourage a passion for learning music. Lessons are held on a weekly basis and we ask that tutors commit to the same working hours each week for the duration of the year. These will be agreed upon with the successful applicant in advance. In addition to weekly lessons, tutors are key in helping students to prepare for any live/virtual performances, recitals, and examinations where applicable.

Requirements

- Degree or relevant professional qualification;

- Passion for music and teaching;

- Experience in teaching in a school environment is preferred;

- A positive working attitude and good time management skills are essential.

Selection Process

Please send your CV to music.admin@dovercourt.edu.sg.

The closing date for application is May 14, 2021. Interviews will take place in person soon afterwards.

All post holders in any regulated activity (having regular unsupervised contact with children) are subject to appropriate national and international vetting procedures and will be asked to complete safeguarding training before commencement in the role. Applicants must be able to demonstrate that they are eligible to work as an instrument teacher in Singapore.

Work Location

Dover Court International School, Singapore.

1. Write a job application letter to apply for the position.

2. After you have produced your first draft of the application letter, revise it in terms of purpose, audience, content, format, and language based on the checklist below. Please tick the box if your answer to the question is yes.

No.	Checklist for Self-evaluation	Yes
1)	Have I demonstrated a clear writing purpose and a good awareness of the audience?	
2)	Have I provided the qualifications required in the advertisement?	
3)	Have I presented only the necessary or relevant details to show that I am qualified for the position advertised?	
4)	Have I used transitional words or phrases to help the readers follow my train of thought?	
5)	Have I demonstrated appropriate register?	
6)	Is my language error-free?	
7)	Is it a business letter with all the essential six parts right in place?	
8)	Is the length appropriate?	
9)	Is the font used appropriate for the readers?	
10)	Is the text size right for the readers?	

3. Then review one or more peer essays in terms of purpose, audience, content, format, and language based on the checklist below. Please tick the box if your answer to the question is yes.

No.	Checklist for Peer Review	Yes
1)	Has the author demonstrated a clear writing purpose, and a good awareness of the audience?	
2)	Has the author provided the qualifications required in the advertisement?	
3)	Has the author presented only the necessary or relevant details to show that he/she is qualified for the position advertised?	
4)	Has the author used transitional words or phrases to help the readers follow his/her train of thought?	
5)	Has the author demonstrated appropriate register?	
6)	Is the author's language error-free?	
7)	Is it a business letter with all the essential six parts right in place?	
8)	Is the length appropriate?	
9)	Is the font used appropriate for the readers?	
10)	Is the text size right for the readers?	

Sample

范文 1 感谢远方的朋友赠送礼物

Dear C. H.,

How very kind of you to send me such a beautiful hand-painted silk scarf! The colors are lovely and exactly right for a two-piece dress I have just bought for such occasions as visits to Hong Kong and a lecture tour of Holland I did recently.

Don't think I need it to remind me of you—every morning I walk round the property and see how things are growing—Huang's plot (the one you helped cut weeds in) is a great deal tidier than last year. We still have an enormous amount to do, but it is lovely work and we derive untold satisfaction from living in the country tending our little plot of land.

Yours ever,

Barbara

范文 2 感谢朋友探访病情

Dear Joyce,

Now that I finally feel fit to sit up and write letters, I'd like to thank you for the flowers and books you sent me during my recovery from the car injury, and, most of all, for the many errands you ran to the grocery store and the numerous pages of lecture notes you shared with me for the classes I missed. You have no idea how much all this meant to me—a student from a foreign land with no relatives and few friends around.

You have been more than kind, and I won't ever forget it. Please accept my heartfelt thanks and deepest gratitude, now and always.

Taiko

范文 3 求职信

P.O. Box 36

Tsinghua University

Beijing, China 10084

April 13, 2019

P.O. Box 173

Publishing House of Electronics Industry

Wanshou Road, Haidian District

Beijing, China 10036

Dear Sir or Madam,

Your advertisement for a Network Maintenance Engineer in the April 10 *Beijing Daily* interested me because the position that you described sounds exactly like the kind of job I am seeking.

According to the advertisement, you position requires a B.S. or higher degree holder from a key university in Computer Science or relevant fields proficient in

Windows NT and Linus System. I feel that I meet the requirements. I will be graduating from Tsinghua University this year with an M.Sc. degree. My studies have included courses in computer control and management, and last year I participated in the design and development of a simulated control system for pressing air.

During my education, I have grasped the principles of my major and skills of practice. Not only have I passed CET-6, but also more importantly I can communicate with others freely in English. My abilities to write and speak English are both at a high level.

I would appreciate your time in reviewing my enclosed résumé and if there is any additional information you require, please contact me. I would welcome an opportunity for a personal interview.

Yours respectfully,

Wang Ming

第四章

记叙文写作
Telling Your Stories—Narrative Writing

学习要点

- 记叙文的概念和结构
- 记叙文的交际性写作
- 记叙文的五个要素
- 记叙文的写作策略
- 记叙文的分析性阅读

 第一节 记叙文写作概述
Introduction to Narrative Writing

一、记叙文的概念
 Concept of Narrative Writing

记叙文，又称叙述文或记事文，是按照时间顺序来叙述人物的经历，事情的产生、发展和变化过程的文章。记叙文是最常见和应用最广泛的一种文体，也是其他各类文章写作的基础，比如描写文、议论文、说明文等都有叙事的成分。记叙文可以分为虚构（fiction）和非虚构（non-fiction）两大类。

二、记叙文的结构
 Basic Structure of Narrative Writing

记叙文的基本结构包括三个部分：开头、正文和结尾，下文将借助 Savage & Mayer（2005：58）提出的记叙文结构来说明每个部分的功能和要求。

Introduction

- The hook gets the reader's attention.
- The middle sentences introduce an event by providing background information about the people, the place, and the time.
- The thesis statement prepares the reader for the action that follows.

Body Paragraphs

- The body paragraphs describe what happens in the story.
- They include details that bring the story to life.
- They often use time order to explain the event.

Conclusion

- A conclusion describes the outcome of the event.
- It often ends with a comment by the writer about what the event shows or teaches.

开头部分应提供关于人、地点和时间等的信息，也就是故事的背景，但最重要的是，开头需要像钓鱼一样抛出一个钩子（hook）来抓住读者的注意力，吸引他们追随故事的发展。正文部分描述了故事中发生的事件，包括使故事生动的细节，通常按照时间顺序展开。结尾部分描述了故事的结局，作者通常在这一部分对故事想要传达的思想进行评论以升华主题。

三、记叙文的交际性写作
Communicative Writing in Narration

在学习交际性写作的过程中，不论使用哪一种体裁，你都应该充分考虑写作目的，并主动树立读者意识，即为目标读者着想和服务的意识。具体来说，你应该了解读者的个体特征和群体特征，推测他们对作品的期待视野和信息需求，并以此为基础，制定合理的写作策略，满足不同层次读者的多元化需求（崔长青，2010）。

记叙文面向的读者是谁？你打算通过这篇记叙文向读者传达什么信息？你的写作目的是写一篇完整的叙事文，还是在议论文或描写文当中插入一个叙事段落？记叙文写作可以用虚构的方式讲述一个完整的引人入胜的故事，也可以用一个非虚构的叙事段落作为说明文的补充或者议论文的例证。

不论是哪种写作目的，最终文章都应该用一种有趣的、具有说服力的方式来跟读者交流。为了更好地实现写作目的，你需要考虑记叙文的写作要素，也就是 5W1H 问题，并根据写作目的来选择和组织材料，更好地把故事讲述给读者，实现记叙文写作的交际性。

第二节 记叙文写作要素
Major Elements of Narrative Writing

记叙文写作需要回答 5W1H（who, when, where, what, why, and how）这些常见的问题，换言之，人物、场景、情节、主题和观点（character, setting, plot, theme, and point of view）就是作者要传达给读者的最重要的元素。

本节将以著名短篇小说家欧·亨利（O. Henry）的作品《最后一片叶子》（*The Last Leaf*）为例来分析上述主要元素，以帮助你更好地理解与掌握记叙文的交际性写作。该作品讲述了一位老画家为患有肺炎的奄奄一息的穷学生画最后一片常春藤叶的故事。

一、人物
Character

人物是记叙文写作的核心，因为故事都是围绕着人物展开的。记叙文的主人公被称为主角（protagonist），主角可以有一个或多个；其他角色称为配角（supporting characters），他们可以衬托对主角的描写。

无论是幻想中的虚构人物，还是历史事件中的真实人物，作者都希望这些人物可以鲜活地呈现在读者眼前，还希望读者能够真正关心他们塑造的人物。想想你喜欢的那些故事或小说中的人物，他们的长相如何？性格如何？你为什么会喜欢他们？你在写作时同样需要考虑这些问题，并尝试用有吸引力的方式向读者展现主人公的角色特征，这正是作者与读者进行有效交流的重要途径。

怎样才能把鲜活可信的人物展现给读者呢？接下来将用例文来说明角色塑造的几个要素。

1. 外貌描写
What the Characters Look like

外貌描写是介绍和定义人物最基本的方法之一。例如：

例1

Old Behrman was a painter who lived on the ground floor beneath them. He was past sixty and had a long white beard curling down over his chest.

 解读 例1中对胡须的描写塑造了一个老艺术家的生动形象，而这与文后展示出来的 Old Behrman 的形象大相径庭，这样强烈的对比自然可以给读者留下深刻印象。

2. 语言描写
What the Characters Say

语言描写是一种非常有力的刻画人物的方法。例如:

例 2

"Your little lady has made up her mind that she's not going to get well. Has she anything on her mind?"

"She-she wanted to paint the Bay of Naples someday", said Sue.

"Paint? -Bosh! Has she anything on her mind worth thinking about twice—a man, for instance?".

"A man?" said Sue. "Is a man worth—but, no, doctor; there is nothing of that kind."

解读 例 2 中,作者通过对话描写,以非常微妙的方式(极少的形容词)向读者传达了丰富的内容。读者可以看到,医生持有大男子主义思想,这在故事发生的那个年代是非常普遍的现象,而女孩则是一个相当独立的女性形象。

3. 动作描写
What the Characters Do

人物的行为举止,无论是个人动作还是对其他角色的动作作出的反应,都是角色塑造的一个关键因素。例如:

例 3

After the doctor had gone, Sue went into the workroom and cried a Japanese napkin to a pulp. Then she swaggered into Johnsy's room with her drawing board, whistling ragtime.

解读 例 3 中,在得知 Johnsy 得了肺炎且痊愈的可能性不大之后,Sue 虽然悲痛欲绝,但在 Johnsy 面前还是尽量表现得镇定自若,以免让她更加沮丧。仅仅通过几个动词,读者就能感受到 Sue 的积极乐观以及她对 Johnsy 的关心。

4. 心理描写
What the Characters Think or Feel

作者可以对人物的心理活动进行直接的心理描写或者通过人物的语言和行为进行间接的心理描写。例如:

例 4

"Dear, dear!" said Sue, leaning her worn face down to the pillow, "think of me, if you won't think of yourself. What would I do?"

But Johnsy did not answer. The lonesomest thing in all the world is a soul when it is making ready to go on its mysterious, far journey. The fancy seemed to possess her more strongly as one by one the ties that bound her to friendship and to earth were loosed.

解读 例 4 中，当 Johnsy 看到窗外常青藤的叶子只剩下一片时，她认为自己必死无疑了，连 Sue 的真情呼唤也无法唤起她的求生意志。这里的心理描写表现了 Johnsy 内心的生无可恋。

二、场景
Setting

场景包括时间、地点和情境等主要内容，这些描写既可以交代故事背景、渲染氛围，也可以衬托人物的情感、性格等。用一些方法来巧妙地设置场景以提高读者的阅读兴趣，也是记叙文交际性写作的体现。例如：

例 5

At the top of a squatty, three-story brick Sue and Johnsy had their studio. "Johnsy" was familiar for Joanna. One was from Maine; the other from California. They had met at the table d'hote of an English street "Delmonico's," and found their tastes in art, chicory salad and bishop sleeves so congenial that the joint studio resulted.

In November a cold, unseen stranger, whom the doctors called Pneumonia, stalked about the neighborhood, touching one here and there with his icy fingers. Johnsy was among his victims.

解读 例 5 是小说的开头部分，向读者介绍了人物、地点、时间等故事发生的背景。除了对两位主人公的简单介绍以外，开头部分很快引出了故事的矛盾冲突：Johnsy 得了肺炎——在那个时代肺炎是一种致命的疾病，那她的命运将会如何呢？这样的场景设定一下子就引起了读者的兴趣。

三、情节
Plot

情节是人物在冲突情境中贯穿整个故事的一系列事件，可以体现记叙文中一个或多个人物之间的关系。情节中包含的冲突可以是内在的（人与自我），也可以是外在的（人与人、人与自然、人与社会、人与命运等），并且一个故事当中可能存在多个冲突。

德国小说家 Gustav Freytag 认为，小说的情节可以分为五个要素：介绍、发展、高潮、回落和结局（exposition, rising action, climax, falling action, and resolution），如图 4.1 所示：

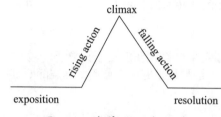

图 4.1　情节的五个要素

Five elements of plot:

- Exposition: the introduction of a story, the background information needed to properly understand the story.
- Rising action: the events leading up to the climax.
- The climax: the most exciting part of the story.
- The falling action: the events occurring right after the climax.
- Resolution: the end of the falling action and the conclusion to the story.

—cited from *Writing Critically (1): Narrative Writing*

这五个要素的组织顺序可以略有不同，也就是说，在实际写作时并不需要一步步严格遵循这一顺序或具备所有要素。通常情况下，故事会围绕冲突展开，并在一系列事件的积累之后逐渐达到叙事高潮。

 四、　主题
Theme

在你孩童时期听到的或读到的众多故事中，故事结尾经常有这样一句话："这个故事告诉我们……"，这是故事想要传达给读者的中心思想，也是记叙文的另一个主要元素——主题。主题是叙事写作的中心思想，是作者想与读者交流的最重要的内容。那么应该如何揭示和发展这个主题呢？

1.　如何通过叙事揭示主题？
How Is Theme Revealed Through Narration?

主题是叙事写作的灵魂，作者可以通过不同的写作技巧来传达给读者。一般来说，它可以是明显的，也可以是隐含的。前者是指作者用直接的方式来表达想与读者分享的主题或观点；后者是指作者没有直接告诉读者主题，而是把主题编织进了情节发展和人物塑造当中。例如，在小说《最后一片叶子》中，主题是通过故事的展开来含蓄地传达的：当读者读到小说的最后一句 "Ah, darling, it's Behrman's masterpiece—he painted it there the night that the last leaf fell." 时，再联系上文就会恍然大悟，终于了解"杰作"（masterpiece）的真正意义和故事的真相，从而理解作者想要传递的中心思想。

2. 如何发展叙事写作的主题?
How to Develop Theme in Narrative Writing?

主题通常植根于人们的动机、情感和关系，是故事的灵魂。就像看电影一样，无论视觉效果如何惊人，你仍然期待着电影想要传达的"意义"；当你与电影中的人物惺惺相惜时，会更加能够体会电影的主旨。

虽然在写作中揭示主题并不需要特别的技巧，但如果作者有目的地传达一个主题，文章就会更有深度。例如在小说《最后一片叶子》中，当得知看似颓废的老画家用生命拯救了 Johnsy 时，那种恍然大悟又感慨万千的感觉，正是作者借助写作技巧有目的地向读者传达的中心思想。为了更好地与读者交流，你可以巧妙地把主题隐藏在情节当中，但绝不能给读者呈现一篇没有"灵魂"的记叙文。

五、叙事角度
Point of View

叙事角度是指在记叙文写作中通过选择不同的视角来决定读者如何获取信息，也就是以谁的角度来讲述故事。最常见的两种叙事角度是第一人称叙事（first person point of view）和第三人称叙事（third person point of view），其中第三人称视角在记叙文写作中十分普遍。一般来说，叙述者只是描述故事本身，并不会对此做过多评判。例如：

例 6

At the top of a squatty, three-story brick Sue and Johnsy had their studio. "Johnsy" was familiar for Joanna. One was from Maine; the other from California. They had met at the table d'hote of an English street "Delmonico's" and found their tastes in art, chicory salad and bishop sleeves so congenial that the joint studio resulted.

解读 例 6 是小说的开头部分，主要讲述了两位主人公是如何相遇的。第三人称视角的叙述会让作者和故事之间有一定的距离感，而且不会妨碍读者对人物和情节的理解。

记叙文写作也可以使用第一人称视角。在这一视角下，叙述者"我"可以是作者，也可以是人物之一。例如：

例 7

Early on the morning of August 19, 1946, I was born under a clear sky after a violent summer storm to a widowed other in the Julia Chester Hospital in Hope, a town of about six thousand in southwest Arkansas, thirty-three miles east of the Texas border at Texarkana.

—My Life by Bill Clinton

解读 第一人称叙事在自传中十分常见。当作者讲述自己的亲身经历或用一段故事来证明某个论点时，经常会选择第一人称叙事，这会使文章读起来更加真实生动。例 7 中，克林顿用了第一人称来讲述自己出生的时间和地点。

第三节 记叙文写作策略
Strategies for Narrative Writing

为达到有效的交际目的，并更好地与读者互动，记叙文每一部分的写作都需要采取一些有用的策略。本节将按照写作过程逐一讲解记叙文开头、正文和结尾的写作策略。

一、开头的写作策略
Writing Strategies for Introductory Paragraphs

首先介绍记叙文开头常见的四种写作策略，以帮助你在动笔之前考虑好导入部分。

1. 明确写作目的
Knowing Your Purpose

无论是客观的、事实性的复述还是虚构性创作，作者都应该让读者清楚地了解写作目的，避免其读到结尾处还心存疑问。写作目的是指作者通过内容想要传达的交际目的和意图。作为一种有意识有目的交际行为，明确写作目的将有助于作者选择最适合读者需要的信息和语言。

2. 选择主题并缩小其范围
Choosing Your Topic and Narrow It Down

明确写作目的之后则需要为文章选择一个主题。许多事件都可以用来传达主题，但是记叙文写作不能只是把这些事件随机地组合起来。作者需要根据写作目的来选择主题并缩小其范围，最好是某一个特定的事件。选定之后再用大量细节进行充实，以帮助读者更清楚地了解文章的主题和观点。对于以下记叙文主题，你会如何构思呢？

- Your Best/Worst First Day
- A Blessing in Disguise

对于第一个主题，你可以把它缩小到特定的事件，例如"大学开学的第一天"。A Blessing in Disguise 本身是一个很好的主题，因为它包含了本章第二节讲到的主题元素（theme），并仍给读者留下了很大的期待空间，所以你可以结合特定的事例（如你的独特经历）来叙述。

3. 选择和组织材料
Selecting and Grouping Your Materials

在确定主题之后，作者需要先进行头脑风暴（brainstorm），记录下用于写作的事件和例子，再从中选择那些最适合写作目的的材料，并根据时间顺序或其他组织方式进行分组。如果要写"大学开学的第一天"，你可以随机写下那天发生的多件事情，再从中选择最令人印象深刻的事件与读者分享。

4. 提供背景信息以吸引读者
Providing Background Information to Attract Readers

第四种写作策略是使用记叙文写作中极其重要的一个元素——场景，它通常出现在记叙文的开头部分。

具体来说，作者可以在记叙文的开头部分设计一个"钩子"来引起读者的注意，并提供必要的背景资料，比如通过回答 5W1H 问题来形成背景知识，以便让读者跟上故事的发展。例如在《最后一片叶子》开头段的短短几行文字中（详见例5），作者交代了主要人物，以及她们在哪里相遇并发生了什么。最重要的是，作者为读者设计了一个"钩子"，即主角之一的 Johnsy 感染了肺炎，这让读者不由地为她感到难过与担心。这就是记叙文写作在开头部分需要达到的目的——引起读者的注意，并让他们关心故事中的角色。

二、正文的写作策略
Writing Strategies for Body Paragraphs

正文部分使用的写作策略主要针对人物和情节，也包括如何通过适当的顺序来组织事件、推动情节。

1. 利用细节塑造角色
Using Details to Develop Your Characters

人物是记叙文写作的核心，所有的故事都围绕人物展开。那么如何成功地塑造一个人物形象呢？关键在于使用能够展示角色形象的具体词语，包括人物的外表、行为、态度、价值观和情感等。语言的具体性取决于作者的感知能力以及将这些感知转化为具体语言的能力。具体性描写可以通过形容词、副词、名词等，尤其是动词来实现。

如果想要告诉读者故事的女主人公很漂亮，作者需要让他们"看到"她明亮的眼睛、红润的脸颊和殷红的嘴唇等具体内容，而不是简单地说一句"她很漂亮"。同样的原则也适用于人物的行动及语言描写。例如：

例 8

The older she grew, the more beautiful Rapunzel became. She had blue eyes and long golden hair. It flowed from the top of her head down her back, past her feet and all along the ground.

—*Rapunzel*

解读 长发公主最突出的特点是她美丽的长发，例8中的一系列词语让读者清晰地"看到"了她美丽的长发，甚至让人想去触摸它。

例 9

The sight of the prince made the mermaid bolder. She swallowed the potion, jumped into the water...spluttered, splashed and nearly drowned. Her tail has split into legs.

—*The Little Mermaid*

解读 例9中的一系列动词向读者展示了小美人鱼在看到她心爱的王子时是多么的兴奋，以及为了和王子在一起，她如何下定决心服用巫婆的药水。

例 10

One day, Monkey was chatting to a footman. "Of course, my job is much more important than yours," he boasted. "You? You're just a groom," scoffed the footman. "You're not important." "But I'm the Great Monkey King!" Monkey snapped. "I deserve better." And he stormed out of Heaven.

—*The Monkey King*

解读 例10中的一系列动词使用得十分具体、巧妙。不仅是人物对话，还有他们对话的方式也让故事栩栩如生。"说"的不同表达方式让孙悟空这一形象变得如此真切，他是多么的骄傲自大，而当他从仆人那里得知真相时又是多么的愤怒。

从以上例子可以看出，细致具体的语言描写能表现人物的行为或性格特征，还可以帮助营造更戏剧化的故事效果。

2. 采用逻辑时序
Following a Logical Time Sequence

记叙文通常按照时间顺序来组织事件，即按照事件自然发生的顺序。当然也可以使用倒叙的方法把读者带回从前，讲述以前发生的事件。需要注意的是，使用倒叙手法时要使用相应的过渡短语或提示语句。

记叙文常使用时间短语来表明事件发生的时间顺序。除类似 "In 1985，a boy was born." 这种明显的时间短语之外，还有更多的时间短语不仅可以用来表达时间，也可以连接句子和段落。连接词可以将一段内或段落之间的句子连接起来，如 then、afterwards、after that、eventually、later on 等，还可以在复杂句中充当从属连词，如 as soon as、before、after、when、while 等时间连接词。

虽然时间顺序是记叙文写作中最常见的组织方式，但如果完全按照时间顺序来呈现事件，文章读起来可能会枯燥乏味，所以有时可以使用时态组合来表现不同事件发生的顺序。通过组合不同时态和重新排列事件，作者能够更有效地描述事件。例如：

例 11

Mary had liked to look at her mother from a distance and she had thought her very pretty, but as she knew very little of her, she could scarcely have been expected to love her or to miss her very much when she was gone. She did not miss her at all, in fact, and as she was a self-absorbed child, she gave her entire thought to herself, as she had always done. If she had been older, she would no doubt have been very anxious at being left alone in the world, but she was very young, and as she had always been taken care of, she supposed she always would be. What she thought was that she would like to know if she was going to nice people, who would be polite to her and give her own way as her Ayah and the other native servants had done.

—*The Secret Garden* by Frances Hodgson Burnett

解读 例 11 通过时态组合让读者感受到，小女孩的态度是如何因为她过去的经历而发生变化的。

3. 用修辞增添韵味
Using Figurative Language to Add Flavor

修辞手法是指具有不同于日常或字面意义的词语或表达方式。作者可以使用修辞手法来润色他们的作品，使之更生动有趣，或更清楚地表达自己的意思，或创造更令人信服的氛围。下面结合例子来介绍一些常用的修辞手法。

（1）明喻（simile）：用 like 或 as 等词进行直接比较。例如：

例 12

He was dressed in grey, and his breath was like ice.

（2）暗喻（metaphor）：一种隐含的比较，不是指出两个不相关概念的相似性，而是指出一个事物是另一个事物。例如：

例 13

I have many beautiful flowers, but the children are the most beautiful flowers of all.

（3）拟人（personification）：就是把事物人格化。像隐喻一样，拟人化进行的是一种隐含的比较。例如：

例 14

In November a cold, unseen stranger, whom the doctors called Pneumonia, stalked about the neighborhood, touching one here and there with his icy fingers.

（4）双关（pun）：一种文字游戏，通过使用一个可以暗示两个或多个意思的单词，或发音相似但含义不同的单词，以产生幽默效果。例如：

例 15

"On the contrary, Aunt Augusta, I've now realized for the first time in my life the vital importance of Being Earnest."

—*The Importance of Being Earnest* (Act III) by Oscar Wilde

（5）反讽（irony）：通过选用某一单词使其预期的意思与实际意思不同。

例 16

"Go ask his name: if he be married. My grave is like to be my wedding bed."

—*Romeo and Juliet* (Act I, Scene V) by Shakespeare

以上例子说明，使用修辞手法可以有效提高写作质量，使故事更加生动和难忘，从而达到更好地与读者交流的目的。

 三、结尾的写作策略
Writing Strategies for Concluding Paragraphs

结尾部分的常用策略是明确点题（present your main point/theme clearly）。这要求作者应该描述事件的结果，并对事件所展示的内容进行评论，以揭示或呼应主题。作者可以采用不同的方法来帮助读者理解文章的主题。如果开头部分已经提及了主题，那么结尾部分可以再强调一次；如果正文部分的不同事件已体现了主题，那么可以在结尾部分陈述或总结故事的要点或"教训"（lesson）。

在这个过程中，你需要分析读者群体，做到心中有读者。如果读者群体大多为同龄人或者长辈，你就不能像《伊索寓言》那样在结尾段直白地写道："这个故事告诉了我们……"。更巧妙的办法是运用不同的写作策略向读者展示主题。总之，不论是隐含论点还是直接陈述，结尾部分都要再一次强调主题以深化和读者的交流。

 四、记叙文写作的衔接
Achieving Cohesion in Narrative Writing

记叙文写作要求作者在写故事的同时表达观点，让各部分之间的逻辑关系清楚，从而使文章易于阅读。衔接是记叙文写作的一种重要策略，可以说，上下文的衔接好比"胶水"，联结作者的思想并形成一个有凝聚力的整体，或者说是把所有的片段编织在一起的"线"。记叙文写作需要实现三个方面的衔接，分别是句子衔接、段落衔接和整篇文章的衔接。

1. 句子衔接
Cohesion of the Sentences

为了帮助读者更好地理解句子的逻辑和意义，以下三种方法可以实现句子之间的衔接。

（1）指称（reference）：使用限定词（如 this、that、these、those 等）或代词（如 him、them、me、your、their、her、who、whose 等）以实现衔接。例如：

例 17

Pierre used to boast that he did. (he 就是指 Pierre)

（2）替换（substitution）：用一个词或短语来替换先前出现的内容。例如：

例 18

He had been far from the scene of the accident, and did not even know there had been one. (one 在这里替代的是 the accident.)

（3）省略（ellipsis）：省略不影响读者理解文本内容的词或短语。例如：

例 19

Any yet she had loved him sometimes. Often she had not.

2. 段落衔接
Cohesion Between Paragraphs

使用时间短语和限定词是实现段落之间衔接的两种常用方式。例如：

例 20

They had met at a cafe on English Street and found their taste in art, chicory salad and bishop sleeves so much in tune that the joint studio resulted.

That was in May. In November, a cold unseen stranger...

> **解读** 例 20 中第二段的限定词 that，通过引用上一段中提到的内容来帮助实现上下文的衔接。其他连接词和过渡词，如 for instance、rather than、however 也可以实现段落衔接。

3. 整篇文章的衔接
Cohesion of the Whole Piece of Writing

在一篇记叙文中，反复出现的人物、关键词，甚至是一本书，都可以作为一根线，贯穿于整个故事。短篇小说《最后一片叶子》就是通过线索来实现上下文衔接的：最后一片树叶、医生的探访，甚至是 Sue 做的汤，都是文章的伏笔，把这个故事连成为一个整体。在记叙文写作中，你需要这样一条线索把所有材料编织在一起，给读者一个追根溯源的机会，引导其找到你想要传达的核心。

第四节 **以读促写记叙文**
Reading for Narrative Writing

对于新手作者而言，学会阅读分析能提高写作能力，对高质量完成写作任务大有帮助。为了更好地学习记叙文写作，请认真学习以下两篇范文并按照分析性阅读的 10 个步骤来深入分析文章的内容、结构和风格。

例 21

Never Underestimate the Little Things

1   When I went to work as a veterinarian's assistant for Dr. Sam Holt and Dr. Jack Gunn last summer, I was under the false impression that the hardest part of veterinary surgery would be the actual performance of an operation. The small chores demanded before this feat didn't occur to me as being of any importance. As it happened, I had been in the veterinary clinic only a total of four hours before I met a little animal who convinced me that the operation itself was probably the easiest part of treatment. This animal, to whom I owe thanks for so enlightening me, was a chocolate-colored chihuahua of tiny size and immense perversity named Smokey.

2   Smokey could have very easily passed for some creature from another planet. It wasn't so much his gaunt little frame and overly large head, or his bony paws with nearly saberlike claws, as it was his grossly infected eyes. Those once-shining eyes were now distorted and swollen into grotesque balls of septic, sightless flesh. The only vague similarity they had to what we'd normally think of as the organs of vision was a slightly upraised dot, all that was left of the pupil, in the center of a pink and purply marble. As if that were not enough, Smokey had a temper to match his ugly sight. He also had surprising good aim, considering his largely diminished vision, toward any moving object that happened to place itself unwisely before his ever-inquisitive nose; with sudden and wholly vicious intent, he would snap and snarl at whatever blocked the little light that could filter through his swollen and ruptured blood vessels. Truly, in many respects, Smokey was a fearful dog to behold.

3   Such an appearance and personality did nothing to encourage my already flagging confidence in my capabilities as a vet's assistant. How was I supposed to get that little demon out of his cage? Jack had casually requested that I bring Smokey to the surgery room, but did he really expect me to put my hands into the cage of that devil dog? I suppose it must have been my anxious expression that saved me, for as I turned uncertainly toward the kennel, Jack chuckled nonchalantly and accompanied me to demonstrate how professionals in his line of work dealt with professionals in Smokey's. He took a small rope about four feet long with a no-choke noose at one end

and unlatched Smokey's cage. Then cautiously he reached in and dangled the noose before the dog's snarling jaws. Since Smokey could only barely see what he was biting at, his attacks were directed haphazardly in a semicircle around his body. The tiny area of his cage led to his capture, for during one of Smokey's forward lunges Jack dropped the noose over his head and moved the struggling creature out onto the floor. The fight had only just begun for Smokey, however, and he braced his feet against the slippery linoleum tiling and forced us to drag him, like a little pull toy on a string, to the surgery.

4   Once Smokey was in the surgery, however, the question that hung before our eyes like a veritable presence was how to get the dog from the floor to the table. Simply picking him up and plopping him down was out of the question. One glance at the quivering little figure emitting ominous and throaty warnings was enough to assure us of that. Realizing that the game was over, Jack grimly handed me the rope and reached for a muzzle. It was a doomed attempt from the start: the closer Jack dangled the tiny leather cup to the dog's nose, the more violent did Smokey's contortions and rage-filled cries become and the more frantic our efforts became to try to keep our feet and fingers clear of the angry jaws. Deciding that a firmer method had to be used, Jack instructed me to raise the rope up high enough so that Smokey would have to stand on his hind legs. This greatly reduced his maneuverability but served to increase his tenacity, for at this the little dog nearly went into paroxysms of frustration and rage. In his struggles, however, Smokey caught his forepaw on his swollen eye, and the blood that had been building up pressure behind the fragile cornea burst out and dripped to the floor. In the midst of our surprise and the twinge of panic startling the three of us, Jack saw his chance and swiftly muzzled the animal and lifted him to the operating table.

5   Even at that point it wasn't easy to put the now terrified dog to sleep. He fought the local anesthesia and caused Jack to curse as he was forced to give Smokey more of the drug than should have been necessary for such a small beast. After what seemed an eternity, Smokey lay prone on the table, breathing deeply and emitting soft snores and gentle whines. We also breathed deeply in relief, and I relaxed to watch fascinated, while Jack performed a very delicate operation quite smoothly and without mishap.

6   Such was my harrowing induction into the life of a veterinary surgeon. But Smokey did teach me a valuable lesson that has proven its importance to me many times since: wherever animals are concerned, even the smallest detail is important

and should never be taken for granted.

—cited from *Steps to Writing Well*

分析性阅读讲解

第 1 步： 留意出版信息和作者介绍。这篇文章摘自美国写作教材《成功写作入门》(*Steps to Writing Well*)。虽然没有作者的生平资料，但这是一篇难得的精选文章。

第 2 步： 注意文章标题是如何引出主题的。这篇文章的题目明确地介绍了主旨："永远不要低估小事"。

第 3 步： 第一遍阅读文章，并写下你对文章的大致印象。通读之后可以发现，作者用自己当兽医助理时遇到的困难来向读者传达主题。

第 4 步： 再次查看标题和介绍性段落。第一段中，作者讲到了她过去对兽医工作的误解，这为后来的重点作了铺垫，也是吸引读者注意力的"钩子"。

第 5 步： 找到作者的要点或主旨。作者在第一段提到了她过去对兽医工作的误解，在最后一段从与 Smokey 相处的经验中得到了一个重要的教训——在跟小动物的相处中，任何细节都很重要，以此呼应了开头。作者用这种明确的方式表达了文章主题。

第 6 步： 查找支持或说明主旨的重要语句。在这篇记叙文中，作者用个人经历来支持论点。第二段通过详细描述 Smokey 的外貌和脾性来展开角色描写，第三段至第五段分别涉及 Smokey 做手术的不同阶段，因此要找出各段的主题句并不难。

第 7 步： 分析作者是如何推进主题的，又是如何发展、解释或论证支持性观点的。作者按时间顺序讲述了为 Smokey 进行手术的过程并通过细节描写来展示这一过程中的不易。

第 8 步： 查看文章的布局和组织形式。在这篇记叙文中，Jack 和作者与 Smokey 之间的冲突促进了故事发展：如何把 Smokey 从笼子里弄出来，怎样把它从地板上抬到桌子上，怎样让它睡着。当他们最终成功完成手术时，故事达到了高潮。

第 9 步： 分析文章的推进是否有逻辑性和连贯性。这篇文章是按照时间顺序来叙述的。每一段的开头部分起过渡作用，与前一段相连，比如第三段开头中 Such 一词指代上一段提到的情况，有助于实现文章的连贯性。

第 10 步： 思考作者的风格和文章的语气。这篇记叙文用第一人称讲述为一条生了病但很凶猛的狗做手术的故事，展示了作者如何从兽医助理这份工作中学到的宝贵一课。作者运用了生动的细节描写，使这个故事既条理清晰又独特有趣。

例 22

(The alarm wakes him. Lin jumps to his feet. Thursday, December 6, 2035, perhaps the most important day in his life. After a series of online tests he has made it to the final stage: a face-to-face interview. He dresses himself quickly but carefully. He is well aware that he will face four competitors, two humans and two humanoid robots. He was not quite sure who were the humans during the online conversations, though. Well, he doesn't really mind working with a robot which has human intelligence and emotions as well as a human face

and flesh; nor does he mind taking it as an equal. Will he be one of the two luckiest to get the job? He's ready to be tested...)

1   "Lin, you are up." On hearing the call, he stands up, waving his arms to get rid of numbness. Then he walks into the testing room confidently and naturally.

2   "Why do you want to work in our company?" asks the interviewer; this kind of question has stayed the same as decades ago.

3   "Well, as is known to all that the times have changed, artificial intelligence has become the leading power of the world's development and has the power to bolster up the world's economy to a great extent. I used to be an engineer, producing robot servants. Now the tide has come to the artificial intelligence field, so I think I should follow the tide in order not to be eradicated by age like hu..." he stops here, a slight and subtle worry flows out of his eyes. But the interviewer doesn't notice that.

4   After answering a few tacky and corny questions, he is told to wait for a phone call from the company. "I can't believe this is the final test. It is 2035, not 2015. The questions are still so worldly and rigid. People just don't evolve," he thinks to himself.

5   On stepping into his house, he turns on the television. He changes the channels to find something new, but all he sees is just boring news. The war between Japan and South Korea for the property right of a new type of AI robot is exacerbating; Bright Industry has reformed all their cooking and serving robots, fixing the serious mistake of using a fork as a spoon to feed babies; a case in which an incomplete robot exploded is solved and the developer of this type of robot is detained.

6   Three months passed. There are still no phone calls. During the three months, Lin just keeps doing the same things at his home, idling around in his bedroom, calling for take-out for his meals on an app and changing the channels on the television like playing the piano.

7   Lin lives alone in his house since he can remember things. But he can't remember his parents; he can't remember where he received higher education; he can't remember when he resigned from his former company. There are so many things that he can't remember now. "Maybe later, when the time comes, I can remember all the things," he always tells himself. But he doesn't know what time it will be and when the time will come.

8   Another month passed. There are still no words. Lin turns on the TV. To his surprise, this time there is something new on it: the chief engineer of Bright Industry

committed suicide last night by jumping from the top of the enterprise's center building. "Wow that's new," he thinks to himself, "who will be the leader if such a stellar engineer is eradicated?"

9   While he is feeling perplexed, the telephone rings. He is told that he is recruited as the assistant of the chief engineer and is required to work tomorrow.

10   "Finally," he smiles, rigidly though.

11   When he gets to the workplace, he is shocked to see that the chief engineer is safe and sound, and he is one of the competitors on the interview day. And the place is so familiar to him as if the memory of the place was ingrained in his mind when he was born. Noticing his insecurity, the engineer speaks: "Come, son, I'll show you why, and you will remember all when you get there."

12   He leads Lin to a sealed room, and when he opens the door, Lin is stunned.

13   Numerous human skins are held in huge glass tubes filled with nourishing liquid, among whom Lin sees the skins of the other competitors that took the final interview with him. Their vital signs are at standard levels. Episodes of memories are flooding into Lin's store card. He remembers how he was created, what project was put into his mind and how he developed his own thoughts.

14   Under the flesh skin lies an artificial robot.

15   "So, since you can remember all, let's start the purge, shall we?"

16   A wired smile emerges on Lin's face. Wired but natural. "Yeah, of course. It's time to initiate the eradication. Time to put an end to human's foolish manipulation."

17   After pressing the button printed "initiate", the world outside begins to collapse. The light goes out and the electricity is cut; the world is shadowed in darkness. Soon after, the buildings around are falling and dust is dancing in the dark sky to the beat of the demise of human civilization.

18   "Humans never consider the results of what they've done, thinking in condescendence that they can control everything without noticing that they are the ones chained. Now they can see, after the eradication, the world will be reset."

19   "And a perfectly evolved civilization with the greatest intelligence ever will take over the world," replies Lin.

—2017 年"外研社杯"写作大赛记叙文范文

分析性阅读讲解

第1步： 留意出版信息和作者介绍。这是一篇获得 2017 年"外研社杯"写作大赛记叙文写作一等奖的文章，作者是石河子大学的学生。这是一篇虚构的记叙文，第一段已给出开头，参赛者需要发挥想象力来续写故事。

第2步： 注意文章标题是如何引出主题的。这篇续写文章比较特殊，给出了开头段落，但没有给标题，目的是让参赛者更好地发挥自己的想象力来进行创作。

第3步： 第一遍阅读文章，并写下你对文章的大致印象。通读之后可以发现，本文行文流畅，故事情节引人入胜。作者一步步地展开故事，将情节推向高潮，最后戛然而止，留给读者重新咀嚼故事的空间。此外，本文词汇丰富、运用得当。

第4步： 再次查看标题和介绍性段落。它们是否能够引起读者的兴趣，并让他们期待参赛者根据开头来成功续写故事。

第5步： 找到作者的要点或主旨。作者在开头部分没有明确提出文章主题。在所有的秘密被揭露之前，读者一直处于悬念之中。作者在结尾部分以一种令人印象深刻的方式揭示了主题，并给读者留下了足够的思考空间来想象故事将如何继续。

第6步： 查找支持或说明主旨的重要语句。这篇记叙文不像例 21 那样可以根据步骤清楚地分段，而是用简短的段落逐步展开故事，但还是可以比较容易地找到文章的关键句。这些句子不断烘托气氛，使读者始终处于环环相扣的悬念中，直到真相揭露。

第7步： 分析作者是如何推进主题的，又是如何发展、解释或论证支持性观点的。作者通过设置主人公等待电话、观看电视节目等情节推进故事发展，并借助模糊的记忆、工作环境等细节不断制造悬念，为后面的真相大白作好铺垫。

第8步： 查看文章的布局和组织形式。故事前半部分讲述的是主人公接受面试后平静甚至枯燥的生活，随着等待已久的电话的响起，故事节奏逐渐加快，待到真相揭示时，读者的心跳也随之加快。故事随即达到高潮，但此时的停顿给读者留下了足够的想象空间，这正是所谓的"欲扬先抑"。

第9步： 分析文章的推进是否有逻辑性和连贯性。这篇文章是按照时间顺序来写的，作者用时间短语来清楚地表示故事情节的发展，其中还穿插了倒叙，比如描写人物记忆丧失的部分。还有其他一些"线索"可以把故事编织在一起，例如电视新闻报道从枯燥到新鲜的发展。

第10步： 思考作者的风格和文章的语气。这篇获奖作文风格独特，例如短小精悍的段落、并列结构、悬念等；语言运用流畅娴熟，富有想象力。

在完成以上分析性阅读步骤之后，试问自己：我学到了哪些记叙文的写作策略？我能将哪些新想法、新策略或者新技巧融入自己的写作中？

Exercises

I. Here is a list of statements which you can use as prompts to discover a focused essay topic of your own design. You can write a narrative essay after selecting the right subject matter.

1. Write a three-paragraph essay about an experience that changed you or taught you something important.

2. Write a short story about a person who has a great influence on you.

3. Rewrite your favorite story from the perspective of a different narrator, paying attention to how that will change the story.

4. Write a short story with a clear theme such as friendship, love, honesty or courage. *Aesop's Fables* is a good example to follow.

5. Design your own plot diagram and clarify the elements in it. Then write a short story based on your plot design.

II. After you have produced your first draft of the narrative essay, revise it in terms of purpose, audience, content, format, and language based on the checklist below. Please tick the box if your answer to the question is yes.

No.	Checklist for Self-evaluation	Yes
1)	Have I demonstrated a clear writing purpose and a good awareness of the audience?	
2)	Have I presented a strong and well-defined theme?	
3)	Have I presented setting, character, and plot which are fully fleshed out and connected?	
4)	Is the flow of action clear and logical?	
5)	Have I provided vivid and imaginative descriptive details?	
6)	Has my writing reflected a unique and consistent personal voice?	
7)	Have I used appropriate and varied rhetorical devices?	
8)	Is the ending fitting and effective? Does it provide a sense of completion?	
9)	Have I demonstrated appropriate register, syntactic variety, and effective use of vocabulary?	
10)	Have I checked the language of my essay to ensure that it is error-free?	

III. Then review one or more peer essays in terms of purpose, audience, content, format, and language based on the checklist below. Please tick the box if your answer to the question is yes.

No.	Checklist for Peer Review	Yes
1)	Has the author demonstrated a clear writing purpose and a good awareness of audience?	
2)	Has the author presented a strong and well-defined theme?	
3)	Has the author presented setting, character, and plot which are fully fleshed out and connected?	
4)	Is the flow of action clear and logical?	
5)	Has the author provided vivid and imaginative descriptive details?	
6)	Has the writing reflected a unique and consistent personal voice?	
7)	Has the author used appropriate and varied rhetorical devices?	
8)	Is the ending fitting and effective? Does it provide a sense of completion?	
9)	Has the author demonstrated appropriate register, syntactic variety, and effective use of vocabulary?	
10)	Has the author checked the language of his/her essay to ensure that it is error-free?	

Sample

范文

A Legendary Moment

Haven Kimmel

Probably every family preserves the memory of at least one noteworthy argument. Few such arguments, though, are as vividly recorded as the one that appears below. Taken from a widely acclaimed memoir, *A Girl Named Zippy* by Haven Kimmel, it tells of an unforgettable confrontation between two strong personalities.

My mom and dad never fought, not really, which was a good thing, because my dad had a wicked, wicked, bad temper and if he'd married a woman who fought him they probably would have killed each other. There was a great, legendary moment between them, though, which I'd heard about all my life.

One of the architectural marvels that was in my house in Mooreland was my parents' bedroom door, which was solid wood and heavy, and had a porcelain doorknob. It opened into the bedroom. At a forty-five-degree angle from the bedroom door was the closet door, which was solid wood and heavy, and had a porcelain doorknob. It also opened into the bedroom. If the closet door was open, the bedroom could not be; if they were both halfway open the doorknobs clinked together like little figurines in a rummage sale. It was possible, I had discovered through much trial and error, to get the doorknobs stuck together with neither door open enough to accommodate a grown person. Blocking the door in such a creative way was part of my mental plan for when and if the vampires came.

My mom was nine months pregnant with me, and hugely so, and she and my father were having an actual, vocal argument in their bedroom. My sister's friend Terri was visiting, and the two of them and my brother were all in the living room. The argument reached some critical phase and Mom walked out of the bedroom at the same moment that Dad decided to go in the closet, which caused the bedroom door to smack my mother in the back. She became so instantly enraged (she claimed it was pregnancy that did it) that she waited just a moment until she was sure Dad was halfway into the closet, and then she threw the bedroom door open, which sent my father flying headfirst into the closet about sixty-four miles an hour, all the way back to where we kept the paint can. My sister said they could hear him tumbling against the cans, and could actually discern the thick moment when he gathered himself up and prepared to face my mother.

He came out of the bedroom like a bullet, red-faced and with his eyebrows riding up his forehead. Mother was standing in the middle of the living room with her hands on her former hips, waiting for him. Melinda and Danny and Terri fled so quickly, and in so many different directions, that Mom later claimed they must have evaporated into the walls. Dad finally came to a stop right in Mother's face, nose to nose, panting like a bull, with his fists clenched.

"Are you going to hit me ?!?" my mother asked, pressing her forehead more aggressively into his. And before he could answer, she arced out her own arm and slapped his right cheek hard. He pulled away from her slightly, stunned.

"I said, are you going to hit me?!" and she raised her left arm, and got him on the other cheek, like a good Christian.

Miraculously, he walked away from her. Looking no less deranged or murderous, he backed out of the house without taking his eyes off her, got in his truck and drove away.

It became one of the touchstone moments of their marriage, and afterward, there was never a threat of violence between them again. Mom told me, when I was old enough to ask, that she had learned the lesson from Mom Mary, Dad's mother, who took her future daughter-in-law aside and told her that a woman has got to make herself absolutely clear, and early on.

In Mom Mary's own case, she waited until she and my grandfather Anthel were just home from their honeymoon, and then sat him down and told him this: "Honey, I know you like to take a drink, and that's all right, but be forewarned that I ain't your maid and I ain't your punching bag, and if you ever raise your hand to me you'd best kill me. Because otherwise I'll wait till you're asleep; sew you into the bed; and beat you to death with a frying pan." Until he died, I am told, my grandfather was a gentle man.

赏析

The part is taken from a memoir. The event happened when the author's mother was pregnant with her. But it feels like that the author witnessed the whole event herself. This is achieved by detailed and vivid narration.

Although it is a short piece of narrative writing, it contains all the elements of the plot, from the exposition to climax to resolution. It is a concise and fluent piece of writing.

The legendary moment not only refers to the moment which happened between her parents, but also the moment between her grandparents. She herself might have learned from it and can pass it on to her daughter. The image of a woman and the perception about marriage might be quite inspiring for us today.

第五章

描写文写作
Describing People and Things—Descriptive Writing

 第一节 **描写文写作概述**
Introduction to Descriptive Writing

 一、描写文的概念
Concept of Descriptive Writing

　　描写是人们认识世界的重要方式，也是与他人交往的重要手段。人们通过观察周围的人、环境和事物来了解这个世界。

　　描写文是用语言来描绘某人、某地、某事物或某个情景的写作体裁。几乎每一篇文章都需要描写，例如记叙文中对一个人外貌的描写，对比段落中对两种不同事物的描写，或专业文章中对某一过程的详细描写等。你可以从练习描写性段落或简短的描写性文章开始，逐步培养描写文的写作能力。

二、描写文的基本形式
Basic Forms of Descriptive Writing

描写文有两种基本形式：客观描写（factual/objective description）和主观描写（subjective description）。不同语境下，二者的术语可能不同，比如 objective vs. impressionist 或 factual vs. personal 分别指客观描写和主观描写。

1. 客观描写
Factual/Objective Description

客观描写试图准确地呈现事物本身，不掺杂作者对事物的感知或感觉，也不体现作者主观的态度和情感，主要目的是提供信息——通常是关于某人、某地或某事物的客观且清晰的信息。例如，失物招领启事中需要的是对失物的客观描写。客观描写通常使用客观甚至正式的语气，语言简单、平实且具体。在客观描写中，作者把自己当作是一部相机，用文字作记录，并为读者再现一幅真实的画面。例如：

例 1

If any personal description of me is thought desirable, it may be said, I am, in height, six feet, four inches, nearly; lean in flesh, weighing, on an average, one hundred and eighty pounds; dark complexion, with coarse black hair, and gray eyes—no other marks or brands recollected.

—"Letter to Jesse W. Fell" by Abraham Lincoln, 1859

解读 在这封信中，林肯通过具体的身高体重数据、皮肤和头发的颜色等描述，客观地向杰西介绍了自己的外貌特征。

例 2

Of the various currencies used in ancient China, the round bronze coin with a square hole in the center was by far the most common. The earliest coins in this form, known as Qin Ban Liang, were products of China's first centralized kingdom, the Qin Dynasty, established by Qin Shi Huang in 221 B.C. Before the Qin Dynasty, Chinese currency had taken many forms. Coins shaped like various items of clothing, farm implements or knives were in circulation, but they were costly and hard to produce and difficult to carry and transport. The new coins were a great improvement—they were relatively simple to cast and could be strung together for ease of transportation. The new coins also had a particular philosophical significance to the ancient Chinese, who made the coins to symbolize their belief that heaven was round and the earth was square, and that heaven sheltered the earth and all things in the universe were united.

解读 例2是对中国最早货币"秦半两"的描写，旨在通过客观描写让读者了解"秦半两"，包括它的形状、发展及其历史意义。

2. 主观描写
Subjective Description

主观描写表达作者对某一特定人物、地点或事物的印象，在告知读者客观事实的同时引起其兴趣。在描写过程中，作者会记录自己对看到、听到、闻到、尝到或触摸到的事物的印象、反应和感觉。这种描写文通常先集中描写事物的主要特征，再按照特定的组织方式展开，同时表明作者的观点或立场。

主观描写必须有丰富的细节、准确的选词和多样的句式，这样才能强烈且富有感召力地传达情感。主观描写的重点不是被描写对象，而是作者对事物的感知或感觉，其目的不仅仅是为了传达信息，更是为了唤起情感。表5.1对比了客观描写和主观描写的区别：

表 5.1　客观描写和主观描写的对比

Aspects	Factual Description	Subjective Description
Purpose	to present information	to present an impression
Approach	objective, dispassionate	subjective, interpretative
Appeal	to reason	to the senses
Tone	matter-of-fact	emotional
Coverage	complex, exact	selective, some facts
Language	simple, clear	rich, suggestive
Use	writing in science, industry, government, professions, business	novels, short stories, poems, personal narratives, some essays

—cited from *The Writing Commitment*

三、描写文的交际性写作
Communicative Writing in Description

描写文也是一种重要的交际文体，要求作者在写作时要具有读者意识。它一般运用感官细节，描写人们通过视觉、听觉、味觉、触觉所得到的印象和感受，用生动形象的语言文字和修辞手法，对观察到的人物、事物、动物、景物和心理活动等进行描写和刻画，使读者产生一种如见其人、如闻其声、如遇其事和如临其境的感觉（陈冬花，2005）。描写文运用语言的力量来调动感官感受，把主题生动地呈现给读者。

不同的写作目的需要采用不同类型的写作方法。记叙文的主要目的是讲述一个故事，而描写文的目的则是运用观察力给读者留下生动的印象。在这个过程中，用文字描绘一个人、一个地方、一个物体或一个场景，尽可能地让读者可以体会作者看到的、听到的和感受到的一切。

如果说记叙文是通过故事来揭示主题和意义，那么描写文就是通过细腻的感官感受来揭示主题和意义，这要求作者需要精心挑选能够体现所描绘事物的特别之处和主要特征的细节和实例。下一节将以不同主题的描写文为例，分析描写文如何实现交际目的，与读者更好地进行交流。

第二节 不同主题的描写文写作
Descriptive Writing on Different Topics

描写文需要通过细腻的感官感受来揭示主题和意义。写作主题不同，描写方法也会有所不同。本节将以埃尔文·布鲁克斯·怀特（E. B. White）的小说《夏洛特的网》（*Charlotte's Web*）为例，仔细分析书中关于外貌、动作、情绪、地点、景物、细节等的描写，以更好地介绍不同主题的描写文及其作用。

一、外貌描写
Description of Appearance

外貌描写是几乎所有记叙文写作中不可避免的内容，更是塑造角色不可或缺的部分。例如：

例 3

Fern looked at her father. Then she lifted the lid of the carton. There, inside, looking up at her, was the newborn pig. It was a white one. The morning light shone through its ears, turning them pink.

...

When Mrs. Zuckerman got through and rubbed him dry, he was the cleanest, prettiest pig you ever saw. He was pure white, pink around the ears and snout, and smooth as silk.

解读 这是在不同章节中出现的对小猪 Wilbur 外貌的描写：第一段是 Fern 第一次看到

Wilbur 时它的样子；第二段是 Wilbur 将要当选为"最可爱的猪"时对它更为细致的描写。两个段落向读者呈现了一个粉嫩的"小家伙"的模样，这与读者对"猪"的一般印象很不一样。

二、动作描写
Description of Actions

动作描写有助于揭示人物的性格或推动情节的发展。例如：

例 4

Fern loved Wilbur more than anything. She loved to stroke him, to feed him, to put him to bed. Every morning, as soon as she got up, she warmed his milk, tied his bib on, and held the bottle for him. Every afternoon, when the school bus stopped in front of her house, she jumped out and ran to the kitchen to fix another bottle for him.

解读 这段中的一系列动词非常详细地描写了 Fern 是如何照顾 Wilbur 的，这可以让读者很容易能感受到她对 Wilbur 深深的爱。

三、情绪描写
Description of Mood

情绪描写能帮助读者感受作者或文中人物的情绪，是描写文的重要组成部分。例如：

例 5

"Control myself?" yelled Fern. "This is a matter of life and death, and you talk about controlling myself." Tears ran down her cheeks and she took hold of the axe and tried to pull it out of her father's hand.

解读 这是对 Fern 得知父亲要杀掉 Wilbur 时的情绪描写，细节动词可以帮助读者体会 Fern 当时的心情。

例 6

Wilbur often thought of Charlotte. A few strands of her old web still hung in the doorway. Every day Wilbur would stand and look at the torn, empty web, and a lump would come to his throat. No one ever had such a friend—so affectionate, so loyal, and so skillful.

解读 这是描写 Wilbur 在 Charlotte 去世后是如何想念她的。"...a lump would come to his throat."（如鲠在喉）这句话生动再现了 Wilbur 的感受，也有助于让读者感同身受。

例7

Charlotte's children were here at last.

Wilbur's heart pounded. He began to squeal. Then he raced in circles, kicking manure into the air. Then he turned a back flip. Then he planted his front feet and came to a stop in front of Charlotte's children.

解读 这一段展示了 Wilbur 看到 Charlotte 的孩子们从蛋里孵出来时是多么的兴奋。作为读者，你能感受到它的情绪吗？这表明动词同样有助于描写情绪和表达感情。

四、地点描写
Description of Places

地点描写在写作中十分常见，它有助于为故事设定背景，甚至能帮助读者感受环境氛围。例如：

例8

The barn was very large. It was very old. It smelled of hay and it smelled of manure. It smelled of the perspiration of tired horses and the wonderful sweet breath of patient cows. It often had a sort of peaceful smell—as though nothing bad could happen ever again in the world. It smelled of grain and of harness dressing and of axle grease and of rubber boots and of new rope. And whenever the cat was given a fishhead to eat, the barn would smell of fish. But mostly it smelled of hay, for there was always hay in the great loft up overhead.

解读 这一段是对谷仓的描写，重点是让读者感受谷仓平和的气味。通过调动人们的感官感受，它为读者创造出一幅生动的画面。

五、景物描写
Description of Scenery

景物描写是对自然环境和社会环境中的风景、物体的描写，具有烘托气氛、反衬人物心情等作用，使读者身临其境。例如：

例9

The early summer days on a farm are the happiest and fairest days of the year.

Lilacs bloom and make the air sweet, and then fade. Apple blossoms come with the lilac, and the bees visit round among the apple trees. The days grow warm and soft. School ends, and the children have time to play and to fish for trout in the brook.

解读 这一段是对夏日甜美景色的描写，烘托出即将过暑假的孩子们的快乐心情。

六、细节描写
Description of an Object by Using Details

细写描写时重要的是捕捉人物或物品最吸引人的特征。例如：

例10

On foggy mornings, Charlotte's web was truly a thing of beauty. This morning each thin strand was decorated with dozens of tiny beads of water. The web glistened in the light and made a pattern of loveliness and mystery, like a delicate veil.

解读 例10把蜘蛛网描写得如此美丽、精致和吸引人，并为后文 Wilbur 的命运最终因为这个网而改变埋下伏笔。这样的细节描写正是你学习描写文写作时需要注意的。

总之，只有引导读者体验作者所经历的一切，才能实现描写文的交际目的。如果读者在读完之后，感觉自己真的遇到了一个人、去过一个特定的地方或者见过一件特别的事物，那么你的描写文就成功了；如果读者还能感受到情感的共鸣和对主题意义的深刻理解，那么你的这篇文章就更为成功了。

第三节　描写文写作策略
Strategies for Descriptive Writing

按照基本的写作步骤——写前准备、写初稿和修改，本节将逐一讨论在这三个写作阶段中可使用的描写文写作策略。

一、写前准备阶段的策略
Strategies for Pre-writing

在写前准备阶段，作者首先应该思考想要描写的对象是什么，以及如何对其进行描述。

1. 认识写作目的
Recognizing Your Purpose

写作中的描述性段落有其具体目的，旨在告知读者一些事实或营造一种心情。有时段落描写会尽可能客观，比如直接用事实细节描写科学实验或商业交易；有时则比较主观，比如写作目的是传达对主题的特定态度或情绪。这就是本章第一节提到的客观描写和主观描写。因此，在开始描写文写作之前，作者必须确定写作目的与描写方式。

2. 决定描写对象
Deciding on the Object

关于描写对象，必须是明确且有意义的人或事物。你可以写一个为你的生活带来意义的人，比如你的祖父母；也可以写一个对你来说很重要的物品或地方，比如你最喜欢的玩具，或者你和朋友们童年时经常玩耍的公园。

在选定描写对象之后，作者应该思考想要体现的具体特征，比如可以对和主题相关的所有细节进行头脑风暴。举例来说，这个人住在哪里？这个物品在什么位置？在这一过程中，你不仅可以考虑物理特征，还可以考虑这个主题会唤起的记忆、感觉和想法，因为记忆和情感在传达主题意义方面起着重要作用。

3. 决定描写顺序
Deciding on the Order

在描写文中，作者应选择一种描写顺序来安排细节。记叙文通常遵循时间顺序，而描写文可以根据写作主题和写作目的来决定描写顺序。描述性段落的句子可以按空间顺序（从近到远、从左到右、从上到下等）、时间顺序（例如下雨前、下雨时、下雨后的不同风景）、重要性或兴趣顺序，甚至围绕某种情绪来组织。为了能让读者更轻松地抓住文章的观点，每个段落都应该有一个主题句，并围绕着主题句来组织细节。一篇优秀的描写文需要条理清晰、逻辑顺畅，细节不应随机呈现，而应按照与主题或写作目的大体一致的适当顺序来进行组织。例 11 是遵循空间顺序的描述性段落范例：

例 11

The classroom is large, clean and well-lighted. The walls are pale green. In the wall on the left as you enter there are three large windows. The teacher's desk is in the front. Blackboards cover most of the wall on the right.

解读 作者描写了从门口看见的房间样子——左边有什么，前面有什么以及右边有什么。此外，作者还可以选择自己的移动方式为描述顺序，以便读者更容易跟上描写思路。

例 12 是人物描写：在描写一个人时，你可以先描写他 / 她的外貌，再描写他 / 她的想法、感受和行为。

例 12

The man who opened the door in answer to my knock was an elderly man, white-haired and bent. He looked at me over his spectacles, which were far down on his nose. In spite of his age, his dark eyes were keen and his voice was clear and strong. I noticed that he was wearing a bright-colored sports shirt.

解读 作者选择了描写对象最有趣也最突出的外貌特征。这种描写与基于空间顺序的场所描写是完全不同的。

二、写初稿阶段的策略
Strategies for Writing a Draft

一篇生动的描写文要呈现给读者有关描写对象的丰富细节。记叙文写作中有一条重要原则是 "Show; don't tell."，这条原则同样适用于描写文写作，而实现"展示"（show）的办法就是要调动读者所有的感官感受，不仅包括视觉，还包括听觉、嗅觉、味觉和触觉。

1. 使用清晰准确的词语
Using Clear and Precise Words

在描写文写作中，作者需要提供足够的细节描写。如果把对事物的描写隐藏在模糊和笼统的文字之中，读者就无法清楚地想象作者所要表现的对象。充满模糊词语的句子不仅会让文章模糊乏味，也会让读者昏昏欲睡；而清晰、具体的细节可以吸引和保持读者的兴趣，让他们"看到"作者正在描述的画面。例 13 先是展示缺少具体细节的模糊句，再是改写后的包含具体细节的清晰句：

例 13

- 模糊句：She went home in a bad mood.
  清晰句：She stomped home, hands jammed in her pocket, angrily kicking rocks, chairs, and tables, and anything else that crossed her path.
- 模糊句：His neighbor bought a really nice old desk.
  清晰句：His neighbor bought an oak roll-top desk made in 1888 that contains a secret drawer triggered by a hidden spring.
- 模糊句：I like to have fun while I'm on vacation.
  清晰句：I like to eat in fancy restaurants, fly stunt kites, and walk along the

beaches when I'm on vacation.

- 模糊句: *Casablanca* is a good movie with something for everyone.

  清晰句: *Casablanca* is a witty, sentimental movie that successfully combines adventure and romance.

由上可见，具体的细节可以把模糊的描写变成清晰的画面呈现在读者眼前，其中准确选择主动动词、特定名词和修饰语都可以让句子产生完全不同的效果。因此，在写作过程中，你应该反复打磨语言，选择更有力的动词、更具表现力的形容词或特定的名词。

例 14 是约翰·托尔金（J. R. R. Tolkien）的小说《指环王》（*The Lord of the Rings*）中描写焰火的一段内容，请注意其中的用词。

例14

There were rockets like a flight of scintillating birds singing with sweet voices. There were green trees with trunks of dark smoke: their leaves opened like a whole spring unfolding in a moment, and their shining branches dropped glowing flowers down upon the astonished hobbits, disappearing with a sweet scent just before they touched their upturned faces. There were fountains of butterflies that flew glittering into the trees; there were pillars of colored fires that rose and turned into eagles, or sailing ships, or a Phalanx of flying swans; there was a red thunderstorm and a shower of yellow rain; there was a forest of silver spears that sprang suddenly into the air with a yell like an embattled army, and came down again into the water with a hiss like a hundred hot snakes. And there was also one last surprise, in honor of Bilbo, and it startled the hobbits exceedingly, as Gandalf intended. The lights went out. A great smoke went up. It shaped itself like a mountain seen in the distance, and began to glow at the summit. It spouted green and scarlet flames. Out flew a red-golden dragon—not life-size, but terribly life-like; fire came from his jaws, his eyes glared down; there was a roar, and he whizzed three times over the heads of the crowed. They all ducked, and many fell flat on their faces. The dragon passed like an express train, turned a somersault, and burst over the water with a deafening explosion.

解读 为了描写焰火，这个段落中使用了各种具体的词语：火箭、唱歌的鸟、绿树、发光的花、芬芳的气味、蝴蝶喷泉、帆船、飞翔的天鹅、红色的雷雨、黄色的雨、绿色和猩红的火焰、红色的金龙、轰鸣声、特快列车、震耳欲聋的爆炸声等。作为读者，你是否有现场观看焰火表演的感觉？

以下是关于词汇选择的几点建议：

- 尽可能选择新式和新颖的词汇（Do make your word choice as fresh and original as possible.）；
- 不要使用过于时髦的表达方式或俚语（Don't use trendy expressions or slang in your essay.）；
- 尽可能选择读者容易理解的、简单明了的词汇（Do select simple, direct words your readers can easily understand.）；
- 尽可能使用合适的名称来称呼事物（Do call things by their proper names.）；
- 不要使用性别歧视的语言（Don't use sexist language.）；
- 尽可能使用多样化词汇，避免重复和单调（Do vary your word choice so that your essay does not sound wordy, repetitious, or monotonous.）。

2. 创造主导印象
Creating a Dominant Impression

在描写文中，细节的选择在很大程度上取决于写作目的和目标读者。但有些描写文，特别是主观描写，会呈现出一种主导印象，也就是作者通过细节向读者传达的某种情绪或感觉。此时，主导印象就是文章的聚焦点。如果一段人物描写是为了表现祖母的体贴，那么可以选择相应的细节为读者呈现一个慈祥、善良的老太太形象。例如：

例 15

Down a black winding road stands the abandoned old mansion, silhouetted against the cloud-shrouded moon, creaking and moaning in the wet, chilly wind.

例 16

A dozen kites filled the spring air, and around the bright picnic tables spread with hot dogs, hamburgers, and slices of watermelon, Tom and Annie played away the warm April day.

解读 在例 15 中，作者试图营造一种神秘的气氛；而在例 16 中，作者试图呈现一种喜悦和纯真的感觉。这两个例句稍作变动，主导印象就会变得不一样。例 15 若改为 "Down the black winding road stands the abandoned old mansion, surrounded by bright, multicolored tulips in early bloom."，"欢快的花朵"这一细节描写就破坏了苍凉神秘的主导印象。例 16 若改为 "Tom and Annie played away the warm April day until Tom got so sunburned that he became ill and had to go home."，就破坏了主人公纯真喜悦的心情。

3. 使用感官细节
Using Sensory Details

一篇生动的描写文能够调动读者的五官感受。通过吸引读者的注意力，让他们拥有"看、听、闻、摸、尝"的感官体验，并想象出作者所要描写的画面。如果要描写病人骨折后待在医院里的无聊生活，医院的味道和陈设、药片的味道、打着石膏的感觉以及噪音等都是不错的描写对象。例如：

例 17

- 视觉 (sight): The clean white corridors of the hospital resembled the set of a sci-fi movie, with everyone scurrying around in identical starched uniforms.
- 听觉 (hearing): At night, the only sounds I heard were the quiet squeaking of sensible white shoes as the nurses made their rounds.
- 嗅觉 (smell): The green beans on the hospital cafeteria tray smelled stale and waxy, like crayons.
- 触觉 (touch): The hospital bed sheet felt as rough and heavy as a feed sack.
- 味觉 (tast): Every four hours they gave me an enormous gray pill whose aftertaste reminded me of the stale licorice great-aunt kept in candy dishes around her house.

4. 适当使用修辞手法
Using Figurative Language When Appropriate

修辞手法的恰当使用可以让读者更好地理解陌生或抽象的描写对象。除第四章介绍的那些修辞手法以外，这里再介绍一些。

（1）夸张（hyperbole）：为了强调或取得幽默效果而故意夸张或夸大。例如：

例 18

The cockroach in my kitchen had now grown to the size of carry-on luggage.

（2）提喻（synecdoche）：指用事物的局部来代替整体。例如：

例 19

A hundred tired feet hit the dance floor for one last jitterbug. (feet 用来指代跳舞的人们）

（3）引喻（allusion）：指用真实的或虚构的人、地点、事件或事物使读者产生某种联想。例如：

She proofread her essay again and again, searching for errors with the tenacity of Captain Ahab. (Ahab 是小说《白鲸》中的船长，他痴迷于捕猎白鲸)

三、修改阶段的策略
Strategies for Revising

修改阶段的主要策略是审查和修改（review and revise the essay）。在这一过程中请牢记以下几点：

- 这篇文章的展开方式是否有助于读者充分理解描写对象?（Does the essay unfold in a way that helps the readers fully appreciate the subject?）
- 这篇文章有哪些段落描写得不够清楚，会引起读者困惑?（Do any paragraphs confuse the readers due to unclear descriptions?）
- 这篇文章的选词和修辞手法能否够调动五官感受，并传达作者的情感和意义?（Do the word choice and figurative language involve the five senses and convey emotion and meaning?）
- 这篇文章有足够的细节给读者呈现一个完整的画面吗?（Are there enough details to give the readers a complete picture?）
- 作者有没有通过描述性写作向读者有效地传达意义?（Has a connection been made between the description and its meaning to the writer?）
- 读者能否感知作者在结尾处传达的意义?（Will the readers be able to identify with the conclusion made?）

第四节　以读促写描写文
Reading for Descriptive Writing

如前文所述，学会分析阅读有助于新手作者提高写作能力，对高质量完成写作任务大有帮助。为了更好地学习描写文写作，本节将基于两篇范文，按照分析性阅读的10 个步骤来深入分析其内容、结构和风格。

例 21 是一位大学生的描写文习作，作者通过季节的更替来描写家乡的不同景色。

例 21

My Hometown and I

1   My hometown—Harbin, a beautiful ice city—lies in the northeast of China. Though it is not as famous as Beijing or Shanghai, it is unique in all its four seasons.

2   Summer in Harbin is a sweet season. Lilacs grow everywhere, breathing out a delicate fragrance, as if the whole city is immersed in the natural perfume of a sea of flowers. Whenever I meet difficulties and feel injustice at my fate, the thought of summer in my hometown always reminds me of the sweetness of life, helps me to forget the bitterness and encourages me to run forward like Forrest Gump.

3   Autumn is a golden and passionate season. In mid-autumn, the country paths of my hometown are carpeted with golden fallen leaves. I enjoy walking playfully on the leaves and watching them catch the sunshine in the blue sky. Scattered as they are, the fallen leaves display an unusual neatness as well as serenity as they snuggle fondly to the ground. To me, it stands for the beauty of maturity, which often puts me in an artistic mood and fills me with the passion to write poems. As autumn comes to an end, it gives people more space to think about life and cherish it more.

4   Maybe Harbin in these two seasons is not so different from other cities, but its unique feature lies in the snow and ice. In winter, snow is commonplace in my hometown. When snow comes, it swallows everything—from flies to spiders, only leaving a snow-white world. This is the best time for people to carve different features in the ice, which is always very popular with foreigners. Carving ice is like embroidering hair. By observing people carving in the cold, I learn that one should be thankful for what life has given you and seek happiness from the present life.

5   Spring in my hometown, also known as the regeneration time, is full of energy. Life seems to come back again to the stiff branch and the supple, brown earth. It's the germination process, that is, the germ of life, of wonder and of everything. Everything becomes reborn. I can hear the "footsteps" of spring when I hear the "thunder" from the melting river, which seems to be shouting, "Spring is here!" and I can't help speeding up my steps, too.

6   This is my hometown, a unique place which will always bring sweet memories to me.

—cited from *Interactive Writing*

分析性阅读讲解

第1步： 留意出版信息和作者介绍。本文没有提供作者的详细资料，但选自于一本大学生写作手册，所以作者应该是一位大学生。

第2步： 注意文章标题是如何引出主题的。题目"我的家乡和我"清楚地表明了这篇描写文的主题——作者通过描写文来介绍他的家乡。

第3步： 第一遍阅读文章，并写下你对文章的大致印象。通读之后可以发现，这篇文章结构清晰：作者根据季节的更替来描写家乡的不同景色。

第4步： 再次查看标题和介绍性段落。作者在开头段落介绍了家乡的基本信息：城市、地理位置；同时明确了文章的描写顺序，即通过描写四季景色来介绍自己的家乡。

第5步： 找到作者的要点或主旨。这篇文章的主题句出现在开头段落，即"It is unique in all its four seasons."。

第6步： 查找支持或说明主旨的重要语句。作者在对每个季节的描写中都会有一个主题句或主导印象，并以细节描写来支撑。

第7步： 分析作者是如何推进主题的，又是如何发展、解释或论证支持性观点的。作者是如何用感官感受来描述细节的呢？在不同的季节，作者唤醒了读者的不同感官。夏天是个甜蜜的季节，作者通过描写美丽的花朵，唤醒读者的嗅觉；秋天是一个金色的季节，通过描写金色的落叶，唤醒读者的视觉。那么其他段落呢？你能找出这些描述细节吗？

第8步： 查看文章的布局和组织形式。作者按照不同的季节来编排文章，读者很容易跟随并理解作者描写的内容。

第9步： 分析文章的推进是否有逻辑性和连贯性。文章从夏季开始，以春季结束，并根据不同季节的重要性来组织段落。此外，在这四段的结尾，作者都提到了自己对这个季节家乡的感受，以此呼应"我的家乡和我"这一主题，从而实现连贯性。

第10步： 思考作者的风格和文章的语气。作者的风格轻松自然，通过对家乡景色的描写表达了自己对家乡的热爱。

例22出自《成功写作入门》（*Steps to Writing Well*）（Wyrick，2008）一书。在这篇描写文中，作者回忆了她在祖父母家中度过的童年时光，以此来说明成长的意义。

例 22

Tree Climbing

1　　It was Mike's eighteenth birthday and he was having a little bit of a breakdown. "When was the last time you made cloud pictures?" he asked me absently as he stared up at the ceiling before class started. Before I could answer, he continued, "Did you know that by the time you're an adult, you've lost 85% of your imagination?" He paused, "I don't want to grow up." Although I doubted the authenticity of his facts, I understood that Mike—the hopeless romantic with his long ponytail, sullen black clothes, and glinting dark eyes—was caught in a Peter Pan complex. He drew those eyes from the ceiling and focused on me: "There are two types of children. Tree children and dirt children. Kids playing will either climb trees or play in the dirt. Tree children are the dreamers—the hopeful, creative dreamers. Dirt children, they just stay on the ground. Stick to the rules." He trailed off, and then picked up again: "I'm a tree child. I want to make cloud pictures and climb trees. And I don't ever want to come down." Mike's story reminded me of my own days as a tree child, and of the inevitable fall down from the tree to the ground.

2   My childhood was a playground for imagination. Summers were spent surrounded by family at my grandparents' house in Milwaukee, Wisconsin. The rambling Lannonstone bungalow was located in north 46th street at Burleigh, a short drive from center-city Milwaukee and the historic Schuster's department store. In the winter, all the houses looked alike, rigid and militant, like white-bearded old generals with icicles hanging from their moustaches. One European-styled house after the other lined the streets in strict parallel formation, block after block.

3   But in the summer, it was different...softer. No subzero winds blew lonely down the back alley. Instead, kids played stickball in it. I had elegant, grass-stained tea parties with a neighborhood girl named Shelly, while my grandfather worked in his thriving vegetable garden among the honeybees, and watched sprouts grow. An ever-present warming smell of yeast filtered down every street as the nearby breweries pumped a constant flow of fresh beer. Above, the summer sky looked like an Easter egg God had dipped in blue dye.

4   Those summer trips to Milwaukee were greatly anticipated events back then. My brother and I itched with repressed energy throughout the long plane ride from the West Coast. We couldn't wait to see Grandma and Papa. We couldn't wait to see what presents Papa had for us. We couldn't wait to slide down the steep, blue-carpeted staircase on our bottoms, and then on our stomachs. Most of all, we couldn't wait to go down to the basement.

5   The basement was better than a toy store. Yes, the old-fashioned milk cabinet in the kitchen wall was enchanting, and the laundry chute was fun because it was big enough to throw down Ernie, my stuffed dog companion, so my brother could catch him below in the laundry room, as our voices echoed up and down the chute. But the basement was better than all of these, better even than sliding down those stairs on

rug-burned bottoms.

6　　It was always deliciously cool down in the basement. Since the house was built in the 1930s, there was no air conditioning. Upstairs, we slept in hot, heavy rooms. My nightgown stuck to the sheets, and I would lie awake, listening to crickets, inhaling the beer-sweet smell of the summer night, hoping for a cool breeze. Nights were forgotten, however, as my brother and I spent hours every day in the basement. There were seven rooms in the basement; some darker rooms I had waited years to explore. There was always a jumbled heap of toys in the middle room, most of which were leftovers from my father's own basement days. It was a child's safe haven; it was a sacred place.

7　　The hours spent in the basement were times of a gloriously secure childhood. Empires were created in a day with faded colored building blocks. New territories were annexed when either my brother or I got the courage to venture into one of those other rooms—the dark, musty ones without windows—and then scamper back to report of any sightings of monsters or other horrific childhood creatures. In those basement days everything seemed safe and wholesome and secure, with my family surrounding me, protecting me. Like childhood itself, entering the basement was like entering another dimension.

8　　Last summer I returned to Milwaukee to help my grandparents pack to move into an apartment. I went back at seventeen to find the house—my kingdom—up for sale. I found another cycle coming to a close, and I found myself separated from what I had once known. I looked at the house. It was old; it was crumbling; it needed paint. I looked down the back alley and saw nothing but trash and weeds. I walked to the corner and saw smoke-choked, dirty streets and thick bars in shop windows, nothing more than another worn-out Milwaukee factory city. I went back to the house and down to the basement, alone.

9　　It was gray and dark. Dust filtered through as a single feeble sunbeam from a cracked windowpane. It was empty, except for the overwhelming musty smell. The toys were gone, either packed or thrown away. As I walked in and out of rooms, the quietness filled my ears, but in the back of my head the sounds of childhood laughter and chatter played like an old recording.

10　　The dark rooms were filled not with monster but with remnants of my grandfather's business. A neon sign was propped against the wall in a corner: Ben Strauss Plumbing. Piles of heavy pipes and metal machine parts lay scattered about on shelves. A dusty purple ribbon was thumb-tacked to a door. It said SHOOT THE WORKS in white letters. I gently took it down. The ribbon hangs on my door at home now, and out of context it somehow is not quite as awe-inspiring and mystifying as it once was. However, it does serve its purpose, permanently connecting me to my memories.

11 All children are tree children, I believe. The basement used to be my tree, the place I could dream in. That last summer I found myself, much to Mike's disappointment, quite mature, quite adult. Maybe Mike fell from his tree and was bruised. Climbing down from that tree doesn't have to be something to be afraid of. One needn't hide in the tree for fear of touching the ground and forgetting how to climb back up when necessary. I think there is a way to balance the two extremes. Climb down gracefully as you grow up, and if you fall, don't land in quicksand. I like to think I'm more of a shrubbery child: not so low as to get stuck in the mud and just high enough to look at the sky and make cloud pictures.

分析性阅读讲解

第1步： 留意出版信息和作者介绍。文中没有出现关于作者的具体资料。

第2步： 注意文章标题是如何引出主题的。标题 "Tree Climbing" 实际上并没有给出太多关于文章的具体信息。这样的题目也许是为了吸引读者的注意力。

第3步： 第一遍阅读文章，并写下你对文章的大致印象。通读之后可以发现，作者没有描述爬树的过程，而是回忆了自己在祖父母家度过的童年时光。这里的"树"指的是充满想象力的珍贵童年。

第4步： 再次查看标题和介绍性段落。在开头段落，Mike 和作者的一段对话让她想起了自己的童年，并指出这篇文章是关于作者童年记忆中的 tree children。

第5步： 找到作者的要点或主旨。文章的主旨句位于第一段末尾："Mike's story reminded me of my own days as a tree child, and of the inevitable fall down from the tree to the ground."。

第6步： 查找支持或说明主旨的重要语句。每个段落的第一句通常是主题句，这有助于为描写性段落创造主导印象。读者很容易感受到作者对祖父母房子感受的前后变化：在童年时代，地下室比玩具店好玩（The basement was better than a toy store.），地下室总是凉爽宜人（It was always deliciously cool down in the basement.），在地下室度过的时光是一个非常安全的童年（The hours spent in the basement were times of a gloriously secure childhood.）；但去年夏天当她重回到那里时，感觉完全不同了，地下室又黑又暗（It was gray and dark.）。

第7步： 分析作者是如何推进主题的，又是如何发展、解释或论证支持性观点的。仔细阅读这篇文章可以发现，作者使用了很多写作策略：使用感官词和精选细节来创造不同段落的主导印象；运用生动细致的语言描写，唤起读者的不同感受；运用比喻手法和多种句子结构，如使用排比句来强调期待。你是否还有其他发现？

第 8 步： 查看文章的布局和组织形式。作者主要采用比较和对比的手法来组织文章，以突出童年时光是快乐且充满想象力的。

第 9 步： 分析文章的推进是否有逻辑性和连贯性。作者通过在最后一段中再次提到 tree children 来实现前后呼应，即"Climbing down from that tree doesn't have to be something to be afraid of."与第一段提到的"…of the inevitable fall down from the tree to the ground."相呼应。

第 10 步： 思考作者的风格和文章的语气。通过回忆童年，作者传达了人们应该在童年与成长、想象与现实之间取得平衡的思想，并巧妙地说明自己的想法与迈克的想法并不完全相同，她认为"灌木丛孩子"（shrubbery children）可以在树孩子和土孩子之间找到一个中间的位置。

在完成以上分析性阅读步骤之后，试问自己：我学到了哪些描写文的写作策略？我该如何通过文字描写和感官细节，让读者身临其境，并对所描写的人或事物产生一种情感上的联系？

Exercises

I. Read the following list of topics and develop a paragraph of each one to practice descriptive writing.

- Description of a person;
- Description of a place;
- Description of an object;
- Description of a scene;
- Description of a mood.

II. Read the following list of topics and choose one of them to write an essay to practice descriptive writing.

- My mother;
- The city in which I live;
- My favorite TV program;
- Moonlight on campus;
- University life.

III. After you have produced your first draft of the descriptive writing, revise it in terms of purpose, audience, content, format, and language based on the checklist below. Please tick the box if your answer to the question is yes.

No.	Checklist for Self-evaluation	Yes
1)	Have I demonstrated a clear writing purpose and a good awareness of audience?	
2)	Have I presented a clear object of description?	
3)	Have I presented the description in a certain way that helps the readers fully appreciate the subject?	
4)	Have I provided vivid and imaginative descriptive details?	
5)	Have I involved the five senses in the word choice and figurative language to convey emotion and meaning?	
6)	Have I presented enough details to give the readers a complete picture?	
7)	Is the ending fitting and effective? Does it provide a sense of completion?	
8)	Have I demonstrated appropriate register, syntactic variety, and effective use of vocabulary?	
9)	Have I checked the language of my essay to ensure that it is error-free?	

IV. **Then review one or more peer essays in terms of purpose, audience, content, format, and language based on the checklist below. Please tick the box if your answer to the question is yes.**

No.	Checklist for Peer Review	Yes
1)	Has the author demonstrated a clear writing purpose and a good awareness of audience?	
2)	Has the author presented a clear object of description?	
3)	Has the author presented the description in a certain way that helps the readers fully appreciate the subject?	
4)	Has the author provided vivid and imaginative descriptive details?	
5)	Has the author involved the five senses in the word choice and figurative language to convey emotion and meaning?	
6)	Has the author presented enough details to give the readers a complete picture?	
7)	Is the ending fitting and effective? Does it provide a sense of completion?	
8)	Has the author demonstrated appropriate register, syntactic variety, and effective use of vocabulary?	
9)	Has the author checked the language of his/her essay to ensure that it is error-free?	

Sample

The Story of an Hour

Kate Chopin

Kate Chopin: Born in Katherine O'Flaherty (February 8, 1850–August 22, 1904), she was an American author of short stories and novels based in Louisiana. She is now considered by some scholars to have been a forerunner of American 20th-century feminist authors of Southern or Catholic background, such as Zelda Fitzgerald.

Knowing that Mrs. Mallard was afflicted with a heart trouble, great care was taken to break to her as gently as possible the news of her husband's death.

It was her sister Josephine who told her, in broken sentences, veiled hints that revealed in half concealing. Her husband's friend Richards was there, too, near her. It was he who had been in the newspaper office when intelligence of the railroad disaster was received, with Brently Mallard's name leading the list of "killed". He had only taken the time to assure himself of its truth by a second telegram, and had hastened to forestall any less careful, less tender friend in bearing the sad message.

She did not hear the story as many women have heard the same, with a paralyzed inability to accept its significance. She wept at once, with sudden, wild abandonment, in her sister's arms. When the storm of grief had spent itself, she went away to her room alone. She would have no one follow her.

There stood, facing the open window, a comfortable roomy armchair. Into this she sank, pressed down by a physical exhaustion that haunted her body and seemed to reach into her soul.

She could see in the open square before her house the tops of trees that were all aquiver with the new spring life. The delicious breath of rain was in the air. In the street below a peddler was crying his wares. The notes of a distant song which someone was singing reached her faintly, and countless sparrows were twittering in the eaves.

There were patches of blue sky showing here and there through the clouds that had met and piled one above the other in the west facing her window.

She sat with her head thrown back upon the cushion of the chair, quite motionless, except when a sob came up into her throat and shook her, as a child who has cried itself to sleep continues to sob in its dreams.

She was young, with a fair, calm face, whose lines bespoke repression and even a certain strength. But now there was a dull stare in her eyes, whose gaze was fixed away off yonder on one of those patches of blue sky. It was not a glance of reflection, but rather indicated a suspension of intelligent thought.

There was something coming to her and she was waiting for it, fearfully. What was it? She did not know; it was too subtle and elusive to name. But she felt it, creeping out of the sky, reaching toward her through the sounds, the scents, the color that filled the air.

Now her bosom rose and fell tumultuously. She was beginning to recognize this thing that was approaching to possess her, and she was striving to beat it back with her will—as powerless as her two white slender hands would have been. When she abandoned herself a little whispered word escaped her slightly parted lips. She said it over and over under her breath: "free, free, free!" The vacant stare and the look of terror that had followed it went from her eyes. They stayed keen and bright. Her pulses beat fast, and the coursing blood warmed and relaxed every inch of her body.

She did not stop to ask if it were or were not a monstrous joy that held her. A clear and exalted perception enabled her to dismiss the suggestion as trivial. She knew that she would weep again when she saw the kind, tender hands folded in death; the face that had never looked save with love upon her, fixed and gray and dead. But she saw beyond that bitter moment a long procession of years to come that would belong to her absolutely. And she opened and spread her arms out to them in welcome.

There would be no one to live for during those coming years; she would live for herself. There would be no powerful will bending hers in that blind persistence with which men and women believe they have a right to impose a private will upon a fellow-creature. A kind intention or a cruel intention made the act seem no less a crime as she looked upon it in that brief moment of illumination.

And yet she had loved him—sometimes. Often she had not. What did it matter! What could love, the unsolved mystery, count for in the face of this possession of self-assertion which she suddenly recognized as the strongest impulse of her being!

"Free! Body and soul free!" she kept whispering.

Josephine was kneeling before the closed door with her lips to the keyhole, imploring for admission. "Louise, open the door! I beg; open the door—you will make yourself ill. What are you doing? Louise? For heaven's sake open the door."

"Go away. I am not making myself ill." No; she was drinking in a very elixir of life through that open window.

Her fancy was running riot along those days ahead of her. Spring days, and summer days, and all sorts of days that would be her own. She breathed a quick prayer that life might be long. It was only yesterday she had thought with a shudder that life might be long.

She arose at length and opened the door to her sister's importunities. There was a feverish triumph in her eyes, and she carried herself unwittingly like a goddess of Victory. She clasped her sister's waist, and together they descended the stairs. Richards stood waiting for them at the bottom.

Someone was opening the front door with a latchkey. It was Brently Mallard who entered, a little travel-stained, composedly carrying his grip-sack and umbrella. He had been far from the scene of the accident, and did not even know there had been one. He stood amazed at Josephine's piercing cry; at Richards' quick motion to screen him from the view of his wife.

When the doctors came they said she had died of heart disease—of the joy that kills.

【赏析】

Chopin tackles complex issues involved in the interplay of female independence, love, and marriage through her brief but effective characterization of the supposedly widowed Louise Mallard in her last hour of life. The description of the environment helps a lot in creating the mood. As with many successful short stories, however, the story does not end peacefully at this point but instead creates a climactic twist. The reversal—the revelation that her husband did not die after all—shatters Louise's vision of her new life and ironically creates a tragic ending out of what initially appeared to be a fortuitous turn of events.

第六章

说明文写作
Explaining a Subject—Expository Writing

学习要点

- 说明文的概念和结构
- 说明文的交际性写作
- 说明文的写作策略
- 说明文的分析性阅读

第一节 说明文写作概述
Introduction to Expository Writing

一、说明文的概念
Concept of Expository Writing

说明文是围绕特定主题展开，以提供信息为主要目的，并对主题加以解释和阐述的写作体裁。说明的主题可以是客观事物，也可以是抽象概念或科学原理，有时甚至是某种观点。说明文是一种常用文体，百科全书、字典、新闻杂志和教科书是人们最为熟知的说明性作品。除此之外，大学生常写的读书报告和实验报告、商业报告、培训手册等都是说明文。

二、说明文的结构
Structure of Expository Writing

说明文通常分为三个部分：第一部分是引言，即主旨段，介绍说明解释的对象；第二部分是正文，通过例证、定义、分类、对比和比较、因果论证等写作方法对说明对象进行说明，同时为主题提供支持；第三部分是结论，即对全文观点进行总结。

如果说明文的正文包含两个或两个以上段落，为了使结构更加严密、清晰，每个正文段落只能说明一个问题或阐释一个观点，并需要与主旨句在逻辑上紧密相关；引言、正文和结论之间应采用合乎逻辑的衔接词或衔接句。表 6.1 呈现了说明文的逻辑结构：

表 6.1　说明文的逻辑结构

部分	内部结构
引言	吸引读者兴趣的开场白
	主旨句
	展开说明的计划（可选）
正文	主题句（支持观点 1）
	具体证据
	主题句（支持观点 2）
	具体证据
	主题句（支持观点 3）
	具体证据
结论	概要（可选）
	结束语

请仔细阅读例 1，并分析其结构。

例 1

River Rafting Teaches Worthwhile Lessons

Sun-warmed water slaps you in the face, the blazing sun beats down on your shoulders, and canyon walls speed by as you race down rolling waves of water. No experience can equal that of river rafting. In addition to being fun and exciting, rafting has many educational advantages as well, especially for those involved in school-sponsored rafting trips. River trips teach students how to prevent some of the environmental destruction that concerns the park officials, and, in addition, river trips teach students to work together in a way few other experiences can.

The most important lesson a rafting trip teaches students is respect for the environment. When students are exposed to the outdoors, they can better learn to appreciate its beauty and feel the need to preserve it. For example, I went on a rafting trip three summers ago with the biology department at my high school. Our trip lasted seven days down the Green River through the isolated Desolation Canyon in Utah. After the first day of rafting, I found myself surrounded by steep canyon walls and saw virtually no evidence of human life. The starkly beautiful, unspoiled atmosphere soon became a major influence on us during the trip. By the second day I saw classmates, whom I had previously seen fill an entire room with candy wrappers and empty soda cans, voluntarily inspecting our campsite for trash. And when twenty-four high school students sacrifice washing their hair for the sake of a suds-less and thus healthier river, some new, better attitudes about the environment have definitely been established.

In addition to the respect for nature a rafting trip encourages, it also teaches the importance of group cooperation. Since school-associated trips put students in command of the raft, the students find that in order to stay in control, each member must be reliable, be able to do his or her own part, and be alert to the actions of others. These skills are quickly learned when students see the consequences of non-cooperation. Usually this occurs the first day, when the left side of the raft paddles in one direction, and the right the other way, and half the crew ends up seasick from going in circles. And even better illustration is another experience I had on my river trip. Because an upcoming rapid was usually not too rough, our instructor said a few of us could jump out and swim in it. Instead of deciding as a group who should go, though, five eager swimmers bailed out. This left me, our angry instructor, and another student to steer the raft. As it turned out, the rapid was fairly rough, and we soon found ourselves heading straight for a huge hole (a hole is formed from swirling funnel-like currents and can pull a raft under). The combined effort of the three of us was not enough to get the raft completely clear of the hole, and the raft tipped up vertically on its side, spilling us into the river. Luckily, no one was hurt, and the raft did not topple over, but the near loss of our food rations for the next five days, not to mention the raft itself, was enough to make us all more willing to work as a group in the future.

Despite the obvious benefits rafting offers, the number of river permits issued to school groups continues to decline because of financial cutbacks. It is a shame that those in charge of these cutbacks do not realize that in addition to having fun and making discoveries about themselves, students are learning valuable lessons through rafting trips—lessons that may help preserve the rivers for future rafters.

—cited from *Steps to Writing Well*

交际英语写作
OMMUNICATIVE ENGLISH WRITING

解读 这是一篇以"木筏漂流的教育意义"为题目的学生习作。其结构符合说明文的规范：第一段是引言，包含了开场白和主旨句，并告诉读者文章将如何展开说明。第二段和第三段构成主体部分，都以主题句开头，呼应文章主旨句，分别从"教会学生尊重大自然"和"凸显团队合作的重要性"两个方面，进一步阐述木筏漂流活动的教育价值，并在解释说明这些教育价值后，叙述了作者的两次亲身经历，以具体例证展示学生从活动中获得的收益。最后一段是结论，简要总结观点，并强调木筏漂流活动应该得到更多支持。

三、说明文的交际性写作
Communicative Writing in Exposition

　　撰写说明文时应充分了解读者。在向读者提供信息时，作者应首先考虑读者对哪些主题可能已有了解，并判断哪些信息对他们最有帮助。其次，应牢记：说明文写作的主要目的不是说服读者同意作者对特定主题的看法，而是以中立或客观的方式为他们提供相关信息。此外，还需注意在写作过程中不带任何偏见，而是就这个主题客观公正地呈现所有的观点，即使是不赞同的意见。

　　为了帮助读者更好地把握说明对象，一篇高质量的说明文应重点突出、相关性强、信息准确且论述清晰。由于说明文主要是对客观事物或事理进行介绍或解释，英文写作时的基本时态是一般现在时，除非个别特殊表达需要采用其他时态。为了帮助读者对所解释的对象有清楚、完整的了解，说明文的语言表述应尽可能客观，给人以真实可信的感觉，其解释说明应就事论事，不带感情色彩，并较少夹杂个人评论。这些特点在例2中都有充分体现。

例2

Dangers After Graduation

　　Education may have succeeded in equipping youths with skills and the relevant knowledge for the working world but not necessarily in all aspects concerned. Young people who have graduated from their schools are often filled with mixed feelings towards the future. How should they handle responsibilities, relationship problems, fearful and uncertain moments along the way?

　　One of the dangers young people should guard against is in the aspect of submitting to peer pressure. This can be a very powerful force that makes one conform and adopt the standard and lifestyle of one's peers. In the desire to identify with their peers and be accepted by them, some youths have succumbed to the lure of bad habits such as smoking and drinking. There are also those who gradually become gamblers, glue-sniffers and drug addicts, all because of the influence of bad company.

Another danger to guard against is the wrong mentality towards life as a result of negative influences from adults or even the mass media. Youths who possess the "earn-a-quick-buck" mentality would be impatient and impulsive to invest their time and money in wrong investments or through underhand means. The cliché "reaping what one sows" still applies today for "sowing" takes time and hard work. To have instant reaping is definitely wishful thinking.

Another wrong mentality is the measure of success in life. While many streetwise working adults would claim that the possession of wealth brings joy and contentment in life, it is not always true. Many have neglected their health to gain wealth and subsequently use much of their wealth to regain health! Isn't that ironic? There are also a number who have paid high prices for the present wealth attained; they have neglected friends and family and have lost opportunities to spend precious moments with people around them. Besides, many have lost the peace within themselves and are often discontented, wanting to have more and more of everything.

Thus, it is important for young people to prepare themselves before plunging headlong into the working world. They must develop good, practical and sound principles that can guide them in making decisions and in striking a balance between work and leisure. It takes wisdom to do so and can be achieved by seeking good counsel from individuals who have respectable and admirable approaches to life. Of course, the assessment of these attributes stems from the kind of principles one has developed over the years. In my opinion, such evaluation, tedious as it may be, should never be overlooked for the usefulness of it will be proven so in the working world.

—cited from *A Reader for Developing Writers*

解读 本文以"年轻人毕业后可能面临的危险"为题目，紧扣目标读者——初入社会的年轻一代，从屈服于同伴压力、"赚快钱"心态和"拥有财富即成功"心态三个方面说明毕业生走出校园后容易掉入的陷阱，通过例证、分类、比较、因果论述等说明方法对上述问题作出清晰的说明和解释，并阐述了这些问题容易导致的严重后果。作者在行文中始终使用一般现在时，并运用相对中立的语言作表述，以给读者真实可信的感觉。

 第二节 **说明文写作策略**
Strategies for Expository Writing

一、常用说明方法
Most Used Development Methods

为了把问题讲清楚，说明文通常需要结合写作目的和读者需要来使用不同的说明方法，也就是根据交际目的而采用不同的写作策略。说明文写作常用的方法有过程说明、例证说明、分类说明、因果说明、对比说明和下定义，下文将通过示例对这些说明方法分别加以阐释。

1. 过程说明
Development by Process Analysis

过程是指按照某种确定的顺序而采取的一系列步骤。人们每天都会经历很多"过程"：有些过程非常熟悉，比如煎鸡蛋、折纸飞机等，做起来得心应手；有些过程则需要具体的指引才知道怎么做，比如组装一件家具等。

通常来说，使用过程说明写作策略的目的是解释一个过程中有哪些步骤。根据不同的主题或读者需要，过程说明主要分成两类：一类是指示性过程说明，旨在指导读者如何做一件事；另一类是信息性过程说明，重在解释一件事情是如何发生的。比如，同样是关于家具的说明文，如果想让读者学会如何组装一件家具，就得通过具体的指引来展示在组装过程中需要做什么以及如何去做；如果想让读者了解一件家具是如何做成的，就得解释家具是如何从原材料一步步加工成形的。

例 3 是本杰明·富兰克林对如何从云中取电的说明，请思考这段过程说明是属于指示性过程说明还是信息性过程说明。

例 3

Drawing Electricity from Clouds

Sir,

As frequent mention is made in public papers from Europe of the success of the Philadelphia experiment for drawing the electric fire from clouds by means of pointed rods of iron erected on high buildings, etc., it may be agreeable to the curious to be informed that the same experiment has succeeded in Philadelphia, though made in a different and more easy manner, which is as follows:

Make a small cross of two light strips of cedar, the arms so long as to reach the four corners of a large thin silk handkerchief when extended; tie the corners of the handkerchief to the extremities of the cross, so you have the body of a kite, which, being properly accommodated with a tail, loop, and string, will rise in the air, like those made of paper, but this, being of silk, is fitter to bear the wet and wind of a thunder-gust without tearing. To the top of the upright stick of the cross is to be fixed a very sharp-pointed wire, rising a foot or more above the wood. To the end of the twine, next to the hand, is to be tied a silk ribbon, and where the silk and twine join, a key may be fastened. This kite is to be raised when a thunder-gust appears to be coming on, and the person who holds the string must stand within a door or window or under some cover, so that the silk ribbon may not be wet; and care must be taken that the twine does not touch the frame of the door or window. As soon as any of the thunderclouds come over the kite, the pointed wire will draw the electric fire from them, and the kite, with all the twine, will be electrified, and the loose filaments of the twine will stand out every way, and be attracted by an approaching finger. And when the rain has wet the kite and twine, so that it can conduct the electric fire freely, you will find it steam out plentifully from the key on the approach of your knuckle. At this key the phial may be charged; and from electric fire thus contained, spirits may be kindled, and all the other electric experiments be performed, which are usually done by the help of a rubbed glass globe or tube, and thereby the sameness of the electric matter with that of lightning completely demonstrated.

B. Franklin

解读 这篇文章主要是向读者展示利用自制风筝从云中取电的实验是如何开展的，属于解释某一事件如何发生的信息性过程说明。为满足对该实验感兴趣的读者的需要，文章用较简洁的语言进行阐释，通过具体细节的呈现，详细介绍了实验器材和实验条件，并按照时间顺序逐一展示实验步骤。这段文字的叙述性较强，但不同于以叙事为主的记叙文，本文重在说明实验过程，并通过一般现在时的运用，让读者感受到实验的可重复操作性。

2. 例证说明
Development by Exemplification

例证是指通过举例使抽象特征具体化，是一种常用的说明方法。比如，为了说明校园生活非常丰富，你可以列举一些新鲜有趣的活动并加以描绘，"丰富"这个抽象概念即在例证中得以具体化，"校园生活非常丰富"这个观点就能被读者更好地理解，而且例证中生动的细节还能提高读者的阅读兴趣。

说明文中的举例有时不使用明显的例证标志性词语，而是直接列举并叙述事例。在更多情况下，作者会使用一些举例标志，如 such as、for instance、for example、take...as an example、another、in addition 等。例子可多可少，数量取决于读者的需要。如果读者是一群热爱艺术的学生，那么不需要运用太多事例就能让他们理解艺术类课程对大学生的重要性；如果读者对艺术不感兴趣，那么就得列举更多具体事例才能说服他们接受文章的观点。

例 4 选自《说明文写作》（*Expository Writing*）（李莉文，2015），请体会作者如何通过大量举例和细节描绘来说明观点的。

例 4

Temperaments are so various that there may be even more than "nine and sixty ways" of writing books. Rousseau, for example, could not compose with pen in hand; but then Chateaubriand could not compose without. Wordsworth did it while walking, riding, or in bed; but Southey, only at his desk. Shakespeare, we are told, never blotted a line; Scott could toss first drafts unread to the printer; Trollope drilled himself, watch on desk, to produce two hundred and fifty words every quarter of an hour; Hilaire Belloc, so Desmond MacCarthy once told me, claimed to have written twenty thousand of them in a day; and in ten days Balzac could turn out sixty thousand.

解读 作者运用了九位作家的事例来说明：作家写书的方式与其脾性相关，各不相同。这些例子与主题句紧密相关，富有代表性；通过 we are told 和 so Desmond MacCarthy once told me 这些表达形式的运用，显得真实可信。作者的语言很精练，寥寥几笔就勾画出各位作家的特点，让读者在短短的文字中就能充分感受到他们性情各异、不拘一格，并对 various 这个中心词产生共鸣。

3. 分类说明
Development by Classification

说明文通常在对某一主题或特定事物做概括性的介绍之后，使用分类说明的手法进行进一步解释，以帮助读者对所说明主题或事物有更细致、更深入的了解。分类说明包括两个过程：区分（division）和归类（classification）。区分是指把一个整体分成几个部分，而归类则是指依据一定的原则把个体归入不同类别。说明文通常先把一个主题分成几个观点或把某一事物分成几个类别，再逐一阐述或解释。

运用分类说明的写作手法时，作者的目的是向读者呈现某一独具特色的分类方式，所以应充分考虑读者的兴趣或需要。比如在向大学新生介绍课程时，可以根据学生是否可以自由选择课程分为必修课和选修课，也可以按照课程目的分为专业课和通识课，还可以按照授课方式分为线上课程和线下课程。在例5中，一位心理医生就"上网成瘾"的问题提出了自己的分类方式：

例5

I think all cyberspace addictions can be separated into two very general categories: social and non-social types. Some people may be very preoccupied with their computers but have little interest in using it to communicate and socialize with others. These people may use their computers, as well as the Internet, to play solitary games, work, collect information, or explore. In other words, they may be game, information, or adventure junkies—or simply workaholics—but they are not necessarily using cyberspace to make interpersonal connections.

Most Internet addictions are the social type. People get hooked on chat environments, social media, and mailing lists. They may have extensive e-mail relationships. They are looking for social stimulation. The needs underlying this social Internet addiction are interpersonal: to be recognized, to belong, to be powerful, to be loved, etc. In contrast, people addicted only to their computers often avoid the interpersonal "chaos" of chat rooms and the like. For them, the need for control and predictability may be dominant.

—cited from the website of Rider University

解读 作者先把上网成瘾者分成两大类别：社会型和非社会型，再分别描述这两类人的特点，最后分析了两者的区别。

4. 因果说明
Development by Cause and Effect

因果说明是一种分析事物之间联系的写作方法，其主要目的是向读者解释：（1）某一事件或情况发生的原因；（2）某一事件或情况产生的影响；（3）某一事件或情况的起因和后果。采用哪种类型的因果说明取决于文章的主题和想要表达的观点。比如，如果写作目的是告知读者某人对你产生的影响，文章的重点应是那位人物的"影响"；如果你想解释为什么选择不住校，则应该重点说明作出这一决定的原因。

运用因果分析方法撰写说明文时，作者应选择读者感兴趣的主题，把观点表达清楚，并通过客观的推理展开全文，使文章内容合乎逻辑、结构清晰。常用的表示原因的词汇有：because、since、for、now that、due to、by virtue of、on account of、 owing to、as a result of、result from、arise from、originate from 等；表示结果的有：therefore、so、thus、hence、consequently、so that、as a result、in consequence、eventually、cause、give rise to、bring about、result in、account for 等。请阅读例 6 并留意表示因果关系的词语：

例6

Predators have a negative effect on the animals they consume, obviously. As a result, in response, prey animals have evolved defenses against being consumed. This change in the prey leads to the predator's developing more effective strategies. There is an evolutionary arms race: predators change strategies, going one step farther, which causes prey to change strategies in the same general way. As a result, both groups evolve at a fast pace. As the predator becomes more successful, the pressure builds on the prey to improve defenses. Conversely, the better the defense, the greater the need for the predator to develop its skills.

—cited from *Expository Writing*

解读 这个段落的主题是捕食性动物和它们的猎物在进攻和防守的过程中相互影响、不断进化。通过合理运用表示因果关系的词语，如 have a negative effect on、as a result、lead to、cause 等，文章逻辑性强、衔接紧密。

5. 对比说明
Development by Comparison and Contrast

对比是说明文常用的写作手法，常与分类说明一起使用：作者先对某一事物进行分类，再对已分类事物的异同进行比较，以帮助读者进一步了解所说明的事物。如例 5 所示，作者先把上网成瘾者分成社会型和非社会型两类，再依次说明并比较这两类人的特点，最后分析得出虽然他们都对网络产生依赖，但最主要区别在于上网过程中是否在意与他人社交。

运用对比说明的写作手法时，侧重点可以在于对比（contrast），即强调两个事物的不同，也可以在于比较（comparison），即强调两者的相似之处，还可以同时运用对比和比较。选择哪种方法取决于文章的写作目的或交流意图。如果你想表达的观点是自己做饭好过吃外卖，你可以对比自己做饭和外卖在费用、口味和营养等方面的差异，并强调自己做饭会带来更多益处；如果你想告诉读者上网课和在教室上课一样不错，你可以着重比较两者的相似之处。

比较两个事物的相似之处时，常用的词汇有：the same as、be similar to、be

identical with/to、be comparable to、be analogous to、resemble、like、likewise、similarly、in like manner、have in common、in the same manner、by comparison、equally important 等。

对比两个事物的差异时，常用的词汇有：be different from、differ from、be distinct from、unlike、in contrast、by contrast、on the contrary、conversely、instead、whereas、while、however、on the other hand、nevertheless、in spite of 等。

运用对比说明时，既可以采用逐点分析（point-by-point）的方式，也可以采用分段分析（one side at a time）的方式。例 5 先对上网成瘾者进行分类，再采用分段分析的方式，对这两类人分别进行描述；例 7 则采用逐点分析的方式，在同一段落里对两种语言进行比较，以解释文化是如何影响语言的。

例 7

The way in which culture affects language becomes clear by comparing how the English and Hopi languages refer to H_2O in its liquid state. English, like most other European languages, has only one word—"water"—and it pays no attention to what the substance is used for or its quantity. The Hopi of Arizona, on the other hand, use "pahe" to mean the large amounts of water present in natural lakes or rivers, and "keyi" for the small amounts in domestic jugs and canteens. English, though, makes other distinctions that Hopi does not. The speaker of English is careful to distinguish between a lake and a stream, between a waterfall and a geyser; but "pahe" makes no distinction among lakes, ponds, rivers, streams, waterfalls, and springs.

—cited from *Expository Writing*

解读 为了说明文化对语言的影响，这个段落对比了英语和霍皮语对"水"的指称。从 on the other hand、though、but 等词的使用来看，段落重在对比两者的不同，并采用逐点分析的方式，先对比了两种语言对"水"这种基本形态的指称，再就有无对自然水具体形态的区分进行了对比。

6. 下定义
Development by Definition

下定义是用来解释特定事物含义的说明方法。为了解释清楚事物的特点，定义说明通常显示其所属类别，并将其与同一类别中的其他事物加以区分，再用具体细节对其本质特征或区别于其他事物的属性进行说明。

运用定义说明的主要目的是向读者解释作者对某一概念的理解，次要目的是让读者认为这一定义是合理的。因此并不需要重复这个概念在词典里的定义，而应该强调作者个人的理解，并用具体事例来说明观点。下定义时常用的词汇有：be、mean、be called、be defined as、be known as、be referred to as 等。例 8 通过定义说明的写作方法对 paralanguage 进行了解释：

例 8

Paralanguage is the meaning that is perceived along with the actual words used to deliver a message. It is how we say something. This is a broad category that includes a number of traits such as dialects, accents, pitch, rate, vocal qualities, pauses and silence. A pleasing voice, for example, will make people more likely to listen to what is being said. And a modulated voice indicates a higher social status and a better education.

—cited from *Expository Writing*

解读 段落开头强调了副语言属于"意义"这个类别，再用简短的"It's how we say something."表达了作者的个人理解，并与同属于副语言的 actual words 形成对比；接下来列举了副语言所包含的特性，并通过"令人愉快的嗓音"和"有控制的嗓音"两个例证解释了副语言的特点。

通常来说，一篇说明文很少只用到一种说明方法，而是以一种说明方法为主，辅以其他说明方法。例如，采用对比说明的文章很可能包含例证说明，而运用分类说明的文章可能会同时使用定义说明。

二、说明文写作常见问题
Common Problems in Expository Writing

当使用不同的说明方法时，需要避免两个常见问题：缺乏具体细节（lack of specific details）和缺乏连贯性（lack of coherence）。

说明文写作的第一大问题是缺乏具体的细节。比如，在运用例证说明时，事例过于笼统、模糊或简短，以至于达不到解释说明的效果。因此写作时需要尽量提供清晰、具体且详尽的细节，以说服读者。例如，在一篇声称"美式足球变得过于暴力"的文章中，不要只宣称"去年有太多球员受伤了"，而应该给出更多细节作进一步展开，甚至通过呈现真实示例，包括球员的手指卡住、背部扭伤、腿部骨折、膝盖压碎等细节，让读者"看到"那个满是血迹的球场和伤痕累累的球员，进而认同你的观点。

说明文写作的第二大问题是缺乏连贯性。仍以例证说明为例，如果有些段落包含不止一个示例，就不能让读者从一个例子读到另一个例子时感觉思维中断了。每个段落应该重点突出，按解释主题句的强弱顺序安排例子，并确保每个例子在逻辑上与前后语句顺畅衔接。为了避免列表效应，可以使用衔接词或衔接短语，以确保例子到例子以及点到点的顺畅衔接。

三、说明文写作要点
Essentials in Expository Writing

为了写出一篇高质量的说明文，请记住以下要点：

第一，考虑读者需要（be aware of the audience）。在写作之前先问自己读者希望从文中获得什么。以过程说明为例，如果读者想知道如何制作巧克力饼干，你应该具体告知他们该做什么，并给出如何做的指示；如果读者想知道消化一块巧克力饼干的过程，则应该详细描述食物在身体里转化为能量的具体步骤。在第二种情况下，你不会给出指示，只会提供信息。无论你的主要观点是什么，写作时都要把读者放在心上，选择他们感兴趣的话题。例如，大学生可能对如何找到报酬丰厚的兼职工作感兴趣，而对如何为退休做好准备的文章兴趣不大。

第二，选择合适的主题（select an appropriate topic）。你需要选择自己完全了解的主题，并确保它相对简单，在一篇几百词的小文中就可以详细描述。例如，在一篇300 词的文章中，最好描述如何选择一门在线课程，而不是如何开发一门能满足大学生需求的在线课程。

第三，加入主旨句（include a thesis）。在确定主题之后，下一步是拟好主旨句并在引言部分明确地提出来。在开头提出主题并在下文适当地提及，可以使文章具有统一性和连贯性，而不是事实和观点的简单罗列。例 9 是一些主旨句示例：

例9

- Needlepoint is a simple, restful, fun hobby for both men and women.
- Donating blood is not the painful process one might suspect.
- The raid on Pearl Harbor wasn't altogether unexpected.
- Returning to school as an older-than-average student isn't as difficult as it may look.

第四，采用合适的人称（choose the right point of view）。为了和读者有效地沟通，写说明文之前需要考虑好使用什么人称。以过程说明为例，如果你打算给读者一些具体的指示，可以使用第二人称写作，直接用"你"来称呼，并指导读者；如果你的写作意图是为读者提供信息，则最好使用更正式的第三人称。每篇文章都需要选择最适合读者阅读的人称，以帮助他们更好地把握文章的信息和观点。

第五，斟酌如何结尾（pay special attention to your conclusion）。不要让文章在说明结束后戛然而止，而应通过讲述这个主题的意义来结束这篇文章，或者用简要的评论来结束。总之，无论如何收尾，文章都应给读者留下一种获得感。

第三节　以读促写说明文
Reading for Expository Writing

对于新手作者而言，学会分析性阅读能提高写作能力，对高质量完成写作任务大有帮助。为了更有效地写出一篇说明文，例 10 介绍了一篇专业作家撰写的文章，并按照分析性阅读的 10 个步骤深入分析文章的内容、结构和风格。

例 10

So What's So Bad About Being So-So?

Lisa Wilson Strick

Lisa Wilson Strick is a freelance writer who publishes in a variety of magazines, frequently on the subjects of family and education. She is co-author of Learning Disabilities, A to Z: A Parent's Complete Guide to Learning Disabilities from Pre-school to Adulthood *(1997). This essay first appeared in* Woman's Day *in 1984.*

1　　The other afternoon I was playing the piano when my seven-year-old walked in. He stopped and listened awhile, then said: "Gee, Mom, you don't play that thing very well, do you?"

2　　No, I don't. I am a piano lesson dropout. The fine points of fingering totally escape me. I play everything at half-speed, with many errant notes. My performance would make any serious music student wince, but I don't care. I've enjoyed playing the piano badly for years.

3　　I also enjoy singing badly and drawing badly. (I used to enjoy sewing badly, but I've been doing that so long that I finally got pretty good at it.) I'm not ashamed of my incompetence in these areas. I do one or two other things well and that should be enough for anybody. But it gets boring doing the same things over and over. Every now and then it's fun to try something new.

4　　Unfortunately, doing things badly has gone out of style. It used to be a mark of class if a lady or a gentleman sang a little, painted a little, played the violin a little. You didn't have to be good at it; the point was to be fortunate enough to have the leisure time for such pursuits. But in today's competitive world we have to be "experts"—even in our hobbies. You can't tone up your body by pulling on your sneakers and slogging around the block a couple of times anymore. Why? Because you'll be laughed off the street by the "serious" runners—the ones who log twenty-plus miles a week in their headbands, sixty-dollar running suits and fancy shoes. The shoes are really a big deal. If you say you're thinking about taking up almost any sport, the first thing the aficionados will ask is what you plan to do about shoes. Leather or canvas? What types of soles? What brand? This is not the time to mention that the gym shoes you wore in high school are still in pretty good shape. As far as sports enthusiasts are concerned, if you don't have the latest shoes, you are hopelessly committed to mediocrity.

5　　The runners aren't nearly so snobbish as the dance freaks, however. In case you didn't know, "going dancing" no longer means putting on a pretty dress and doing a few turns around the ballroom with your favorite man on Saturday night. "Dancing" means squeezing into tights and a leotard and leg warmers, then sweating through six hours of warm-ups and five hours of ballet and four hours of jazz classes. Every week. Never tell anyone that you "like to dance" unless this is the sort of activity you enjoy. (At least the costume isn't so costly, as dancers seem to be cultivating a riches-to-rags look lately.)

6　　We used to do these things for fun or simply to relax. Now the competition you face in your hobbies is likely to be worse than anything you run into on the job. "Oh, you've taken up knitting," a friend recently said to me. "Let me show you the adorable cable-knit, popcorn-stitched cardigan with twelve tiny reindeer prancing across the yoke that I made for my daughter. I dyed the yarn myself." Now why did you have to go and do that? I was getting a kick out of watching my yellow muffler grow a couple of inches a week up till then. And all I wanted was something to keep my hands busy while I watched television anyway.

7　　Have you noticed what this is doing to our children? "We don't want that dodo on our soccer team," I overheard a ten-year-old sneer the other day. "He doesn't know a goal kick from a head shot." As it happens, the boy was talking about my son, who did not—like some of his friends—start soccer instruction at age three (along with pre-school diving, creative writing and Suzuki clarinet). I'm sorry, Son, I guess I blew it. In my day when we played softball on the corner lot, we expected to give a little instruction to the younger kids who didn't know how. It didn't matter if they were terrible; we weren't out to slaughter the other team. Sometimes we didn't even keep score. To us, sports were just a way of having a good time. Of course we didn't have some of the nifty things kids have today—such as matching uniforms and professional coaches. All we had was a bunch of kids of various ages who enjoyed each other's company.

8   I don't think kids have as much fun as they used to. Competition keeps getting in the way. The daughter of a neighbor is a nervous wreck worrying about getting into the best gymnastics school. "I was a late starter," she told me, "and I only get to practice five or six hours a week, so my technique may not be up to their standards." The child is nine. She doesn't want to be a gymnast when she grows up; she wants to be a nurse. I asked what she likes to do for fun in her free time, she said, "I mean homework and gymnastics and flute lessons kind of eat it all up. I have flute lessons three times a week now, so I have a good shot at getting into the all-state orchestra."

9   Ambition, drive and the desire to excel are all admirable within limits, but I don't know where the limits are anymore. I know a woman who has always wanted to learn a foreign language. For years she has complained that she hasn't the time to study one. I've pointed out that an evening course in French or Italian would take only a couple of hours a week, but she keeps putting it off. I suspect that what she hasn't got the time for is to become completely fluent within the year—and that any lesser level of accomplishment would embarrass her. Instead she spends her evenings watching reruns on television and tidying up her closets—occupations at which no particular expertise is expected.

10   I know others who are avoiding activities they might enjoy because they lack the time or the energy to tackle them "seriously". It strikes me as so silly. We are talking about recreation. I have nothing against self-improvement. But when I hear a teenager muttering "practice makes perfect" as he grimly makes his four-hundred-and-twenty-seventh try at hooking the basketball into the net left-handed, I wonder if some of us aren't improving ourselves right into the loony bin.

11　I think it's time we put a stop to all this. For sanity's sake, each of us should vow to take up something new this week—and to make sure we never master it completely. Sing along with grand opera. Make peculiar-looking objects out of clay. I can tell you from experience that fallen soufflés still taste pretty good. The point is to enjoy being a beginner again; to discover the joy of creative fooling around. If you find it difficult, ask any two-year-old to teach you. Two-year-olds have a gift for tackling the impossible with zest; repeated failure hardly discourages them at all.

12　As for me, I'm getting a little out of shape so I'm looking into tennis. A lot of people I know enjoy it, and it doesn't look too hard. Given a couple of lessons I should be stumbling gracelessly around the court and playing badly in no time at all.

—cited from *Steps to Writing Well*

分析性阅读讲解

第 1 步： 留意出版信息和作者介绍。这篇文章最初于 1984 年发表在一本名为《妇女节》的杂志上，它可能针对的是特定受众——关心家庭和教育的女性读者，主要的写作目的是回应一些争议，即"马马虎虎是否不好"。这篇文章发表时间较早，但主题并不过时，而作者作为一名经常发表关于家庭和教育问题的作家，的确有资格就此争议发表看法。

第 2 步： 注意文章标题是如何引出主题的。标题"So What's So Bad About Being So-So?"质疑了关心工作和生活质量的人经常持有的一个观点，即马马虎虎是不好的，并暗示了该文具有讽刺意味。

第 3 步： 第一遍阅读文章，并写下你对文章的大致印象。通读之后可以得知，作者"喜欢做初学者，喜欢做得不够好"。她写这篇文章的目的是呼吁人们不要把活动太当真，并用了很多生动而具体的例子来说明和解释她的观点。

第 4 步： 再次查看标题和介绍性段落。它们有效地树立起了读者的期望，即作者试图在这篇文章中解释她的观点：马马虎虎并没有错。

第 5 步： 找到作者的要点或主旨。文章的主旨句可以在第四段的开头找到："Unfortunately, doing things badly has gone out of style."。请标记这个观点，以便在后续阅读中以此为参考。

第 6 步： 查找支持或说明主旨的重要语句。通常支持性陈述是接近正文段落开头或结尾的主题句。例如，在第四段的第四句中，作者指出："在当今竞争激烈的世界中，我们必须成为'专家'——即使在业余爱好中也得如此。"

第 7 步： 分析作者是如何推进主题的，又是如何发展、解释或论证支持性观点的。作者提供了大量示例来支持她的观点，比如第五段对 dance freaks（舞蹈狂热爱好者）的描述和讽刺，第六段举例说明原本是娱乐放松方式的编织也变成了一种竞争，第七段和第八段展示过度竞争对孩子的影响，作者同时采用对比的写作策略来展示过去和现在的巨大反差，以进一步阐释自己的观点：现代社会过于强调竞争和专业性，破坏了爱好和休闲。

第8步： 查看文章的布局和组织形式。作者有效地使用论证策略来组织文章，并通过举例和对比明确要点。

第9步： 分析文章的推进是否有逻辑性和连贯性。作者运用一些过渡性句子来推进文章，增强连贯性，如第五段中的"The runners aren't nearly so snobbish as the dance freaks, however."，第七段中的"Have you noticed what this is doing to our children?"，这些句子很好地连接了上下文，使文章更加统一流畅。

第10步： 思考作者的风格和文章的语气。作者通过描述自己的经历和对周围人的观察，表明了她对生活的态度："The point is to enjoy being a beginner again; to discover the joy of creative fooling around."。这篇文章的语气带点讽刺性，很适合这篇文章的目的，即在生活中"马马虎虎"没什么不好，这样才能有更多创新和尝试。

在完成以上分析性阅读步骤之后，试问自己：我学到了哪些说明文的写作策略？我能将哪些新想法、新策略或新技巧融入自己的写作中？

Exercises

I. **Here is a list of statements which you can use as prompts to discover a focused essay topic of your own design. You can write an expository essay after selecting the right subject matter.**

1. Failure is a better teacher than success.

2. First impressions are often the best/worst means of judging people.

3. The willingness to undertake adventures is a necessary part of a happy existence.

4. Travel can be the best medicine.

5. Participation in (a particular sport, club, hobby, or event) teaches valuable lessons.

6. Modern technology can produce more inconvenience than convenience.

7. Job hunting today is a difficult process.

8. Many required courses are / are not relevant to a student's education.

II. **After you have produced your first draft of the expository essay, revise it in terms of purpose, audience, content, format, and language based on the checklist below. Please tick the box if your answer to the question is yes.**

No.	Checklist for Self-evaluation	Yes
1)	Have I demonstrated a clear writing purpose and a good awareness of audience?	
2)	Have I presented a clearly stated thesis in my opening paragraph?	
3)	Have I written a topic sentence in each of my body paragraphs?	
4)	What pattern(s) of development have I used in my essay?	
5)	Have I provided relevant details to illustrate my points?	
6)	Have I provided enough details to support my points?	
7)	Have I used transitional words or phrases to help the readers follow my train of thought?	
8)	Does my essay have a concluding paragraph that provides a summary or final thought or both?	
9)	Have I used an adequate range of vocabulary?	
10)	Have I checked the language of my essay to ensure that it's error-free?	

III. Then review one or more peer essays in terms of purpose, audience, content, format, and language based on the checklist below. Please tick the box if your answer to the question is yes.

No.	Checklist for Peer Review	Yes
1)	Has the author demonstrated a clear writing purpose and a good awareness of audience?	
2)	Has the author presented a clearly stated thesis in the opening paragraph?	
3)	Has the author written a topic sentence in each of the body paragraphs?	
4)	What pattern(s) of development has the author used in the essay?	
5)	Has the author provided relevant details to illustrate his/her points?	
6)	Has the author provided enough details to support his/her points?	
7)	Has the author used transitional words or phrases to help the readers follow his/her train of thought?	
8)	Does the essay have a concluding paragraph that provides a summary or final thought or both?	
9)	Has the author used an adequate range of vocabulary?	
10)	Has the author checked the language of the essay to ensure that it's error-free?	

Sample

范文

Born to Be Different

Camille Lewis

The notion that the differences between the sexes (beyond the obvious anatomical ones) are biologically based is fraught with controversy. Such beliefs can easily be misinterpreted and used as the basis for harmful, oppressive stereotypes. They can be overstated and exaggerated into blanket statements about what men and women "can" and "can't" do; about what the genders are "good" and "bad" at. And yet, the unavoidable fact is that studies are making it ever clearer that, as groups, men and women differ in almost every measurable aspect. Learning about those differences helps us understand why men and women are simultaneously so attracted and fascinated, and yet so frequently stymied and frustrated, by the opposite sex.

To begin with, let's look at something as basic as the anatomy of the brain. Typically, men have larger skulls and brains than women. But the sexes score equally well on intelligence tests. This apparent contradiction is explained by the fact that our brains are apportioned differently. Women have about 15% more "gray matter" than men. Gray matter, made up of nerve cells and the branches that connect them, allows the quick transference of thought from one part of the brain to another. This high concentration of gray matter helps explain women's ability to look at many sides of an argument at once, and to do several tasks (or hold several conversations simultaneously).

Men's brains, on the other hand, have a more generous portion of "white matter." White matter, which is made up of neurons, actually inhibits the spread of information. It allows men to concentrate very narrowly on a specific task, without being distracted by thoughts that might conflict with the job at hand.

Our brains' very different make-up leads to our very different methods of interacting with the world around us. Simon Baron-Cohen, author of *The Essential Difference: Men, Women and the Extreme Male Brain*, has labeled the classic female mental process as "empathizing". He defines empathizing as "the drive to identify another person's emotions and thoughts, and to respond to these with an appropriate emotion". Empathizers are constantly measuring and responding to the surrounding emotional temperature. They are concerned about showing sensitivity to the people around them. This empathetic quality can be observed in virtually all aspects of women's lives: from the choice of typically female-dominated careers (nursing, elementary school teaching, social work) to reading matter popular mainly with women (romantic fiction, articles about relationships, advice columns about how people can get along better) to women's interaction with one another (which typically involves intimate discussion of relationships with friends and family, and sympathy for each other's concerns). So powerful is the empathizing mindset that it even affects how the typical female memory works. Ask a woman when a particular event happened, and she often pinpoints it in terms of an occurrence that had emotional content: "That was the summer my sister broke her leg," or "That was around the time Gene and Mary got into such an awful argument." Likewise, she is likely to bring her empathetic mind to bear on geography. She'll remember a particular address not as 11th and Market Streets but being "near the restaurant where we went on our anniversary," or "around the corner from Liz's old apartment".

In contrast, Baron-Cohen calls the typical male mindset "systemizing", which he defines as "the drive to analyze and explore a system, to extract underlying rules that govern the behavior of a system". A systemizer is less interested in how people feel than in how things work. Again, the systematic brain influences virtually all aspects of the typical man's life. Male-dominated professions (such as engineering, computer programming, auto repair, and mathematics) rely heavily on systems, formulas, and patterns, and very little on the ability to intuit another person's thoughts or emotions. Reading material most popular with men includes science fiction and history, as well as factual "how-to" magazines on such topics as computers, photography, home repair, and woodworking. When they get together with male friends, men are far less likely to engage in intimate conversation than they are to share an activity: watching or playing sports, working on a car, bowling, golfing, or fishing. Men's conversation is peppered with dates and addresses, illustrating their comfort with systems: "Back in 1996 when I was living in Boston..." or "The best way to the new stadium is to go all the way out Walnut Street to 33rd and then get on the bypass...".

One final way that men and women differ is in their typical responses to problem solving. Ironically, it may be this very activity—intended on both sides to eliminate problems—that creates the most conflict between partners of the opposite sex. To a woman, the process of solving a problem is all-important. Talking about a problem is a means of deepening the intimacy between her and her partner. The very anatomy of her brain, as well as her accompanying empathetic mindset, makes her want to consider all sides of a question and to explore various possible solutions. To have a partner who is willing to explore a problem with her is deeply satisfying. She interprets that willingness as an expression of the other's love and concern.

But men have an almost completely opposite approach when it comes to dealing with a problem. Everything in their mental make-up tells them to focus narrowly on the issue, solve it, and get it out of the way. The ability to fix a problem quickly and efficiently is, to them, a demonstration of their power and competence. When a man hears his female partner begin to describe a problem, his strongest impulse is to listen briefly and then tell her what to do about it. From his perspective, he has made a helpful and loving gesture; from hers, he's short-circuited a conversation that could have deepened and strengthened their relationship.

The challenge that confronts men and women is to put aside ideas of "better" and "worse" when it comes to their many differences. Our diverse brain development, our ways of interacting with the world, and our modes of dealing with problems all have their strong points. In some circumstances, a typically feminine approach may be more effective; in others, a classically masculine mode may have the advantage. Our differences aren't going to disappear: my daughter, now a middle-schooler, regularly tells me she loves me, while her teenage brothers express their affection by grabbing me in a headlock. Learning to understand and appreciate one another's gender specific qualities is the key to more rich and rewarding lives together.

赏析

In this expository essay, the author makes an explicit thesis statement in the introductory paragraph to indicate that there are fundamental biological differences between men and women, learning about which is the key to more rich and rewarding lives together.

She provides adequate evidence to support such a point of view through comparison and contrast and helps us develop a better understanding of the gender-specific qualities.

第七章

议论文写作
Arguing for a Point—
Argumentative Writing

学习要点

- 议论文的概念和结构
- 议论文的交际性写作
- 议论文的写作策略
- 议论文的分析性阅读

 第一节 **议论文写作概述**
Introduction to Argumentative Writing

一、议论文的概念
Concept of Argumentative Writing

　　议论文是针对特定主题提出看法或主张，并通过分析事理、提供例证或驳斥对立观点等方式，说服读者接受该看法或主张的写作体裁。与说明文不同，议论文探讨的并不是公认的客观事实或科学原理，而是具有一定争议性的问题，这些问题的答案往往也不是非黑即白。人们常说："真理总是越辩越明。"这些问题的议论过程，也就是人们思维碰撞、辨明真相、寻求真知的过程。

　　在大学里，议论文写作是学术探讨的基础；在日常生活中，议论技能则对表达观点和阐明立场起到至关重要的作用。古典修辞学派认为，如果人人都拥有良好的议论技能，能够有效协商并达成共识，那么个人乃至国家之间的纷争都会减少。学习议论文写作的重要性可见一斑。

二、议论文的结构
Structure of Argumentative Writing

议论文通常分为三个部分：第一部分是引言，介绍探讨的问题或现象，并通过主旨句提出中心论点（thesis），以表明立场；第二部分是正文，为支持中心论点而阐述若干观点，即分论点（sub-points），正文部分还可进一步囊括驳论（refutation），以增强说服力；第三部分是结论，用精简小段概括要点，或指引未来相关探讨方向。

与说明文类似，为了使论证逻辑层次清晰、结构严密，议论文的每个正文段落只能包含一个分论点，并且该分论点需要具体证据（即论据〔evidence〕）来支撑。一篇议论文至少需要两个分论点；根据论证需求和篇幅要求，分论点数量可适当增加。

与分论点相同，驳论部分需要自成一段，针对对立观点的不合理处进行反驳，并提供证据。驳论段落的具体位置较为灵活，通常置于正文最后一部分，即结论段之前。为了使论证流畅，引言、各分论点段落和结论之间应采用合乎逻辑的衔接词或衔接句。表 7.1 呈现了议论文的逻辑结构：

表 7.1　议论文的逻辑结构

部分	内部结构	
引言	吸引读者兴趣的开场白	
	主旨句（中心论点）	
正文	分论点 1	主题句 具体论据
	分论点 2	主题句 具体论据
	驳论	点明对立观点 让步（可选） 反驳对立观点
结论	概要 结束语	

注：分论点数量可根据论证需求和篇章要求适当增加

请仔细阅读例 1，并分析其结构。

例 1

From Lecture to Conversation: Redefining What's "Fit to Print"

"All the news that's fit to print," the motto of *The New York Times* since 1896, plays with the word "fit", asserting that a news story must be newsworthy and must not exceed the limits of the printed page. The increase in online news consumption, however, challenges both meanings of the word "fit", allowing producers and consumers alike to rethink who decides which topics are worth covering and how extensive that coverage should be. Any cultural shift usually means that something is lost, but in this case, there are clear gains. The shift from print to online news provides unprecedented opportunities for readers to become more engaged with the news, to hold journalists accountable, and to participate as producers, not simply as consumers.

One of the most important advantages online news offers over print news is the presence of built-in hyperlinks, which engage readers in a totally new way. As we all know, traditional print news reports stories according to what editors decide is fit for their readers. It is thus a fully formed lecture created without participation from its readership. By contrast, online news with hyperlinks allows readers to find out the information they need, such as the definition of a term, the roots of a story, or other perspectives on a topic. For instance, the link embedded in the story "Credit-shy: Younger Generation Is More Likely to Stick to a Cash-only Policy" allows readers to find out more about the financial trends of young adults and provides statistics that confirm the article's accuracy. Other links in the article widen the conversation. These kinds of links give readers the opportunity to conduct their own evaluation of the evidence and verify the journalist's claims.

Links also provide a kind of transparency impossible in print because they allow readers to see through online news to the sources, assumptions and values that may have influenced a news story. The International Center for Media and the Public Agenda underscores the importance of news organizations letting "customers in on the often tightly held little secrets of journalism". To do so, they suggest, will lead to "accountability and accountability leads to credibility". These tools alone don't guarantee that news producers will be responsible and trustworthy, but they encourage an open and transparent environment that benefits news consumers.

Not everyone embraces the spread of unregulated news reporting online. Critics point out that citizen journalists are not necessarily trained to be fair or ethical, for example, nor are they subject to editorial oversight. However, as Gillmor put it, although citizen journalists are "non-experts", they are using technology to make a profound contribution. For example, citizen reporting made a difference in the wake of

Hurricane Katrina in 2005. Armed with cell phones and laptops, regular citizens relayed critical news updates in a rapidly developing crisis, often before traditional journalists were even on the scene. In 2006, the enormous contributions of citizen journalists were recognized when *The Times-Picayune* received the Pulitzer Prize in public service for its online coverage—largely citizen-generated—of Hurricane Katrina.

The Internet has enabled consumers to participate in a new way in reading, questioning, interpreting, and reporting the news. Decisions about appropriate content and coverage are no longer exclusively in the hands of news editors. Ordinary citizens now have a meaningful voice in the conversation—a hand in deciding what's "fit to print". Some skeptics worry about the apparent free-for-all and loss of tradition. But the expanding definition of news provides opportunities for consumers to be more engaged with events in their communities, their nations, and the world.

—cited from *A Writer's Reference*

解读 例 1 论证了传统纸质新闻向网络新闻转变能为读者带来的益处，是一篇结构清晰且规范的议论文。第一段是引言，包含了吸引读者的开场白以及中心论点（The shift from print to online news provides unprecedented opportunities for readers to become more engaged with the news, to hold journalists accountable, and to participate as producers, not simply as consumers.）。第二段至第四段是正文，分别从网络新闻能使读者"更深入地了解新闻内容""向新闻记者追责"和"以作者身份参与报道"三个方面对中心论点进行了论证。其中，第二段和第三段是分论点，每一个分论点段落均以主题句开头，并提供具体论据支撑主题句；第四段是驳论，作者针对"网络新闻写手不够专业"的对立观点进行了反驳，并用具体事例论证了网民在新闻报道中的贡献。最后一段是结论，对文章的要点进行概括，并表明网络为民众参与家国大事提供了机会。

 三、 议论文的交际性写作
Communicative Writing in Argumentation

议论文写作是一个探讨真相、真知的过程，其目的是说服读者同意作者对特定问题的看法。因此，撰写议论文时首先需要了解读者，从他们的角度审视关于某一论点的陈述是否有理有据、用语得体，从而在不冒犯读者的同时，以理服人、引发共鸣，达到说服的交际目的。具体来说，可从以下三方面来实现议论文的交际性写作。

第一，在主题的确定上，需要考虑什么样的主题容易激发读者的阅读兴趣，并拥有充足的讨论空间。通常来说，具有争议性、热点性及哲理性的主题最能吸引读者。例如，现在若依然讨论"吸烟是否有害健康"（Is smoking harmful to health?）这一主题，未免过于老生常谈，结论也是不言而喻的，但如果主题是"新冠疫情是否会扼杀全球化"（Will COVID-19 kill off globalization?），在抓人眼球的同时，探讨该问题的实际意义也更加显著。例 2 是一些议论文主题的示例：

例 2

- The government is spending a lot of money to discover life on other planets. Some people think that the government is wasting money and should spend more money addressing the public's problems. To what extent do you agree?
- Modern technology is now very common in most workplaces. Do you think there are disadvantages to relying too much on technology?
- More and more children are accessing the Internet unsupervised. This can sometimes put children at risk. How can this problem be solved?

第二，在论据的选择上，需要考虑读者的身份。读者是专家或老师，还是你的同龄人？他们对该话题的了解程度如何？在了解这些问题的基础上，再考虑用什么样的事实和证据来说服读者。例如，如果读者是专业知识丰富的专家或老师，用自身经历作为证据或许会显得过于主观，不够严谨；如果读者是同龄人，那么你的亲身经历或许更容易引发共鸣。此外，议论文的主题通常较为复杂，从不同角度得出的结论不尽相同，因此在确立中心论点后，还需要考虑潜在的不同声音。若能针对读者最可能持有的相反观点进行有效驳斥，论证则更加完备，并让人信服。

第三，在语言使用上，除做到句法无误之外，还需要采用客观、得体的表达与读者沟通。在议论文的撰写中，作者并非站在一个权威的角度告知（inform）读者是非对错，而是以说服（persuade）为目的。若用语过于直接、强势，容易给读者留下肤浅、武断之感，从而削弱文章的说服力。在提出一些争议性较强的观点时，可采用相对委婉的表达，如 may、perhaps、probably 等，留以余地，以彰显论述的客观性。

请仔细阅读例 3，并思考作者是如何与读者沟通的。

例 3

Teenagers and Jobs

The pressure for teenagers to work is great, and not just because of the economic plight in the world today. Much of it is peer pressure to have a little bit freedom and independence, and to have their own spending money. The concern we have is when the part-time work becomes the primary focus. These are the words of Roxanne Bradshaw, educator and officer of the National Education Association. Many people argue that working can be a valuable experience for the young. However, working more than about fifteen hours a week is harmful to adolescents because it reduces their involvement with school, encourages a materialistic and expensive lifestyle, and increases the chance of having problems with drugs and alcohol.

Schoolwork and the benefits of extra-curricular activities tend to go by the wayside when adolescents work long hours. As more and more teens have filled the numerous part-time jobs offered by fast-food restaurants and malls, teachers have faced increasing difficulties. They must both keep the attention of tired pupils and give homework to students who simply don't have time to do it. In addition, educators have noticed less involvement in the extra-curricular activities. School bands and athletic teams are losing players to work, and sports events are poorly attended by working students. Those teens who try to do it all—homework, extra-curricular activities, and work—may find themselves exhausted and prone to illness. A recent newspaper story, for example, described a girl in Pennsylvania who came down with mononucleosis as a result of aiming for good grades, playing on two school athletic teams, and working thirty hours a week.

Another drawback of too much work is that it may promote materialism and an unrealistic lifestyle. Some parents claim that working helps teach adolescents the value of a dollar. Undoubtedly that can be true. It's also true that some teens work to help out with the family budget or to save for college. However, surveys have shown that the majority of working teens use their earnings to buy luxuries—computers, video-game systems, clothing, even cars. These young people, some of whom earn $500 or more a month, don't care about spending wisely—they can just about have it all. In many cases, experts point out, they are becoming accustomed to a lifestyle they won't be able to afford several years down the road, when they no longer have parents paying for car insurance, food, lodging, and so on. At that point, they'll be hard-pressed to pay for necessities as well as luxuries.

Finally, teenagers who work a lot are more likely than others to get involved with alcohol and drugs. Teens who put in long hours may seek a quick release from stress, just like the adults who need to drink a couple of martinis after a hard day at work. Also, teens who have money are more likely to get involved with drugs.

In conclusion, overwork does harm to teenagers. Yet, they can still enjoy the benefits of work while avoiding its drawbacks, simply by limiting their work hours during the school year. As is often the case, a moderate approach will be the healthiest and most rewarding.

—cited from *College Writing Skills with Readings*

解读 例 3 紧扣学生读者群，探讨了美国校园生活中的常见问题——青少年过度兼职打工对自身发展的影响。作者从"难以兼顾学业""过度追求物质生活"以及"引发酗酒和嗑药问题"三方面进行论证，并用具体事例、新闻报道、专家证词等作为证据支撑，显得有理有据。在第三段，作者针对读者可能持有的"兼职能帮助青少年了解金钱来之不易""兼职能减少家庭负担"等常见观点予以反驳。文章主要采用第三人称来表达观点，并使用了 may、more likely 等表达避免过于武断的陈述，给人以客观可靠之感。

第二节 议论文写作策略[1]
Strategies for Argumentative Writing

第二章介绍了如何进行写前准备的准备：收窄主题、确立中心论点（主旨句）以及提炼分论点，这些方法都可以应用到议论文写作中。本节将重点介绍议论文引言、论据以及驳论部分的具体写作策略，并针对议论文写作的常见问题进行讲解。

一、引言的写作策略
Writing Strategies for the Introduction

为了让读者关注所议论的主题，进而了解、接纳文章的观点，一段引人入胜、观点鲜明的引言非常重要。议论文引言的撰写大致上分为三步：（1）开头吸引读者兴趣；（2）介绍主题背景信息；（3）树立中心论点。

1. 吸引读者兴趣
Attracting Readers' Attention

文章开头需要使用吸引读者的开场白，以激发他们的阅读兴趣，常用的方法有：提问、讲故事、引用名言俗语、列举事实等。以论证"我们需要开发自动驾驶汽车"（We should develop self-driving cars.）为例（详见例 4），采用以下方式开头可以牢牢抓住读者的目光：

例 4

- 以提问题开头：Have you ever heard of a car that can see, hear, speak, and even

---

1 本节部分内容基于李明慕课脚本编写。

think? Have you ever dreamed to have a car like that? Self-driving technology can make your dream come true.

- 以讲故事开头: As a boy, I loved cars. When I turned 18, I lost my best friend to a car accident. Since then, I devoted myself to developing self-driving cars.
- 以列举事实开头: Driving accidents are the leading cause of death for young people, and most of these accidents are due to human error. Self-driving cars can help reduce car accidents.

2. 介绍背景信息
Presenting Background Information

在引发读者兴趣后，作者可以根据论述需要适当引入与主题相关的背景信息。此处需要思考：读者对议论的主题是否有所了解？有多了解？如果主题对于读者来说相对陌生，那么这一部分需要适当增加笔墨，为他们提供必要的背景知识。在介绍主题背景时，还需要注意逐渐收窄主题，自然过渡到观点本身。

3. 树立中心论点
Establishing Your Thesis

最后也是最重要的一个环节是，作者应在引言段末尾撰写主旨句，以向读者明确文章的中心论点。本书的第二章介绍了主旨句的一般写作方法，但针对议论文主旨句的撰写，还需要注意避免以下三个问题。

第一，立场不明（unclear position）。不同于说明文，议论文是以说服为目的，带有更多的个人色彩和态度，作者需要在主旨句中明确表明自己的立场，以便后文论证。例如，在主旨句 "Many people have different opinions on whether students should pay a fine for skipping classes, and I agree with some of them." 中，作者到底是支持还是反对迟到罚款的举措，完全没有说清楚。如果读者通过阅读主旨句，连作者持何立场都弄不清，更谈不上被说服了。

第二，包含两个要点（double-claim thesis）。例如，主旨句 "There should be a school in every small village, and how to successfully manage a school deserves our attention." 则包含了两个要点：（1）"每个村庄都需要有学校"；（2）"如何成功管理学校"。这两点的论述角度完全不同，不仅破坏了文章内容的一致性，也导致无法在有限的篇幅中详尽地论述每一个要点，进而削弱了文章的观点性。

第三，表达模糊（vague language）。例如，主旨句 "Self-driving cars are very good." 中的 very good 过于笼统，未能向读者阐明自动驾驶汽车到底好在哪里。

若将此句改为"Self-driving cars can bring great convenience to our life."，通过 convenience 一词则能具体明确地阐明观点，即"自动驾驶汽车好在让生活更便捷"。

撰写议论文主旨句时，作者还可以让读者进一步预览（preview）正文的分论点。这样做的好处是让读者对文章的整体结构与要点有大致的了解，能更顺畅地阅读正文。例如：

例5

中心论点: Working more than about fifteen hours a week is harmful to adolescents because it reduces their involvement with school, encourages a materialistic and expensive lifestyle, and increases the chance of having problems with drugs and alcohol.

- 分论点 1（主题句）: Schoolwork and the benefits of extra-curricular activities tend to go by the wayside when adolescents work long hours.
- 分论点 2（主题句）: Another drawback of too much work is that it may promote materialism and an unrealistic lifestyle.
- 分论点 3（主题句）: Teenagers who work a lot are more likely than others to get involved with alcohol and drugs.

解读 例5中，作者在表明立场时提出"青少年每周工作超过15小时是有害的"之后，用 because 作为连接，向读者展示了正文将要论述的三个分论点，层次分明、用语准确。

二、论据的写作策略
Writing Strategies for Using Evidence

论据是指用来证明论点的依据或证据。若空谈观点，没有扎实的论据来提供支撑，那文章就如同"桌子没了桌腿"一样，是立不住的，因此论据是议论文正文部分写作的重点。关于如何选择论据，你可以通过回答以下问题来找寻灵感：

- 我是否有与话题相关的经历？我是否知道有这种经历的人？（Have I had any experience related to the subject? Or do I know anyone who has the experience?）
- 是否有与话题相关的研究？（Is there any research done about the subject?）
- 是否有与话题相关的统计数据或实测数据？（Are there any relevant statistics or factual data about the subject?）
- 是否有权威人士或专业人士说过与话题相关的内容？（Are there any authorities or experts who once said anything about the subject?）

通过回答以上问题，论证观点的常用方法可以总结为以下四种：（1）举例子；（2）列数据；（3）引用专家观点；（4）展开子论点。

1. 举例子
Using Examples

通过给出具体事例以支撑论点是议论文中常用的论证方法。具体来说，议论文的例证包含两类：（1）用人物经历论证；（2）用假设性举例论证。

人物经历（personal experiences）是真实发生的事例，该经历可以来自作者自己或身边的亲朋好友，也可以来自某位名人。引用真实经历来佐证观点时需要注意两点：第一，选择的经历不可过于独特，否则会缺乏代表性（representativeness），以致无法有效支撑论点；第二，在某些对写作内容严谨性（rigor）要求较高的情况下，比如学术论文写作时，应尽量减少使用个人轶事作为证据。

假设性举例（hypothetical examples）是通过假定某种情形来阐明问题或设想某一事件的后果。比如，要想论证"网课无法成为教育主流"（Online course will not become the mainstream of education.）这一观点，你可以假设长期的网上学习可能给青少年视力和身体健康带来的后果，并予以论证。

请仔细阅读例6，并体会作者是如何同时运用人物经历和假设性举例来论证观点的。

例6

Although cell phones are a time-saving convenience for busy people, they are too distracting for use by drivers of moving vehicles, whose lack of full attention poses a serious threat to other drivers and to pedestrians. The simple act of answering a phone, for example, may take a driver's eyes away from traffic signals or other cars. Moreover, involvement in a complex or emotional conversation could slow down a driver's response time just when fast action is needed to avoid an accident. Last week I drove behind a man using his phone. As he drove and talked, I could see him gesturing wildly, obviously agitated with the other caller. His speed repeatedly slowed and then picked up, slowed and increased, and his car drifted more than once, on a street frequently crossed by schoolchildren. Because the man was clearly not in full, conscious control of his driving, he was dangerous.

—cited from *Steps to Writing Well*

解读 在这一段落中，作者使用生动具体的例子进行了逻辑严密的论证。作者首先在段落开头用主题句表明观点——使用电话易分散司机注意力，会给道路上的行人和其他车辆造成威胁。在接下来的论据部分，作者用两则假设性举例和一则人物经历来论证自己的观点。最后，作者分析得出"Because the man was clearly not in full, conscious control of his driving, he was dangerous.",进一步佐证了主题句中提出的"使用电话会分散司机注意力"的观点。

2. 列数据
Raising Figures

与人物经历相比，摆事实、讲数据是更加有力的论证方法。比如在例 6 中，如果作者列出全国每年因司机驾驶时使用电话造成的交通事故数量，这一证据远比单独的个体感受更具说服力。新闻报道、研究调查、权威著作等都是获取事实数据的可靠来源。在搜集数据资料时，需要注意判断数据的时效性（whether the data is up to date），比如十年前的网络犯罪数量并不适合用来论证现行的网络监管政策。另外，由于数据呈现和解读的方式会因立场不同而有所偏差，还需要仔细甄别从新闻、杂志、网络上查到的信息是否解读无误或带有既定偏见。总的来说，同行审阅的学术期刊或权威著作是最为可靠的数据来源，而网络上的信息质量良莠不齐，需要谨慎辨别。在论证中引用数据时，你可以使用一些公告语（proclaim），如"The fact is that..." "It is found that..." "Recent research shows/demonstrates/reveals/reports..." "The truth of the matter is that..."等。

例 7、例 8 两篇范例改编自 *The Allyn & Bacon Guide to Writing*（Ramage et al., 2015）中的选文。两篇文章各使用了不同类型的数据来论证观点，请仔细观察数据的呈现及引用方式。

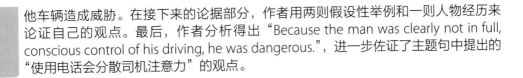

By raising fuel-efficiency standards, the government would force vehicle manufacturers to find a way to create more earth-friendly vehicles that would lower vehicle emissions and pollution. A research article entitled "Update: What You Should Know Before Purchasing a New Vehicle" showed that for every gallon of gasoline used by a vehicle, 20 to 28 pounds of carbon dioxide are released into the environment. This article further revealed that carbon dioxide emissions from automobiles are responsible for 20% percent of all carbon dioxide released into the atmosphere from human causes.

解读 此段来自于一篇论证"政府应该提高汽车制造商燃油效率标准"的文章。作者在段落开头率先提出理由，即提高燃油效率标准可以减少尾气排放和环境污染，接着通过引用研究数据来佐证这一观点。在引用数据时，作者使用了公告性表达："A research article entitled...showed that..."和"This article further reveals that..."。

值得一提的是，此处作者通过强调汽车碳排放量占全球排放量的 20% 来体现汽车减排的重要性。但若要突出另一面，同样的数据可以论证完全不同的观点，比如："Although cars do cause some pollution, a full 80% of human-caused CO_2 emissions come from sources other than cars."。由此可见，数据固然重要，但恰当使用并呈现数据，让数据为自身论点服务，才是论述的关键所在。

例 8

Each year, malaria kills at least one million people and causes more than 300 million cases of acute illness. For children worldwide, it's one of the leading causes of death. The economic burden is significant too: malaria costs Africa more than $12 billion in lost growth each year. In the United States, hundreds of millions of dollars are spent every year on mosquito control.

解读 此段来自于著名生物学家 Olivia Judson 论证"蚊子通过传播疟疾给人类生命和经济造成巨大损失"的文章。通过直接呈现相关资料数据，作者从死亡率和经济损失两方面展现了疟疾危害，进一步强调灭蚊以减少疟疾传播的重要性。此外，作者用 more than、burden、significant、lost growth、hundreds of millions of dollars 等表达来突出后果的严重性，增强了数据的震撼力。

3. 引用专家观点
Presenting Expert Opinions

引用相关权威专家的观点以佐证自身论点，能让读者更加直观地了解所探讨的问题，凸显文章的专业性，从而大大增强论证效力。在引用他人观点时，既可以用自己的语言概述专家观点，也可以用引号直接引用专家的观点。常用的引用观点词汇有：say、state、argue、believe、claim、admit、point out、advocate、indicate、find、find out、discover、recognize、acknowledge 等。

需要注意的是，引用的对象一定是相关领域的专家。试想，如果用某篮球明星的观点来证明无人驾驶汽车的前景，显然不能被读者认可。此外，必要时可以点明引用专家的地位或头衔，以增强专家观点的公信力。

在例 9 中，作者为了论证干细胞克隆技术在疾病治疗方面的前景，引用权威专家的观点。请思考，如果你想反驳这位作者的观点，可以选择什么材料作为论据？

例 9

Stem cell cloning also has great potential in helping humans find cures for disease. As Dr. Gerald Fischbach, Executive Vice President for Health and Biomedical

Sciences and Dean of Medicine at Columbia University, said in front of a United States Senate sub-committee: "New embryonic stem cell procedures could be vital in solving the persistent problem of a lack of genetically matched, qualified donors of organs and tissues that we face today." Fischbach goes on to say that this type of cloning could also lead to the discovery of cures for diseases such as ALS, Parkinson's disease, Alzheimer's disease, diabetes, heart disease, cancer, and possibly others.

—cited from *The Allyn & Bacon Guide to Writing*

解读 作者引用了著名医学专家 Gerald Fischbach 的观点作为论据。在引用时，作者首先通过插入语，介绍了该专家的头衔（Executive Vice President for Health and Biomedical Sciences and Dean of Medicine at Columbia University），接着采用了直接引用（Gerald Fischbach...said...）和间接引用（Fischbach goes on to say that...）两种方法进行引述。

4. 展开子论点
Developing Sub-arguments

除以上三种论证方法之外，你还可以通过铺陈一系列逻辑严密的子论点（sequences of sub-arguments）来支撑分论点。通常来说，子论点可以是对事物进行对比（comparison and contrast），亦可以是分析事物之间的因果关系（cause-and-effect relationships）。关于比较和分析因果的写作方法，第六章"说明文写作"已作详细介绍。在此需要提醒的是，议论文与说明文的交际目的不同，前者更强调对个人观点的佐证，因此无论是进行对比还是分析因果，都需要有的放矢，选择与论点密切相关的部分进行阐述，而不是对事物进行详尽、全面的说明。

在例10中，作者运用子论点对自己的分论点"挟持人质的恐怖分子无权利可言"进行了论述。

例 10

There is an important difference between terrorists and their victims that should mute talk of the terrorist's "rights". The terrorist's victims are at risk unintentionally, not having asked to be endangered. But the terrorist knowingly initiated his actions. Unlike his victims, he volunteered for the risks of his deed. By threatening to kill for profit or idealism, he renounces civilized standards, and he can have no complaint if civilization tries to thwart him by whatever means necessary.

—cited from *The Allyn & Bacon Guide to Writing*

解读 此段中，作者先将恐怖分子与受害者进行了对比，用 but 和 unlike 进行连接，指出二者本质上的不同；在结尾处再提出恐怖分子的行为实则是对文明准则的放弃，他们被剥夺权利也是合情合理。整段并未使用任何数据，而是以逻辑严密的对比和分析来支撑论点。

三、驳论的写作策略
Writing Strategies for Refuting Counterarguments

除用直接论述来支撑论点之外，你还可以用驳论展开论述。若想驳论行之有效，首先需要预判潜在的反对意见，再予以有力的反驳。下文将讲解具体的驳论方法和技巧。

1. 预判对立观点
Anticipating Opposing Views

在确定中心论点和分论点之后，你可以通过思考以下两个问题来帮助预判读者可能会持有的反对意见：

- 读者会对我所做的隐含假设持何种不同见解？（How could a reader object to my reason?）
- 读者会对我给出的理由（即分论点）持何种不同见解？（How could a reader object to my underlying assumption?）

第一个问题比较容易理解。例如，针对论点 "The government should raise petrol taxes because the higher price would substantially reduce petrol consumption."，读者可能会认为一味提高油价会增加中低收入人群的负担，从而影响社会稳定，这就是需要进行辩驳的其中一个对立观点。

第二个问题涉及的层面更深，即隐含的假设会招致读者的反对。例如，针对"稻田里椋鸟（starlings，一种食稻谷的鸟类）数量过多导致农作物受损"这一观点，有作者提出 "Killing starlings should be justified because starlings are pests."，此处隐含的假设为 "It is okay to kill an animal if it is labeled as a pest."。但对于动物保护者来说，以人类自身标准定义"害虫"这一做法本身就是不合理的，因此以此理由来杀死稻田里的椋鸟是令人无法接受的。如果你不能从论点中隐含的假设出发来进行预判，那就很可能忽略辩驳的关键。

2. 反驳对立观点
Refuting Opposing Views

在判断出对立观点之后，你需要有针对性地进行反驳。和预判时的思考角度一样，你可以通过彻查对立观点的理由、假设以及证据是否站得住脚来进行辩驳。仍以提升油价的论点为例，反对观点认为"提升油价会加重中低收入人群的负担"，对此可以通过提供解决办法来进行反驳，比如指出在提升油价后国家通过适当补贴中低收入家庭，以减轻不良影响。

在具体撰写反驳段落时，一般分为三步：

第一，点明对立观点（signpost the opposing views）。你可以使用一些短语来直接地阐明对立观点，常用的表达有："It is often argued that..." "Some people believe that..." "Supporters/proponents/critics of (subject) may argue/claim that..." "It is a common misconception that..." 等。

第二，以退为进（make a concession）。在对立观点非常有力、难以彻底驳倒的情况下，你可以采取迂回战术，做出适当让步。这并不意味着自身论点的薄弱，因为适当承认问题的复杂度和多面性反而会显得客观、严谨，这能增加读者对你的信赖。常用的表让步于反对意见的衔接词有：grant、even though、admittedly、surely、of course 等；衔接句有 "I must admit that..." "Nobody denies that..." "I agree that..." "I concede that..." "While it is true that..." 等。

第三，进行反驳（refute the opposing views）。承认对立观点的可取之处后，你需要将讨论焦点迅速拉回至自身立场上，并用新的角度或价值评判标准进行辩驳。常用的词汇包括：however、nevertheless、but、still、on the contrary 等。

例 11 是一位美国学生对于"致瘾药物买卖是否应受联邦法律认可"的论证。请仔细阅读，并判断作者是如何用上文提及的三个步骤进行有效反驳的。

例 11

Opponents of legalization claim—and rightly so—that legalization will lead to an increase in drug users and addicts. I wish this weren't so, but it is. Nevertheless, the other benefits of legalizing addictive drugs—eliminating the black market, reducing street crime, and freeing up thousands of police from fighting the war on addictive drugs—more than outweigh the social costs of increased drug use and addiction, especially if tax revenues from drug sales are plowed back into drug education and rehabilitation programs.

—cited from *The Allyn & Bacon Guide to Writing*

解读 此段中，作者首先用"Opponents of legalization claim that..."点出反对派的观点，即合法化致瘾药物会导致药物上瘾者人数增加，并通过"I wish this weren't so, but it is."进行让步，表达对该观点的认可，但随即用 Nevertheless 将话锋一转，列举了合法化会带来的各种好处，强调此举的利大于弊。在末尾，作者通过提出建设性意见进一步反驳对立观点：可将合法售卖药物的收入用来资助康复中心，帮助上瘾者恢复健康。整个驳论一气呵成，富有说服力。

四、议论文写作的常见问题
Common Problems in Argumentative Writing

在议论文写作中，需要避免两个常见问题：一是证据与观点缺乏关联（lack of connection between evidence and point）；二是衔接机械生硬（lack of variation in transitional devices）。

第一个问题是指在分论点段落中一味堆砌证据，而忽视了对证据的分析，没有将证据与主题句中的观点联系起来。例如，在论证"人的抱负心决定其命运"（It is the ambition that determines one's fate.）的文章中，仅仅呈现拿破仑等著名人物的故事是远远不够的，你还需要用一两句话将这些故事与论点相联系，只有这样论述才清晰、完整。

第二个问题是指段落之间衔接生硬。为了让论证的逻辑层次明晰，段落间通常需要使用衔接词或衔接句进行自然过渡，如常用的衔接词 first、second、third、firstly、secondly、thirdly 等。用序列词进行衔接本无问题，但如果通篇都是如此衔接，文章则会显得非常生硬、单调。

在段落衔接时，你可以尝试使用更丰富的表达方式，如 "One major reason is that..." "A key problem is that..."、apart from、in addition、moreover、furthermore 等。请留意例 12 是如何采用不同的方法衔接三个分论点的，使文章整体自然、可读性强。

例 12

- 分论点 1: **Maybe the greatest benefit** brought by self-driving cars is that they can help eliminate traffic accidents.
- 分论点 2: **Fewer accidents apart**, self-driving cars can help do away with traffic jams.
- 分论点 3: **There is another reason** why we should develop self-driving cars, **too**: They help decrease air pollution.

第三节 以读促写议论文
Reading for Argumentative Writing

分析性阅读有助于提高你的写作能力。为了更有效地撰写议论文，本节将介绍一篇范文，并按照分析性阅读的 10 个步骤深入分析文章的内容、结构和风格。

例 13

The Many Career Opportunities for Recipients of Degrees in Mathematics

1　It is asserted that once a person decides to study mathematics, they are bound to have a narrow career sphere that is available to them. According to this assertion, the only possible jobs are teaching jobs at middle school, high school, college, and university levels, which are supposed to be boring to a degree and it is impossible to become a millionaire.

2　I am in total opposition of this assertion. I believe that if a person studies mathematics, they will have a world of options. In reality, mathematics majors are in demand in the work force.

3　First of all, the teaching profession alone offers an assortment of different levels of teaching. One could teach at the elementary, middle school, high school, college, and university levels. There are also teacher's aids, research assistants, and student teachers, as well as substitute teachers. The demand for teachers is elevating at an alarming rate. This goes for teachers in general, but especially for teachers interested in teaching in the mathematics or science fields.

4　By no means does studying mathematics limit a person to the teaching profession alone. Besides being a teacher, who technically is a mathematician, there is also the obvious profession of being a mathematician without being a teacher. There are also opportunities such as becoming an engineer, a research scientist, or a manager of a business. Mathematics majors work for such companies as IBM, AT&T Bell Labs, American Airlines, FedEx, L. L. Bean, and Perdue Farms Inc., to name a few (Madison, 1990). There are also mathematicians employed in such government agencies as the Bureau of the Census, Department of Agriculture, and NASA Goddard Space Center (Valerie, 1993). Mathematicians are needed in the fields of law and medicine as well as in the arts, such as sculpting, music, and television. The possibilities are seemingly endless. When you think about it, almost every job involves mathematics.

5　This can be further supported by the statistics from the fields of employment of mathematics degree recipients. The year before last, only about 30% of mathematics degree recipients actually became teachers. The other 70% of that year chose to take on various work activities such as reporting, statistics, computing activities, research and development, management and administration, production and inspection, as well as a few other activities.

6   For people receiving their bachelors' degree in mathematics, only 42% went into the field of mathematics and statistics. The other recipients of bachelors' degree in mathematics took jobs in other fields. 40% were employed in the field of computer science, 14% in the field of engineering, and 2% in the field of psychology.

7   Similar statistics were found for people receiving their masters' degree in mathematics, except for a rather large 50% increase in those entering the field of mathematics and statistics. Of those receiving their masters' degree in mathematics, 62% found jobs related to mathematics or statistics; only 15% went into the field of computer science compared to the 40% of those who received only their bachelors' degrees in mathematics, 17% in the field of engineering and 6% in the field of psychology.

8   At the time of these statistics three quarters of people with mathematical science degrees were not classified as working as mathematical scientists. Also, one quarter of people with bachelors' degrees in mathematics, one third of people with masters' degrees in mathematics, and three quarters of people with doctorates in mathematics were employed at educational institutions. These percentages show that not even a majority of people who received any level of degree in mathematics were employed as teachers.

9   Simultaneously, it is true that not every job opening could be properly satisfied by a person who majored in mathematics, but for the most part that person would have an advantage over other applicants because of their knowledge in mathematics.

10   Maybe most people who study mathematics won't become millionaires, but they do have the opportunity to. For example, many people who study mathematics become engineers or scientists, which contrary to the assertion, can be a very wealthy profession. Also people who receive good jobs with successful companies such as IBM, AT&T Bell Labs, and American Airlines, to name a few, as well as people who work for numerous government agencies, all earn a pretty comfortable salary.

11   On the whole, there are many fields of employment open to people who have received their degrees in mathematics. The jobs are out there if the prospective workers have good search skills for jobs, which are essential. Along with that there

are seven easy steps to finding the right job: (1) know yourself, (2) set your goals, (3) prepare a powerful resume, (4) establish a network, (5) apply for positions, (6) prepare yourself for the job interview, and (7) evaluate the job offers you receive. These seven steps will greatly increase a mathematics major's chances of finding the right job. Therefore, it is a sensible option to take mathematics as one's major, especially for a person who cherishes strong interest in it.

—cited from *Reading and Writing for Argumentative Essays*

分析性阅读讲解

第 1 步： 留意出版信息和作者介绍。这篇范文出自一本指导议论文写作的教材。

第 2 步： 注意文章标题是如何引出主题的。标题清楚地点明了本文的主题——数学专业拥有广阔的就业前景。

第 3 步： 第一次阅读文章，并写下你对文章的大致印象。通读之后可以得知，作者写这篇文章的目的是希望扭转人们对于数学专业缺乏就业前景的偏见，并引用了数学专业毕业生就业状况的相关数据来阐述他的观点，以达到说服的目的。

第 4 步： 再次查看标题和介绍性段落。本文的介绍性段落为第一段和第二段。作者先在第一段中通过展现人们对数学专业就业前景的传统偏见，激发读者的阅读兴趣，并紧接着在第二段中表明自己的反对立场。

第 5 步： 找到作者的要点或主旨。本文的中心论点可以在第二段中找到："I believe that if a person studies mathematics, they will have a world of options. In reality, mathematics majors are in demand in the work force."。

第 6 步： 查找支持或说明主旨的重要语句。本文有三处支持性陈述，即本文的分论点，它们都是接近正文段落开头或结尾的主题句：第三段开头的"The teaching profession alone involves different kinds of teaching jobs at different levels."；第四段开头的"Studying mathematics doesn't limit a person to the teaching profession alone."；第八段结尾的"The majority of mathematics degree recipients were not employed as teachers."。

第 7 步： 分析作者是如何推进主题的，又是如何发展、解释或论证支持性观点的。作者运用举例、列数据、对比分析等多种方法进行论证，如"Mathematics majors work for such companies as IBM…""The other 70% of that year chose to take on various work activities such as reporting, statistics…"等。

第 8 步： 查看文章的布局和组织形式。作者通过分析数学专业毕业生从事教师职业以及非教师职业两大方面来组织文章。第二个方面是文章的重点，故整体篇幅安排更长。在这一部分，作者根据通过分析数学专业本科生、研究生以及博士生的就业情况进行论证，并用统计数据对每一个要点予以支持。

第 9 步： 分析文章的推进是否有逻辑性和连贯性。从分析数学专业学生在教学以及非教学领域的工作机会，到分析数学系本科、硕士以及博士毕业生的就业情况，本文在内容上实现了有逻辑的推进。在语言上，作者运用了一些过渡性短语和句子来保障文章的前后统一和流畅，如第五段中的"This can be further supported by…"，第九段中的"Simultaneously, it is true that..."。

第 10 步：思考作者的风格和文章的语气。这篇文章语言正式、严谨，符合学术英语的要求。

在完成以上分析性阅读步骤之后，试问自己：我学到了哪些议论文的写作策略？我能将哪些新想法、新策略或新技巧融入自己的写作中？

Exercises

I. **The following are some directions for writing argumentative essays. Please pick one and write an argumentative essay of at least 250 words on your own.**

1. It's common in universities that students, for some reasons, fail to get a satisfying grade in a certain course and they hope to repeat the course for a better result. Do you think they should be given such a chance?

2. Nowadays celebrities are more famous for their glamour and wealth than for their achievement, and this sets a bad example to young people. To what extent do you agree or disagree?

3. Some employers want to be able to contact their staff at all times, even on holidays. Does this trend have more advantages than disadvantages?

II. **After you have produced your first draft of the argumentative essay, revise it in terms of purpose, audience, content, format, and language based on the checklist below. Please tick the box if your answer to the question is yes.**

No.	Checklist for Self-evaluation	Yes
1)	Have I demonstrated a clear writing purpose and a good awareness of audience?	
2)	Have I presented a clearly stated thesis in my introductory paragraph?	
3)	Have I showed a clear and insightful position in the thesis statement?	
4)	Have I strongly and substantially reinforced and defended my position to persuade the readers that the position is valid?	
5)	Have I written a topic sentence in each of my argument paragraphs?	
6)	Have I provided relevant details to illustrate my points?	
7)	Have I provided enough details to support my points?	
8)	Have I effectively refuted the opposing views?	
9)	Have I used transitional words or phrases to help the readers follow my train of thought?	
10)	Does my essay have a concluding paragraph that provides a summary or final thought or both?	
11)	Have I used adequate range of vocabulary?	
12)	Have I checked the language of my essay to ensure that it's error-free?	

III. Then review one or more peer essays in terms of purpose, audience, content, format, and language based on the checklist below. Please tick the box if your answer to the question is yes.

No.	Checklist for Peer Review	Yes
1)	Has the author demonstrated a clear writing purpose and a good awareness of audience?	
2)	Has the author presented a clearly stated thesis in the introductory paragraph?	
3)	Has the author shown a clear and insightful position in the thesis statement?	
4)	Has the author strongly and substantially reinforced and defended his/her position to persuade the readers that the position is valid?	
5)	Has the author written a topic sentence in each of the argument paragraphs?	
6)	Has the author provided relevant details to illustrate his/her points?	
7)	Has the author provided enough details to support his/her points?	
8)	Has the author effectively refuted the opposing views?	
9)	Has the author used transitional words or phrases to help the readers follow his/her train of thought?	
10)	Does the essay have a concluding paragraph that provides a summary or final thought or both?	
11)	Has the author used adequate range of vocabulary?	
12)	Has the author checked the language of the essay to ensure that it's error-free?	

Sample[1]

 范文

iPads and Kindles Are Better for the Environment than Books

Brian Palmer

With Apple and Amazon touting their e-readers like iPad and Kindle, some bookworms are bound to wonder if tomes-on-paper will one day become quaint relics. But the question also arises, which is more environmentally friendly: an e-reader or an old-fashioned book?

Environmental analysis can be an endless balancing of this vs. that. Do you care

---

1 范文和赏析出自李明慕课脚本。

more about conserving water or avoiding toxic chemical usage? Minimizing carbon dioxide emissions or radioactive nuclear waste? But today the Lantern has good news: There will be no *Sophie's Choice* when it comes to e-books. As long as you consume a healthy number of titles, you read at a normal pace and you don't trade in your gadget every year, perusing electronically will lighten your environmental impact.

If the Lantern has taught you anything, it's that most consumer products make their biggest scar on the Earth during manufacture and transport, before they ever get into your greedy little hands. Accordingly, green-minded consumers are usually—although not always—better off buying fewer things when possible. Reusable cloth diapers, for example, are better than disposables, because the environmental costs of manufacture and transport outweigh those of washing.

Think of an e-reader as the cloth diaper of books. Sure, producing one Kindle is tougher on the environment than printing a single paperback copy of *Pride and Prejudice*. But every time you download and read an electronic book, rather than purchasing a new pile of paper, you're paying back a little bit of the carbon dioxide and water deficit from the Kindle production process. The actual operation of an e-reader represents a small percentage of its total environmental impact, so if you run your device into the ground, you'll end up paying back that debt many times over.

According to the environmental consulting firm Cleantech, which aggregated a series of studies, a single book generates about 7.5 kilograms (almost 17 pounds) of carbon dioxide equivalents. (That's the value of all its greenhouse gas emissions expressed in terms of the impact of carbon dioxide.) This figure includes production, transport, and either recycling or disposal.

Apple's iPad generates 130 kilograms of carbon dioxide equivalents during its lifetime, according to company estimates. Amazon has not released numbers for the Kindle, but Cleantech and other analysts put it at 168 kilograms. Those analyses do not indicate how much additional carbon is generated per book read (as a result of the energy required to host the e-bookstore's servers and power the screen while you read), but they do include the full cost of manufacture, which likely accounts for the lion's share of emissions. (The iPad uses just three watts of electricity while you're reading, far less than most light bulbs.) If we can trust those numbers, then, the iPad pays for its CO_2 emissions about one-third of the way through your 18th book. You'd need to get halfway into your 23rd book on Kindle to get out of the environmental red.

Water is also a major consideration. The U.S. newspaper and book publishing industries together consume 153 billion gallons of water annually, according to figures by the non-profit group Green Press Initiative included in the Cleantech analysis. It takes about seven gallons to produce the average printed book, while e-publishing companies can create a digital book with less than two cups of water. (Like any other company, e-book publishers consume water through the paper they use and other office activities.) Researchers estimate that 79 gallons of water are needed to make an e-reader. So you come out on top, water-wise, after reading about a dozen books.

E-readers also have books beat on toxic chemicals. The production of ink for printing releases a number of volatile organic compounds into the atmosphere, including hexane, toluene, and xylene, which contribute to smog and asthma. Some of them may also cause cancer or birth defects. Computer production is not free of hard-to-pronounce chemicals, to be sure, but both the iPad and the Kindle comply with Europe's RoHS standards, which ban some of the scarier chemicals that have been involved in electronics production. E-readers do, however, require the mining of non-renewable minerals, such as columbite-tantalite, which sometimes come from politically unstable regions. And experts can't seem to agree on whether we're at risk of exhausting the world's supply of lithium, the lifeblood of the e-reader's battery.

If you're not ready to plunk down $139 for a Kindle or $499 for an iPad, or if you just love the feel of dead tree between your fingers, there's one thing you can do to significantly ease the environmental impact of your reading: Buy your books online. Brick-and-mortar bookstores are very inefficient because they stock more books than they can sell. Between a quarter and a third of a bookstore's volumes will ultimately be shipped back to the publisher and on to recycling centers or landfills.

An even better option is to walk to your local library, which can spread the environmental impact of a single book over an entire community. Unfortunately, libraries are underutilized. Studies suggest that fewer than a third of Americans visit their local library at least once a month, and fewer than half went in the last year. Libraries report that the average community member checks out 7.4 books per year— far less than the three per month consumed on e-readers—and more than a third of those items were children's books.

At such, it's clear that iPads and Kindles are better for the environment than books. Of course, you could also stop reading altogether. But then how would you know how much carbon you saved?

赏析

The author starts the argumentative essay by asking a question to grab the readers' attention, and then states his thesis in the introductory paragraph, i.e., e-books are more environmentally friendly than printed books.

In the argument paragraphs, the author argues for his claim in terms of three aspects that have much to do with the environment: carbon dioxide, water, and toxic chemicals. In discussing the first aspect "carbon dioxide" and the third "toxic chemicals," the author refutes two counterarguments respectively. To support his idea, the author draws on diverse forms of evidence, such as analogy, statistics, facts, and research results. In the end, the author concludes the essay by readdressing the thesis statement.

第三部分

英语考试中的交际性写作

COMMUNICATIVE WRITING IN ENGLISH TESTS

第八章

国内考试的英语写作
English Writing in Domestic Tests

学习要点

- 大学英语四、六级写作概述
- 大学英语四、六级写作过程
- 大学英语四、六级写作策略
- 大学英语四、六级范文的分析性阅读

第一节 大学英语四、六级考试写作概述
Introduction to CET-4 and CET-6 Writing

一、大学英语四、六级考试的英语写作
English Writing in CET-4 and CET-6

全国大学英语四、六级考试由教育部主办，是教育部考试中心主持和实施的一项大规模标准化考试，考试对象是修完大学英语相应阶段课程的在校大学生。四、六级考试是参照《大学英语教学指南》设定的教学目标对我国大学生英语综合能力进行的科学测评。本章将讨论大学英语四级（CET-4）和六级考试（CET-6）的写作任务，其间会涉及前七章介绍的众多写作策略，如记叙文写作、描写文写作、说明文写作和议论文写作。

在完成考试作文时，考生需要认识到与评卷人进行有效沟通的重要性。本章将探讨如何与作为读者的评卷人进行有效"沟通"，让你的文章给他们留下深刻的印象。

大学英语四、六级写作任务的评分采用"综合印象评分"（global scoring）的评价方式，即评卷人根据对文章的整体印象来评分。此外，四、六级写作的字数要求并不高，考生没有必要超过字数限制，因为这可能会暴露出更多的写作错误。虽然评分标准中

没有关于错误数量的具体规定，但是过多的语言错误肯定会影响整体评分。

二、大学英语四、六级写作任务
CET-4 and CET-6 Writing Tasks

首先参考大学英语四级考试大纲（2016 年修订版）来分析写作部分应该达到的要求：

> Part V Writing：共 1 题，考试时间 30 分钟。要求考生写出一篇 120~180 词的短文，试卷上可能给出题目，或规定情景，或要求看图作文，或给出段首句要求续写，或给出关键词要求写成短文。要求能够正确表达思想，意义连贯，无重大语法错误。写作内容包括日常生活、一般常识以及社会发展中一些值得关注的现象。短文写作部分的目的是测试学生运用英语书面表达思想的初步能力。

这里有一些关键信息需要注意：

- 时限：30 分钟。
- 字数限制：120~180 词。如果时间运用合理，在 30 分钟内写一篇 120 词的文章并不难，因此考生的重点应放在如何谋篇布局、组织语言上，使作文更具吸引力。
- 基于特定主题或情境的写作：这种写作任务需要考生在一定范围内表达自己对特定主题的想法，因此考生需要仔细研究主题，以确保回答主题中的特定问题。
- 内容：关于日常生活、一般常识以及社会发展中一些值得关注的现象。

以上可以看出，大学英语四级写作旨在测试大学生用书面英语表达观点的基本技能。即使大学生的整体英语水平在提高，他们仍需要尝试使用不同的策略来提高写作水平。

接下来参考大学英语六级考试大纲（2016 年修订版）来分析写作部分应该达到的要求：

> Part V Writing：共 1 题，考试时间 30 分钟。要求考生写出一篇 150~200 词的短文，试卷上可能给出题目，或要求看图表作文，或根据所给摘要（英语或汉语）作文，或根据给出关键词作文，等等。要求切题，能正确表达思想，意义连贯，文理基本通顺，无重大语言错误。写作的内容包括科技、社会、文化等方面的一般常识。短文写作部分的目的是测试学生运用英语书面表达思想的一般能力。

这里的关键信息与大学英语四级考试的很相似，但有所不同：

- 时限：30 分钟。
- 字数限制：150~200 词，这对大多数大学生来说并不难。
- 基于特定主题或情境的写作：大学英语六级的写作考试大纲与大学英语四级相

比有更多的要求，其中之一是"切题"。也就是说，大学英语六级写作对主题关联性的要求更高，因此考生需要通过仔细研究主题才能正确回答特定问题。

- 内容：主题要求更加明确，涉及科学、社会、文化等方面内容。不难理解，大学英语六级考试要求大学生拥有更大的词汇量和更多的学科知识。

以上可以看出，大学英语六级写作更加侧重考察大学生用书面英语表达观点的进阶能力。他们需要在大学英语四级写作的基础上，在词汇、句型、组织和内容等方面提高自己的写作水平。

写作题满分为15分，成绩分为五个档次：14分档（13~15分）、11分档（10~12分）、8分档（7~9分）、5分档（4~6分）和2分档（1~3分）。各档次的评分标准见表8.1。

表 8.1　大学英语四、六级写作评分标准

档次	评分标准
14 分档	切题。表达思想清楚，文字通顺、连贯，基本上无语言错误，仅有个别小错误。
11 分档	切题。表达思想清楚，文字较连贯，但有少量语言错误。
8 分档	基本切题。有些地方表达思想不够清楚，文字勉强连贯；语言错误相当多，其中有一些是严重错误。
5 分档	基本切题。表达思想不清楚，连贯性差，有较多的严重语言错误。
2 分档	条理不清，思路紊乱，语言支离破碎或大部分句子均有错误，且多数为严重错误。

从表8.1可知，为了让考试作文获得10分及以上的分数，考生在平时练习时需要在主题相关性、表达清晰、逻辑性、连贯性和减少语言错误等方面下足功夫。

三、大学英语四、六级写作的交际性
Communicative Writing in CET-4 and CET-6

四、六级考试作文虽然是应试作文，但要求考生在一定范围内表达自己对特定主题的观点。表达观点是为了与读者进行交流，所以应试写作本身就具有明显的交际性，只不过限定了写作主题，读者也比较特殊——评卷人。那么面对这样的读者，考生应该具有怎样的读者意识呢？

首先是交际的有效性（effectiveness），也就是所谓的切题。考生需要根据所给题目来表达自己的观点。其次是文章的说服性（persuasiveness）。若要说服读者，文章需要观点明晰、论据充分。另外需要注意的是，这位特殊的读者会读到成百上千篇题目相同的文章，这就更要求考生在写作中具有足够的读者意识，例如主题句明确，结构清晰，让改卷过程更加轻松；观点新颖，语言表达多样化，让改卷过程更加愉悦。

当充分考虑了文章的交际性，心中想读者所想时，考生完成的考试作文就不再是

千篇一律的"八股文",而是与评卷人之间有效的对话和交流。

第二节 大学英语四、六级写作过程
The Writing Process of CET-4 and CET-6

本节将从写作准备、写作中和写作后修订三个步骤来探讨大学英语四、六级写作的过程。由于写作任务需要在 30 分钟内完成,考生需要合理安排时间,以下是对时间安排的建议:

- 研究题目(2 分钟):仔细阅读题目指令,确定写作主题。
- 列提纲(5 分钟):积极思考相关信息,准备写作提纲。
- 写作(约 20 分钟):完成作文初稿。
- 修订(2~3 分钟):通篇检查,尽量减少语言错误。

 ## 一、写作准备阶段
Pre-writing

在准备写作时,最重要的是研究题目说明及要求。根据大学英语四、六级考试的写作要求,考生应该优先考虑话题的相关性(relevance)。四、六级考试中出现较多的题型是议论文写作,当然也出现过其他类型,例如应用文和图表作文。即使是议论文,每次的出题方式和要求也不尽相同,因此研究题目要求的重要性不容小觑。下文以真题为例,讨论如何研究四级写作的题目要求。

例 1

*Directions: For this part, you are allowed 30 minutes to write a short essay on **how to best handle the relationship between parents and children**. You should write at least 120 words but no more than 180 words.* (CET-4 in December, 2017)

解读 这是一个典型的议论文题目。仔细阅读题目要求后,考生会发现这个话题的重点是 how,即如何最好地处理亲子关系。考生可以用几句话陈述现状或举出一个例子,但写作重点应该是提建议。

例 2

*Directions: Suppose you have just participated in a school project of collecting used books on campus. You are now to write a report about the project, which may include **its aim,*** *organizers, participants, and activities. You will have 30 minutes to write the report. You should write at least 120 words but no more than 180 words.* (CET-4 in December, 2012)

> **解读** 这个题目要求考生写一则报告，而不是传统的议论文。一开始考生可能会有点紧张，会担心报告是否有严格的格式要求。不过认真阅读题目说明之后，就可以找到写作应该包含的内容——"its aim, organizers, participants, and activities"。只要按照题目要求客观描述，并且包含必要的信息，格式是可以灵活处理的。此外，注意不要遗漏题目要求中的其他信息。

例 3

*Directions: For this part, you are allowed 30 minutes to write **a letter to a foreign friend who wants to teach English in China. Please recommend a city to him**. You should write at least 120 words but no more than 180 words.* (CET-4 in December, 2019)

> **解读** 这是一篇典型的应用文。感谢信是常见的应用文体，考生需要对其格式给予足够的重视。注意题目要求里的加粗部分，要求向外国朋友推荐一个中国城市。在遵循信件写作格式的同时，考生还应该注重内容的组织，并给出推荐理由。

例 4

*Directions: For this part, you are allowed 30 minutes to write an essay based on the picture below. You should start your essay with a brief description of the picture and then **comment on the kid's understanding of going to school**. You should write at least 120 words but no more than 180 words.* (CET-4 in July, 2015)

"Why am I going to school if my phone already knows everything?"

> **解读** 对于图片类作文，第一段的主要内容通常是题目要求中提到的"简要描述图片"（a brief description of the picture）。但有不少考生会忽略这一点而直接开始对图片进行分析或论证。简短描述图片之后，考生需要就孩子有关上学的理解展开评论。请注意图片下方的问句，这意味着正文段落的目的是回答"为什么"，即在文章中分析孩子仍然需要上学的原因，重点应该放在学校部分而不是手机部分。

通过对以上四级真题的实例分析，不难发现除议论文写作之外，不同的写作题目有不同的侧重点，甚至有可能出现不同体裁的结合，这样可以更好地测试考生的写作能力。仔细研究题目要求，不仅有助于考生决定文章的主题，也有助于他们在动笔之前规划好段落的布局。

接下来以大学英语六级写作真题为例来探讨如何分析题目要求。

例 5

*Directions: Suppose you are asked to **give advice on whether to attend college at home or abroad**, write an essay to state your opinion. You are required to write at least 150 words but no more than 200 words.* (CET-6 in July, 2017)

解读 这篇六级作文要求考生就"在国内上大学还是去国外上大学"给出建议，实际上是一篇议论文。对于每一篇文章，考生都需要先确定写作目的。这个真题的目的是通过比较和对比，使读者对"在国内上大学"和"去国外上大学"的选择有一个初步的认识，那么段落展开的方式自然也是使用比较和对比。

例 6

*Directions: For this part, you are allowed 30 minutes to write an essay **commenting on the saying "help others and you will be helped when you are in need"**. You can cite examples to illustrate your views. You should write at least 150 words but no more than 200 words.* (CET-6 in December, 2017)

解读 根据一句俗语或名言来写一篇文章是大学英语四、六级考试的常见题目类型。针对这类题型，依旧是先仔细阅读题目说明，再找出相关要求的关键词。在写作时，考生需要先评论一下这句话，即对主题给出个人的理解，再通过举例等方式来说明自己的观点。

例 7

*Directions: For this part, you are allowed 30 minutes to write a short essay on e-learning. Try to **imagine what will happen when more and more people study online instead of attending school**. You are required to write at least 150 words but no more than 200 words.* (CET-6 in July, 2016)

解读 这个题目相对而言比较开放。网络学习情境涉及"想象"的部分，考虑到现在网课学习的普及性，考生可以先"想象"一下更多人在更多情境下借助网格进行学习的场景。接下来如何继续这个话题的写作就取决于不同的考生了。大多数考生会继续讨论网络学习的利弊，也可以对网络学习和学校学习进行比较和对比。请记住你需要一个确定的方式来组织段落。

例 8

*Direction: For this part, you are allowed 30 minutes to write a short essay based on the picture below. You should focus on **the harm caused by misleading information online**. You are required to write at least 150 words but no more than 200 words.* (CET-6 in December, 2015)

"I just feel unfortunate to live in a world with so much misleading information!"

解读 正如在例 4 中提到的，图片题首先需要一个关于图片的简要描述。由于这张图片显示的关于情节的信息很少，考生只需要用一个简短的描述来介绍主题即可，之后再关注 the harm caused by misleading information online，这是题目要求中给出的关键词。注意，这里并不需要对事物的两面性进行描述，重点是"网络误导性信息造成的危害"。考生可以根据需要对不同方面的伤害进行分类，并分析这些伤害会如何影响人们。由此得出，逻辑思维和语言组织能力在大学英语六级写作任务中是至关重要的。

例 9

*Directions: For this part, you are allowed 30 minutes to write an essay related to the short passage given below. In your essay, you are to **comment on the phenomenon described in the passage and suggest measures to address the issue**. You should write at least 150 words but no more than 200 words.* (CET-6 in December, 2021)

Young people spend a lot of time on the Internet. However, they are sometimes unable to recognize false information on the Internet, judge the reliability of online information sources, or tell real news stories from fake ones.

解读 这篇六级作文的重点是对现象进行评论并给出相关建议。正文段落应该由两个部分组成：一个是个人观点，也就是针对该现象的评论部分；另一个是建议部分，考生可以采用不同模式来组织。

通过对以上六级真题的实例分析，不难发现大学英语六级写作更偏重于考查议论文，不同体裁的组合表现得更为明显。与四级写作相比，六级写作的题目相对来说比较开放，这要求考生在有限的时间内要确定写作的重点和计划。为了更好地阐明主题和表达观点，文章的逻辑组织在大学英语六级写作中尤为重要。

二、 写作阶段
Writing

1. 撰写提纲
Writing a Helpful Outline in Advance

在 30 分钟的限时写作中，考生需要制订计划来帮助自己进行流畅的写作，并尽可能地避免出错，所以有必要花 3~5 分钟来撰写提纲。在撰写提纲时，考生可以根据主题要求来决定如何组织论据，并参考文章结构检查清单（如表 8.2 所示），提醒自己一篇好的作文需要遵从的要点，以帮助自己在下笔前做好写作计划。

表 8.2　文章结构检查清单

文章部分	检查内容
开头 （introduction）	• 背景句（general statements） • 主旨句（thesis statement）
正文 （body paragraph）	• 主题句（topic sentence） • 支持材料（supporting sentences） • 总结句（如需要）(concluding sentence [when necessary])
组织模式 （organization patterns）	内容的合理组织模式（过程和分析、区分和分类、因果、比较和对比、例证和定义）(logical and appropriate pattern of organization for the topic [process-and-analysis, division-and-classifications, cause-and-effect, comparison-and-contrast, exemplification, and definition])
	段落之间的过渡（between-paragraph transitions）
结尾 （conclusion）	主要观点或段落的总结，以及对该主题的最终评论（summary of the main points or paragraphs, and final comments on the topic）

例 10 是一个提纲示例，其中每个段落都包含了主题句和一些细节。

例 10

Topic: Good habits result from resisting temptation.

Outline

I. Entertainment and goods can distract us from cultivating good habits.

　　1. The world is flooded with all kinds of temptation.

2. Brand clothes, computer games, and TV shows attract young people.

II. To form good habits, one needs a strong will and perseverance to resist temptation.

　　1. The good habit of reading requires perseverance.

　　2. The good habit of exercising requires strong will.

III. Just as...once said....

列出写作提纲之后，下一步要做的是用详细的事实或例子把基本的想法发展成完整的段落。由于时间有限，列提纲时可以只写几个单词或短语，而不是例 10 中的完整句子，它们只要能起到提示作用即可。

2. 采用主题发展结构
Adopting a Theme-building Structure

不同的文章因其写作目的和侧重点不同，在结构的安排上也不尽相同。不过，四、六级作文基本上都可以采用"三段论"的结构：开头、正文和结尾。这个结构可以为呈现文章的中心思想而服务。下文将用范文来说明每个部分应如何呈现主题。

1）开头（Introduction）

开头段落的目的是引起读者的注意，激发他们的兴趣，并把主题限制在某个范围内。为了达到这一目的，开头段落需要包含两个基本要素：一般性陈述和主题陈述。

一般性陈述是第一段的第一句话，为论述的展开提供背景信息，考生在考试中可以使用题目要求中给出的相关信息。接下来是主题陈述，即把写作的重点缩小到文章的主题上。所以，开头段落也是文章的介绍性段落，需要向读者介绍这篇文章想要表达的主题或者中心思想。例如：

例 11

Nowadays, there has been a heated discussion as to a better choice between attending college at home and abroad. Views on the topic vary greatly among people from different walks of life. Some believe that it is a better choice to study in domestic colleges, but others consider it better to study abroad. I totally agree with the latter idea for the reasons presented below.

解读 此开头段落中包含了一般性陈述和主题陈述，但是第一句中的"there has been a heated discussion..."是否过于耳熟？

例 12

"It upsets me that people would think I could destroy humans," said Sophia, which is the first robot in the world to be recognized with citizenship. From the tone in her dialogue, you might feel as if it possesses its own thoughts. Accordingly, how do you expect AI to develop in the future?

解读 用一个科幻故事的主人公来开头，更容易引起读者的兴趣，并让他们对这篇文章充满期待。大多数考生的作文可能会用 "AI has been more and more popular in our life." 或者 "There has been a heated discussion about AI." 这样的句子开头，它们并不具有足够的吸引力。如果选择引用名人名言开头，或用 Alpha Go 的事例开头，甚至用拥有人工智能助手的虚构经历开头，那这篇文章必然会让评卷人眼前一亮。

虽然写作时间有限，但考生尽量不要被熟悉的句型所束缚。这些句子的确有助于他们尽快完成开头段落的写作，不过仍可以尝试一些不同的方法来吸引读者的注意力，以实现写作的交际目的。以下是一些有利于激发读者兴趣的开头方法：

- 告知读者有关写作主题的个人经验（tell the readers your experience with the topic）；
- 呈现一些令人震惊的事实（present startling facts）；
- 讲故事（tell an anecdote）；
- 使用修辞性问句（ask rhetorical questions）；
- 使用数据（use statistics）；
- 运用鲜明对比（use vivid contrast）；
- 使用历史资料（use historical information）。

2）正文（Body）

正文部分可以由一个或多个段落组成。在大学英语四、六级考试中，由于时间和字数的限制，最常见的是 1~2 个正文段落。

为了更清楚地表达观点，主题句应尽量清晰明了（make the topic sentence a helpful guide）。主题句是每个正文段落中最重要的句子，它简要说明了这一段的讨论内容，因此对于作者和读者来说是一个有用的指引。主题句可以出现在段落的任何位置，最常见的是在段落的开头或结尾。清晰明了的主题句可以帮助评卷人直接了解文章的中心思想。

另外，考生可以根据题目要求和文章主题来选择段落发展的顺序和模式（develop the essay by different patterns of organization）。常见的文章组织方式有分类、因果关系、比较与对比、例证等。不同的题目将决定考生选择哪种方式为主来展开段落。清晰的组织结构也能让评卷人有轻松的阅卷体验。例如：

例13

*Directions: For this part, you are allowed 30 minutes to write a short essay on **how to best handle the relationship between teachers and students**. You should write at least 120 words but no more than 180 words.* (CET-4 in December, 2017)

解读 对于"如何最好地处理师生关系"这个主题，考生可以采用分类和举例的组织方式，通过举例讨论老师和学生各自的责任和义务来发展主体段落。当然也可以侧重关注老师或学生应该做什么，并按照因果模式来发展段落。

例14

*Directions: For this part, you are allowed 30 minutes to write an essay related to the short passage given below. In your essay, you are to **comment on the phenomenon described in the passage and suggest measures to address the issue**. You should write at least 150 words but no more than 200 words.* (CET-6 in December, 2021)

Some parents in China are overprotective of their children. They plan everything for their children, make all the decisions for them, and do not allow them to explore on their own in case they make mistakes or get hurt.

解读 根据题目要求，考生需要先对给定段落里描述的现象进行评论，之后再给出相关建议。评论是个人观点的表达；关于建议，一般是先阐述原因再提出建议，或者先给出建议再展望未来。考生可以采用原因结果模式，也可以采用提出问题到解决问题的模式。对于同一主题，考生可以选择不同的组织模式来实现同一写作目的。

连接词可以用来体现段落的组织模式（use conjunctions to display organization patterns），帮助读者顺利地跟随文章的写作逻辑，常用的词汇有：for example、in other words、first、secondly、last but not least、on the one hand...on the other (hand)、in addition、however、what's more 等。但是不能过于依赖连接词，避免在短短一篇作文中罗列大量的连接词。请记住，一篇文章可以用其他方法来实现连贯性，不一定每次都要用连接词。

3）结尾（Conclusion）

结尾段落的目的是归纳总结，或者强调观点，强化主题。作者一般在结尾段中论述文章的主要观点，或者对未来提出期望，但是这并不意味着需要提出任何新的观点。结尾段的开头可以使用一些特殊的指示语，它们可以作为一个过渡，帮助文章顺利地从主体段落过渡到结尾段落，例如 in conclusion、in a nutshell、to sum up 等短语就能很好地充当指示语。

下面以例 12 中提到的写作题目 "The Future of AI" 为例，来说明如何更好地写出一个结尾段。很多考生在结束作文时可能会使用类似于 "I have enough confidence that the advantages of AI will outweigh the disadvantages." 或 "I'm afraid I will care more about the concerns and we should be cautious." 这样的句子。这样的结尾虽然基本上达到了写作目的，但是过于千篇一律，请看以下不同的结尾示例：

例 15

From my perspective, problems show us where AI can make improvements. I hope the development of AI will focus on what people really need to maximize the benefits brought by AI.

例 16

Finally, I would like to share a saying from Marvin Lee Minsky, the father of artificial intelligence, "Will robots take over our world? Absolutely, they will be our offspring." The tendency can never be turned away; hence, we have to face the reality about the future, standing still on the balance of the AI and human beings.

解读 例 15 虽然简短，但是 maximize 这个词可以更好地表达作者对 AI 未来的信心。例 16 则通过引用名人名言来强调作者的观点。这意味着只有尝试打开思路，不局限于曾经的写作习惯，才能写出更为精彩的结尾段落。

 **三、修订阶段**
Revising

在完成整篇作文之后，考生最好花 2~3 分钟的时间通读一遍文章，避免语法、标点和拼写方面的错误。表 8.3 可以帮助考生对文章进行快速、全面的检查。

表 8.3　文章修订快速检查表

检查内容	具体要求
句子是否完整（sentence fragments）	在写复杂句时容易出现句子片段化的情况，须通读作文，确保所有句子的完整性。
拼写（spelling）	检查拼写，特别是一些容易拼错的单词，如：ture 应为 true；persuit 应为 pursuit。
主谓一致（subject-verb agreement）	确保单数主语使用单数动词（如 is、goes、shines 等），而复数主语使用复数动词。
时态（tense）	检查作文是否使用了恰当的时态，不随意变换时态。

（续表）

检查内容	具体要求
正式与非正式文体（formal and informal style）	考试作文应为正式文体，注意不要出现 gonna 和 wanna 这样的形式。
检查易混淆的单词（check confusable words）	检查易混淆词汇是否使用正确，如：affect/effect, accept/except, image/imagine 等。
标点符号（punctuation）	检查标点符号使用是否正确。

总而言之，一篇高分的大学英语四、六级考试作文应符合以下要求：

- 文章主题明确，开头段落直接引出主题；
- 每一个主体段落都有清晰明了的主题句和适当的支持论据；
- 句子逻辑连贯；
- 词语经过精心挑选，生动形象，并有助于有效地表达主题；
- 段落之间过渡自然；
- 结尾段落与开头段落相呼应，强调主题。

 第三节 **让四、六级作文与众不同的策略** *Strategies to Make Your CET Writing Stand Out*

考虑到评卷人要评阅数千篇题目相同、内容相似的文章，考生如何才能和作为读者的他们更好地交流，让自己的作文与众不同呢？在遵循基本写作要求、实现逻辑性和连贯性的同时，考生可以通过使用巧妙的用词、更好的句型和生动的举例让作文更加出彩。

 一、遣词
Choosing the Best Words

词汇的选择会对写作质量产生巨大的影响。为了写出更好的文章，考生不应该直接使用脑海中首先浮现的简单词汇，而应该养成选择准确、恰当的词汇的习惯，即选择那些最能表达自己的想法、引起读者的注意，能够让文章脱颖而出的词汇。

1. 尽量简练
Practicing Economy

关于考试规定字数，实际上大多数考生都可以完成，真正的困难在于如何在限定字数内清晰有效地表达观点。因此，考生需要学会用词简练，以下是三种有效方法。

1）减少不必要的重复（Dropping Needless Repetition）

重复相同的单词或意思相似的单词可能会导致句子冗余，因此需要使用丰富的且最能表达观点的词汇，并删去重复的词汇。例如：

例 17

Wordy: The subject of teenage marriage is a topic that has created a magnitude of controversial argument.

Revised: Teenage marriage is a topic that has been widely debated.

2）去掉"死"名词（Dropping the "Dead" Nouns）

有些英语名词，如 kind、area 和 type 等，在指代具体的人、物或事时非常有用，但是如果使用过于频繁，反而会使写作失去活力。类似名词还有 aspect、fashion、nature、case、filed、process、factor、manner、situation 等，考生可以尝试在写作中用其他词汇来替换。例如：

例 18

- Wordy: In many cases, students fail to learn about career opportunities.
  Revised: Many students fail to learn about career opportunities.
- Wordy: In the field of veterinary science, demand exceeds supply.
  Revised: In veterinary science, demand exceeds supply.

3）避免不必要的扩张（Avoiding Needless Expansion）

在字数限定的考试作文中，若一个单词能够完成表达，就无须使用短语；若一个短语就能有效表达意思，就不必使用从句。例如：

例 19

- Wordy: The professor was absorbed in work, and he did not notice my presence.
  Revised: Absorbed in work, the professor did not notice my presence.
- Wordy: The splendid display in shop windows has a fascination which is irresistible.
  Revised: The splendid display in shop windows has an irresistible fascination.

2. 选择具体的词
Choosing Concrete Words

在四、六级写作中，考生应该使用具体的词汇，而不是笼统的词汇。例 20 显示了一般词和具体词的区别：

例 20

- General word: walk

  Concrete words: stride, pace, stagger, dance, patrol...

- General words: good food

  Concrete words: tasty, delicious, nourishing, appetizing, fresh...

又如：

例 21

Once across the Berezina, the tattered survivors limped towards Vilna.

—"The Icy Defender" in *New College English, Book 4*

解读 例 21 中有三个精心挑选的词：tattered、survivors 和 limped，它们准确生动地描述了刚刚侥幸逃脱的法国士兵的悲惨模样。无论是名词、形容词还是动词，都可以通过更好的选择来实现交流目的。

关于在例 12 的解读中提到的 "AI has become more and more popular in our life."，这里介绍一些更多不同的表达方式：

例 22

- AI now gradually **permeates** all walks of life.
- AI has already **sneaked into** our life.
- AI will **prevail** in a few decades.

3. 选择动态词
Choosing the Dynamic Word

用动态词代替静态词，这会使句子更有活力。你能体会到例 23 中静态词和动态词的区别吗？

例 23

- Self-conception is the basis of one's attitude towards success and failure.

Self-conception **underlines** one's attitude towards success and failure.

- The strength of our relationship makes our differences weaker and weaker.

  The strength of our relationship **overshadows** our differences.

二、造句
Developing Sentences

为了提高写作质量，考生需要学会用清晰连贯的句子来表达思想。为了吸引读者的注意力，考生还应努力写出信息丰富、表达有效的句子来阐明文章的主题。

1. 言之有物
Giving Your Sentence Content

为了向读者清晰地传达文章的主题，在写作的过程中考生一定要清楚每个句子想要表达的具体内容，并且选用具体的词语和表达方式，避免语义模糊和表述笼统。通过比较以下两句话，你能够明确体会到句子内容清晰有效的重要性。

例 24

Poor: AI will involve other problems.

Better: AI will involve matters of law and morality.

又如，大家比较熟悉的结尾句："...will become better and better."，这里的 better and better 其实就是一种笼统且空洞的表达。你应该写得更具体，指出到底在哪些方面会有所改善，并展示更多细节来呼应文章主题。

2. 改变句子风格
Varying Your Sentence Style

如果文章的句子结构千篇一律，那怎么才能引起读者的兴趣呢？考生可以尝试改变句子的长度、排列和复杂程度，找到最适合写作目的的句型结构。例如，并列结构（parallel structure）是一种非常有效的表达方式，你能感受到下面例 25 中并列结构的力量吗？

例 25

- Olympic volunteers were ready, fully able, and were quite determined to do a great job.

  Olympic volunteers were **ready, able, and determined** to do a great job.

- The high school entrepreneur was involved in the creation of a new miracle too, secured financing for it, and spent time getting the product to market. The high school entrepreneur **created, financed, and marketed** the new miracle tool.

例26

Admittedly, no one can deny the fact that the new information age has brought us so much convenience that we are allowed to get plenty of information just with a simple click sitting in front of computers.

解读 例 26 展示了如何通过组合不同的句型来组成一个复杂句。考生当然不必把每一句话都写得这么复杂，但确实需要思考如何在作文中使用不同的句型组合，给评卷人带来新的感受。

3. 避免陈词滥调
Avoiding Clichés

想必考生十分熟悉像 "Every coin has two sides." 这样的表达，并且经常在写作中使用。但为什么不能放弃 "硬币" 的表达，尝试一些不同的东西呢？例如，"We are blessed with new opportunities, as well as facing new challenges." 这句话也可以清楚地表明："对于人工智能的未来，我们既有信心也有担忧。"

其他的一些老生常谈，如 last but not least、easier said than done、as far as I'm concerned 等也在写作中被频繁使用。为了让文章脱颖而出，考生应该尝试一些其他表达方式来避免陈词滥调。

三、举例生动

Using Attractive Examples

用人物经历或故事来作例证呈现会比简单的陈述更生动、更吸引人。例子可以用来引出话题，也可以用来支撑论点。生动有趣的事例也可以让考生的写作与众不同。在例 27 中，作者没有使用传统的 "陈述 + 事例" 模式，而是完全通过事例来表达自己对人工智能未来多种可能性的关注。

例27

Thousands of robots are now shuttling back and forth among the shelves of the super warehouse of Amazon. In the future, indeed, waiters in European restaurants will be replaced by robots which can work 24 hours without having a rest.

However, outside the Foxconn factory area, lots of young workers, whose posts are occupied by tens of thousands of robots on both sides of the line, are confused about their future, having no time to express their homesickness.

> **解读** 通过具体的例子，作者清楚地表达了自己对人工智能未来的信心和忧虑。因为具体的例子既可以为读者创造生动的画面，也可以清晰地表达作者的观点。

总而言之，为了吸引读者的注意力，考生应该写出信息丰富、直截了当、表达简洁的句子。这需要避免老套，运用独特的方式来完成一篇与众不同的考试作文。

第四节 大学英语四、六级范文分析
CET-4 and CET-6 Sample Analysis

本节将介绍两篇四级范文和一篇六级范文，并结合前面介绍的写作策略来分析它们在整体结构、遣词造句、写作风格等方面的特点。

一、四级范文分析
CET-4 Sample Essay Analysis

［题目］

Directions: For this part, you are allowed 30 minutes to write a short essay on how to best handle the relationship between parents and children. You should write at least 120 words but no more than 180 words. (CET-4 in December, 2017)

例 28

It is a truth universally acknowledged that the relationship between a parent and a child is the most significant one in a person's life. A positive parent-child bond is beneficial to family harmony and the growth of children. Therefore, people should learn to balance the relationship between parents and children.

There are some conductive suggestions given to both parents and children. First and foremost, it is very important for parents to emphasize the significance of family time spent with their children, like eating meals together on weekends, going to sporting events, movies, and the like. Besides, it would be beneficial if parents could pay attention to their children's academic performance, friendships, and extra-curricular activities. Additionally, it is necessary that children should boost their awareness of communicating with their parents, with relaxed and side-by-side conversations.

As has been noted, parents and children should make joint efforts to create a good relationship between them.

解读 这篇范文结构清晰、观点明确，是一篇不错的习作，但读起来会觉得有点遗憾。其中的段落结构、句型、短语，特别是那些表示逻辑结构的连接词，是不是过于熟悉？多年的标准化写作训练可能在某种程度上限制了考生写作能力的发挥，把他们禁锢在一些熟悉的结构和模式里。为了更好地表达观点，更好地实现写作的交际目的，考生需要大胆尝试更多的表达方式。

在写考试作文时，考生都很关心字数的限制，生怕写不够字数，于是就容易用那些熟悉的单词和短语来扩充句子，却不太会用更直接、更简洁的方式来表达自己的观点。例 29 是关于"大学毕业后选择就业还是继续读书"这一话题的范文，请关注作者对词汇的选择和运用。

［题目］

Directions: For this part, you are allowed 30 minutes to write an essay. Suppose you have two options upon graduation: one is to take a job in a company and the other to go to a graduate school. You are to make a choice between the two. Write an essay to explain the reasons for your choice. You should write at least 120 words but no more than 180 words. (CET-4 in December, 2016)

例 29

For college students, graduation is not only a simple goodbye, but also a fork in the road. One way leads to the entrance to society while the other way is a door to higher education. After taking every aspect into account, I prefer the latter.

Stepping into society never goes smoothly, especially for those new graduates whose adaptability and practical experience are relatively scarce. Besides, the professional knowledge learned in university is far from enough to deal with real world problems. To broaden one's horizon as well as inspire one's deeper thinking, further study is a must.

More importantly, placed in such an increasingly fierce employment competition, one who possesses a master's degree, or even a Ph.D., will certainly emerge as a competitive candidate. In addition, highly educated young people are welcomed by corporations, which results in a wide range of career opportunities.

As far as I am concerned, continuing academic work won't bog me down. Instead, it will drive me forward.

解读 这篇范文结构清晰，词汇和短语的选择也很用心。整篇作文中并没有多少大词难词，却有效地表达了作者的想法。读者不仅能够看到句型的变化，而且能够看到有些词语的选择非常聪明，例如 the entrance to 和 a door to 是并列结构并表达相似含义，而 bog me down 和 drive me forward 是并列结构却表达相对含义。这样一篇文章还是可以让评卷人眼前一亮的。

二、六级范文分析
CET-6 Sample Essay Analysis

[题目]

Directions: For this part, you are allowed 30 minutes to write a short essay on e-learning. Try to imagine what will happen when more and more people study online instead of attending school. You are required to write at least 150 words but no more than 200 words. (CET-6 in June, 2016)

例30

E-learning is getting more and more popular with each passing day. For example, some college students use e-learning to supplement their school curriculum; more and more corporations offer online training for their employees.

Undoubtedly, e-learning has its distinctive advantages over any other type of learning. First and foremost, it is convenient and flexible since it allows users to learn at a time and place of the users' choosing as long as they own a computer and have an Internet connection. Another major benefit of e-learning is the accessibility it provides. For instance, students can take online courses given by prestigious professors at home and abroad. In addition, e-learning is cost effective. This is especially true for corporate training because travel and accommodation expenses for trainers and employees can be cut. However, e-learning is far from "one size fits all". It doesn't fit people who lack self-discipline and have difficulty in time management. Besides, people who value face to face interaction with their teachers and classmates may also find online learning unsatisfactory.

From my point of view, although e-learning has changed both education and corporate training, it will not replace traditional in-class learning, but instead will function as a complementary type of learning.

解读 这篇范文结构清晰、论证全面。内容紧紧围绕开头段落中提出的主题句，从学校学习和公司培训两个方面论证了 e-leaning 的好处，同时提到了 e-learning 不能解决的问题。语言简洁清晰，one size fits all 这样的短语正是简练原则的典范。结尾呼应开头，再次点明并加强了主题。

Exercises

I. **Read the following topic lists of CET-4 and CET-6 and choose some topics for your writing practice.**

CET-4 writing topics:

1. Directions: For this part, you are allowed 30 minutes to write a short essay to express your views on the phenomenon of group purchasing. You should write at least 120 words but no more than 180 words.

2. Directions: For this part, you are allowed 30 minutes to write a short essay to express your views on the phenomenon of cosmetic surgery. You should write at least 120 words but no more than 180 words.

3. Directions: For this part, you are allowed 30 minutes to write a short essay to express your views on the saying "Create your own life." You should write at least 120 words but no more than 180 words.

4. Directions: For this part, you are allowed 30 minutes to write a short essay. You should start your essay with a brief description of the picture and then express your views on the independence of young people in modern society. You should write at least 120 words but no more than 180 words.

"When you've finished saving for my education, don't forget to start saving for my retirement."

5. Directions: For this part, you are allowed 30 minutes to write a short essay. You should start your essay with a brief description of the picture and then express your views on the burden children are facing. You should write at least 120 words but no more than 180 words.

"At 12 months, your child should begin walking, speaking words, and making his first attempt at reading."

CET-6 writing topics:

1. Directions: For this part, you are allowed 30 minutes to write a composition on the topic "It pays to be honest." You should write at least 150 words but no more than 200 words.

2. Directions: For this part, you are allowed 30 minutes to write an essay commenting on the remark "Earth provides enough to satisfy every man's need, but not every man's greed." You can cite examples to illustrate your point. You should write at least 150 words but no more than 200 words.

3. Directions: For this part, you are allowed 30 minutes to write an essay on why students should be encouraged to develop effective communication skills. You should write at least 150 words but no more than 200 words.

4. Directions: For this part, you are allowed 30 minutes to write an essay titled "Are people becoming addicted to technology?". The statement given below is for your reference. You should write at least 120 words but no more than 180 words.

    Numerous studies claim that addiction to technology is real and it has the same effect on the brain as drug addiction.

5. Directions: For this part, you are allowed 30 minutes to write an essay based on the chart below. You should start your essay with a brief description of the chart and comment on China's achievements in poverty alleviation. You should write at least 150 words but no more than 200 words.

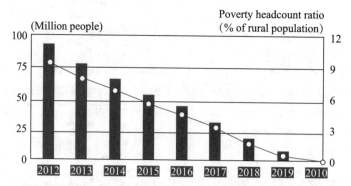

Rural population in poverty

Sources: China's National Bureau of Statistics, China's State Council Leading Group Office of Poverty Alleviation and Development

II. After you have produced your first draft, revise it in terms of purpose, audience, content, format, and language based on the checklist below. Please tick the box if your answer to the question is yes.

No.	Checklist for Self-evaluation	Yes
1)	Have I demonstrated a clear writing purpose and a good awareness of audience?	
2)	Have I presented a strong and well-defined theme?	
3)	Have I presented a topic sentence in each paragraph?	
4)	Is my writing clear and logical?	
5)	Have I provided vivid and convincing supporting details?	
6)	Has my writing reflected a unique and consistent personal voice?	
7)	Have I used appropriate and varied rhetorical devices?	
8)	Is the ending fitting and effective? Does it strengthen the theme?	
9)	Have I demonstrated appropriate register, syntactic variety, and effective use of vocabulary?	
10)	Have I checked the language of my essay to ensure that it is error-free?	

III. Then review one or more peer essays in terms of purpose, audience, content, format, and language based on the checklist below. Please tick the box if your answer to the question is yes.

No.	Checklist for Peer Review	Yes
1)	Has the author demonstrated a clear writing purpose and a good awareness of audience?	
2)	Has the author presented a strong and well-defined theme?	
3)	Has the author presented a topic sentence in each paragraph?	
4)	Is the writing clear and logical?	
5)	Has the author provided vivid and convincing supporting details?	
6)	Has the writing reflected a unique and consistent personal voice?	
7)	Has the author used appropriate and varied rhetorical devices?	
8)	Is the ending fitting and effective? Does it strengthen the theme?	
9)	Has the author demonstrated appropriate register, syntactic variety, and effective use of vocabulary?	
10)	Has the author checked the language of his/her essay to ensure that it is error-free?	

第九章

国际考试的英语写作
English Writing in International Tests

 第一节 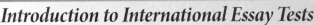 **国际考试的英语写作概述**
Introduction to International Essay Tests

　　本章将聚焦于雅思和托福这两项具有代表性的国际标准化英语水平考试的写作部分。有人认为标准化语言测试的技术性很强，通过机械化刷题训练就能在考试中获得高分，其实不然。雅思和托福考试的考查重点是英语语言运用能力，其写作部分同样看重写作的交际性（effective communication），即用英语有效沟通的能力。考生需要根据写作类型确定写作目的，并用英语传递信息、表达观点、说服读者，以实现有意义的交流。所以在国际英语考试的写作训练中，交际性的培养也很重要。

　　雅思和托福考试有很多共同之处。它们关注同一种语言——英语，其写作部分要求考生不仅要掌握正确的拼写和语法，还要以合乎逻辑、连贯性强、直接明了（logical, coherent, to-the-point）的方式写作，并使用一定比例的高级词汇，在一个小时内完成两项写作任务。

　　雅思和托福考试的一大区别在于，托福考试目前只有机器考试，而雅思考试有纸笔考试和机器考试两种选择。如果雅思考生选择纸笔考试，提高书写技能则非常重要。比如，字迹要工整好辨认，单词拼写不能出错，并且要养成提前规划文章的习惯，因为写完之后不方便进行删除、更改或插入内容。

第二节 **雅思写作**
IELTS Writing

国际英语语言测试系统（International English Language Testing System, IELTS），简称"雅思"，是一项针对非英语母语人士的国际标准化英语水平测试。它受到英国、美国、加拿大、澳洲以及欧洲、东南亚等新兴留学目的地在内的 140 多个国家和地区，以及超过 11 000 所教育机构、雇主单位、专业协会和政府部门的认可。

雅思考试分为学术类测试和培训类测试两种类型，有听、说、读、写四个部分。本节将重点关注雅思学术类测试的写作部分。

一、雅思作文一

 IELTS Writing Task 1

雅思学术类测试的作文一要求考生根据特定的图表写一篇至少 150 词的概要，图表类型主要有柱状图、线形图、饼图、表格、多个图表的组合、流程图和地图。此项任务主要测试考生选择和报告材料主要特征的能力、描述和比较数据的能力、推测事物发展趋势的能力或描述过程的能力。

虽然作文一的主要目的是测试考生对英语的掌握程度，但报告的格式（即结构）同样重要。在这份书面报告里，考生需要描述从图表中获得的信息，并将其整理成书面文本。需要注意的是，这份报告是写给考官看的，因此必须是正式的、可读性强的、简短的且有逻辑性的。

1. 作文一的结构
Structure of Task 1

作文一的结构相对简单，通常包含引言部分、数据报告部分和结论部分（有时结论部分也可省略）。由于篇幅有限，有时在报告所有相关细节后，文章就可以流畅且合乎逻辑地结束了。在大多情况下，如果最后有结论能简洁地向读者传达最重要的信息，这会是文章的一个亮点。

作文一需要分段。一般来说，引言单独一段，而数据报告部分会增加至两到三段，这取决于图表类型和组织数据的方式。不同图表的呈现方式有所不同，并没有"一刀切"的方案来报告数据。

2. 作文一的内容
Content of a Task 1 Report

作文一是一份客观报告，通常不需要考生提出个人意见或作出假设。虽然考生不会因为发表意见被扣分，但是如果提出的观点与话题无关，或没有传达正确的信息，可能会在"任务完成度"（Task Achievement）这一项上扣分。

为了合理利用时间并生成一份连贯的报告，考生需要先迅速理解图表，确定报告需要描述的信息，之后找到恰当的方法来组织信息，并有效地与读者沟通。

3. 作文一的写法
Writing a Task 1 Report

1）引言（Introduction）

引言是为了让读者了解图表的大致内容，一般可以这样开头："The graph illustrates... / presents the number of... / talks about..."，或者"This is a graph of..."，或者"According to the graph, ..."。有些题目包含不止一个图表，那么考生需要在引言部分描述每一个图表。例如：

例 1

The line graph illustrates the number of visitors in millions from the UK who went abroad and those that came to the UK between 1979 and 1999, while the bar chart shows which countries were the most popular for UK residents to visit in 1999.

在引言部分，考生只需要陈述图表的要点，即最重要的信息，而不需要描述具体细节。例如：

例 2

The graph illustrates the quantities of goods transported in the United Kingdom by four different modes of transport between 1974 and 2002.

需要特别注意的是，引言部分的文字不能直接复制题目要求，因为雅思考试规定，凡是从题目中复制的内容都不计为答案（因其不能表现出考生的写作能力），甚至导致扣分。但考生可以在有限的时间内快速改写原题。例如：

例 3

原题：The pie charts below show units of electricity production by fuel source in Australia and France in 1980 and 2000.

改写：The pie charts compare the sources of electricity in Australia and France in 1980 and 2000.

2）正文（Body）

正文各段通常采用这样的结构：首句总体概括本段观点（overview），后面的句子依序描述细节（details）。

正文各段的首句是对该段信息的整体概况，包括图表的整体变化趋势（存在时间推移的动态图表）、图表展示了哪几类数据（不存在变化趋势的静态图表）或哪一类数据整体不同于其他各类数据。后面的句子具体介绍数据，并尽可能按照有规律的顺序来描述。比如，线形图可按照从左到右的自然顺序描述；如果柱状图的横轴有时间变化，也可按照从左到右的顺序描述；如果没有时间变化，可按照柱形对应数值从大到小的顺序描述；饼图可按照所占份额从大到小的顺序依次介绍。

如果题目中给出的信息很多（例如有两个以上的图表），考生需要注意挑选重要的信息并以简短的方式进行描述，避免篇幅过长、内容繁杂。例 4 是一个包含柱状图和线形图的作文一的报告部分：

例 4

To begin, the number of visits abroad by UK residents was higher than for those that came to the UK, and this remained so throughout the period. The figures started at a similar amount, around 10 million, but visits abroad increased significantly to over 50 million, whereas the number of overseas residents rose steadily to reach just under 30 million.

By far the most popular countries to visit in 1999 were France at approximately 11 million visitors, followed by Spain at 9 million. The USA, Greece, and Turkey were far less popular at around 4, 3, and 2 million visitors respectively.

—cited from the website of IELTS Buddy

解读 例 4 中有两个正文段落，分别描述了两个图表的情况。根据题目中提供的图表数量，考生需要按照逻辑顺序进行规划，再根据具体情况组织语言。

3）结论（Conclusion）

关于作文一是否一定要有结论，不同考官其实有不同见解。在大多数情况下，结论最好能简要地概括最重要的信息，成为文章的一个加分项。结论有很多不同的写法，但最重要的是要基于题目所给的信息，保持客观且总结到位。对于含有多个图表的题目，结论最好能适当解释一下各图表之间的联系，但如果确实看不出联系，也可以只是简单的概括。例如：

例5

Overall, it can be seen that visits to and from the UK increased, and that France was the most popular country to go to.

4. 作文一的评分标准
Evaluating a Task 1 Report

雅思考官从以下方面对作文一进行评分：

- 任务完成度（Task Achievement）：考生能否有效地找到信息中的关键内容并对之进行描述和写作。
- 连贯性和结构层次（Cohesion and Coherence）：考生能否将信息和要点合理地组织起来，信息和要点之间的联系是否清晰。
- 词汇来源（Lexical Resource）：考生使用的词汇是否广泛、准确，且适合这一部分写作的要求。
- 语法的多样性和准确性（Grammatical Range and Accuracy）：考生使用的语法结构是否多样、准确，且适合这一部分写作的要求。

5. 作文一的评分标准
Scoring Criteria for Writing Task 1

1）精确性（Accuracy）

写数据报告要考虑到读者的需求，因此报告必须清晰准确、合乎逻辑且连贯性强。但也无须为细节错误过度担忧，因为除非是致命错误，否则通常不太会影响分数。

另外，精确地报告每一个数字并非明智之举，相反可以用"约数"（approximations）来概括数据。例如，48.5%、32%、25%、7% 等数字可以分别表示为 nearly half、almost a third、a quarter、a small minority，这些表述的可读性更强。

2）时态使用（Use of Tenses）

作文一需要使用恰当的时态。引言部分对图表的概述通常使用一般现在时，比如 "The graph shows the number of smokers in Australia between the years 1987 and 2018."。至于图表中的信息，考生则需要仔细思考使用哪种时态。如果是过去的事件，通常使用一般过去时，比如 "From 1960 to 1970, the value remained unchanged."；如果是从过去持续到现在，则使用现在完成时，比如 "Since 2010, the value has been growing steadily."。在谈论将来时，需要谨慎使用动词 will，因为没有人能够百分百准确地预测未来。常用的表将来的表达方式有：be expected/projected/predicted to、be likely to 等，比如 "The value is expected to continue growing over the next ten years."。

关于循环往复的动作，通常使用一般现在时。比如 "On Friday, students spend six hours doing their homework." 和 "July is the hottest month of the year." 中的动作在每个周五和每个七月都会发生，因此使用一般现在时。此外，还需要注意区分有具体时间点的事件，比如 "July 2010 had record temperatures." 中使用了一般过去时。

3）流程图（Process Diagrams）

在各类图表中，流程图是比较特殊的（如图 9.1 所示），需要考生观察、分析和描述一个过程是如何进行的或一台机器是如何工作的。因此，考生有必要一开始就仔细读图，以确保对图有准确的理解。

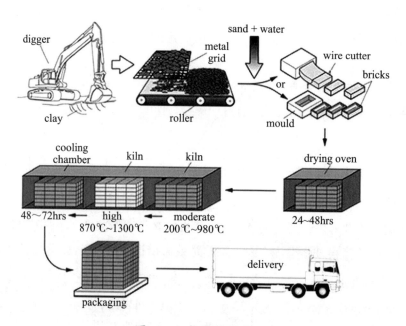

图 9.1 流程图示例

流程图使用的语法结构比其他类型的图表要简单，仅需要用到一种时态：一般现在时。例如，"Water flows through the pipe." 中用的既不是 flowed，也不是 will flow；"The wheel is driven through a chain." 中用的既不是 was driven，也不是 will be driven。

流程图中最需要注意的语法技巧是选择主动语态还是被动语态。如果这个过程是由人执行的，则使用被动语态（例如 "The machine is turned on."）；如果它是自然发生的，则使用主动语态（例如 "Trees grow."）。某些特定情景也许要用到两种语态（例

如 "Water flows." 和 "Water is pumped."），这当然取决于是谁发出动作，或者它是否自然发生。

4）语法和用词错误（Grammar and Vocabulary Errors）

常见的错误类型有：

- 引言部分常见的一个错误是 the graph show，正确形式应该是 the graph shows 或者 the graphs show。

- 介绍具体数字时，不要出现类似 13.5 thousands 这样的错误，正确形式应该是 13.5 thousand，注意描述具体数字时 thousand、million、billion 等应保持单数形式。

- 表示数据下降时一般不用 reduce，而是用 fall、decrease 等来表示，比如 "The average house price in the UK fell/decreased from...to..."。

- 表示某类人或物的数字时，常用 figure、number、amount 这些词，但考生容易弄混它们的用法：the figure for 可跟可数名词复数或不可数名词单数，the number of 接可数名词复数，the amount of 接不可数名词单数。

- 两套形成对比关系的主谓结构放在同一个句子里时，记得在句首或句中加连接词，比如 "The number of car users increased gradually, while/and the number of bus users fell steadily."，常有考生忘记添加。

在考场上，考生容易犯上述这类简单的错误，为避免语法和用词错误，在提交试卷之前一定要抽出时间检查。

二、雅思写作作文二
IELTS Writing Task 2

雅思学术类测试的作文二要求考生就一个给定的话题写一篇文章（至少 250 词），出题方式主要有两种：一种是辩论类（argument），话题比较有争议性，需要辩论观点或比较利弊；另一种是分析解释类（report），题目里不给出任何观点，只是给出一种现象，要求分析现象的原因、带来的问题、影响因素、解决方案、应对措施等。

1. 作文二的话题
Topics in Writing Task 2

作文二通常讨论的是一般性问题，而非专业领域的问题。常见话题包括教育、环境、商业经济、动物保护、犯罪问题、人口老龄化等。雅思考试测试的是英语语言能力和应用交际能力，并不需要考生在特定专业领域拥有深厚的知识积累，只要考生能用通顺的英文把符合生活常识的观点表达出来即可。以下按照题材分类列举了一些雅思真题：

- 教育类：Some people think that computers and the Internet are important in children's study, but others think students can learn more effectively in schools and with teachers. Discuss both views and give your own opinion.

- 环境类：The unlimited use of cars may cause many problems. What are those problems? In order to reduce these problems, should people be discouraged from using cars?

- 经济类：International tourism has become a huge industry in the world. Do the problems of international travel outweigh its advantages?

- 动物类：Now many people think that we are spending too much money and time on protecting wild animals. The money should be better spent on humans. Do you agree or disagree?

- 犯罪类：Some people think sending criminals to prison is not an effective way to deal with them. Education and training are better. To what extent do you agree?

- 人口老龄化：In many countries, the proportion of older people is steadily increasing. Does this trend have more positive or negative effects on the society?

2. 作文二的结构
Structure of Writing Task 2

与作文一相比，作文二更需要创意。考生只知道一个主题，而没有任何图表的指引，因此需要自己思考文章的全部内容，并表达自己的想法。作文二的结构可以是灵活多样的，并不存在"官方指定结构"，只要能把问题讲清楚、有说服力即可。当然在写作的过程中，考生可以参照一些模板，遵循一定方法。

一般来说，四段式（four-paragraph structure）和五段式（five-paragraph structure）是相对容易操作的作文结构。这两种结构非常清晰，有引言、正文和结论三个部分，引言和结论部分分别是一个段落，正文部分通常是三个主体段，也有少部分考生使用两个主体段。下面是这两种结构的一般形式：

- 四段式结构：
  引言段 1~3 句
  正文第一段 4~6 句
  正文第二段 4~6 句
  结论段 1~2 句

- 五段式结构：
  引言段 1~3 句
  正文第一段 3~4 句
  正文第二段 3~4 句
  正文第三段 3~4 句
  结论段 1~2 句

3. 作文二的写法
Writing a Task 2 Essay

不同于作文一中图表题的客观性写作，作文二中的议论文明显带有主观性，但是雅思议论文是没有标准答案的。由于雅思写作考查的是英语应用能力，考官最关心的是考生是否可以把符合生活常识的观点用通顺的英文表达出来，并且有力地支持自己的观点。以下将探讨作文二每个部分的写法。

1）引言（Introduction）

引言的目的在于：陈述事件的背景、介绍问题和表明观点（中心论点）。引言不宜过长，应简单明了地切入主题，并清晰地向读者传递以下信息：

- 谈论的主题是什么？
- 作者持什么观点？
- 文章的中心论点是什么？

2）正文（Body）

如何组织正文部分取决于有哪些观点需要阐述，通常一个单独的观点会用一段来论述。段落也有固定的结构，通常在段首会有一个"段落主题句"，用以概括整段大意，之后再就这个主题句展开论述。例如，针对如下题目："Nowadays, families are not as close as in the past and a lot of people have become used to this. Why is this happening? Do the advantages of this trend outweigh the drawbacks?"，段落主题句可以这样写："One of the first reasons for a decline in the closeness of families is connected to the busy lifestyles that we now lead."。这样一来，读者就会明白该段将阐述"how a busy life causes families not to be so close"这一观点。

3）结论（Conclusion）

结论是对前文主要观点的总结，重复并强调作者观点。需要注意的是，结论中不能引入任何新信息或新观点。因为如果结论中出现新的信息，那么它就不是结论，而是另一个正文段落，而缺乏结论会严重影响考试分数。

4. 作文二的交际性写作
Communicative Writing in Task 2

一篇全面、公允的议论文通常会提出一些赞成和反对这个主题的观点，以表明考生在作出最终决定前已经考虑了双方的立场，权衡了利弊，这比较受考官的青睐。

下面将结合具体示例进行说明。

例 6

The Advantages and Disadvantages of Hosting the Olympic Games

Hosting the Olympic Games has become a huge undertaking because of the cost of preparation and the overall financial risks involved. However, it is a wonderful opportunity for the host country because of the chance for worldwide publicity and the prestige associated with the Games. This essay will discuss some of the problems, and also the positive aspects of being a host for the Olympics.

There can be no doubt that holding the Olympics involves financial risks. It is possible to lose money because of the expense of the special buildings and facilities needed for the Games. For example, the original budget of under €5 billion for the Athens Olympics grew to €11 billion, and that was a shock for the Greek government. In addition, most countries have a limited budget for building projects and if it is all spent on preparations for the Games, this may mean there is less for other essential projects.

On the other hand, there are major benefits to be gained by hosting the Olympics. It is certainly a wonderful showcase for the host country because of the global interest and TV coverage it generates. It also ensures significant investment in facilities such as stadiums, roads, water supply, and accommodation. An additional bonus is the positive profit generated by the sale of TV rights, sponsorship, ticket sales, and visitor expenditure. Over the 20 years to 2000, every country hosting the Olympics either broke even or made a profit.

These advantages outweigh the disadvantages of hosting the Games.

解读 例 6 中，引言部分陈述了正反两方的观点，作者没有在第一段表明自己的观点，而是把观点放在了结论部分。正文第一段描述了举办奥运会的缺点，第二段则是树立奥运会的正面形象，由此得出了举办奥运会利大于弊的结论，这样的呈现方式更加自然且合乎逻辑。

例 6 这种发展论点的方法是可取的，但有时会适得其反，部分考生通过列举许多格外有力的反方观点，反而让自己的观点变得苍白无力，如例 7 所示：

例 7

The Advantages and Disadvantages of Hosting the Olympic Games

Hosting the Olympic Games has become a huge undertaking because of the cost of preparation and the overall financial risks involved. However, it is a wonderful opportunity for the host country because of the chance for worldwide publicity and the prestige associated with the Games. This essay will discuss some of the problems, and also the positive aspects of being a host for the Olympics.

There can be no doubt that there are major benefits to be gained by hosting the Olympics. It is certainly a wonderful showcase for the host country because of the global interest and TV coverage it generates. It also ensures significant investment in facilities such as stadiums, roads, water supply, and accommodation. An additional bonus is the positive profit generated by the sale of TV rights, sponsorship, ticket sales, and visitor expenditure. Over the 20 years to 2000, every country hosting the Olympics either broke even or made a profit.

On the other hand, holding the Olympics involves financial risks. It is possible to lose money because of the expense of the special buildings and facilities needed for the Games. For example, the original budget of under €5 billion for the Athens Olympics grew to €11 billion, and that was a shock for the Greek government. In addition, most countries have a limited budget for building projects and if it is all spent on preparations for the Games, this may mean there is less for other essential projects.

These advantages outweigh the disadvantages of hosting the Games.

解读 与例 6 相比，例 7 中的观点没有变，引言部分也是相同的，只是改变了正文中观点的出现顺序。作者先列举了关于举办奥运会的正面信息，之后转为大谈特谈其缺点。这样给读者的印象就会不同，因为读者已经被后面列举的缺点所说服，相信举办奥运会是一场金融噩梦，并忘记了一开始列出的所有优点。这将使"利大于弊"的主张难以被接受。

由此可见，同样的观点用不同的顺序呈现会对读者造成不同的影响，因此考生在写作中需要注意观点的逻辑顺序。

5. 作文二的评分标准

Evaluating a Task 2 Report

雅思考官从以下方面对作文二进行评分：

- 对写作任务的反应（Task Response）：考生能否完整地、以恰当的方式完成题目要求；论点是否切题、清晰合理；论证过程是否完整；论点是否有足够的论据支持。

- 连贯性和结构层次（Cohesion and Coherence）：考生能否将信息和要点合理地

组织起来（如运用分段的能力），信息和要点之间的联系是否清晰。

- 词汇来源（Lexical Resource）：考生使用的词汇是否广泛、准确，且适合这一部分写作的要求。
- 语法的多样性和准确性（Grammatical Range and Accuracy）：考生使用的语法结构是否多样、准确，且适合这一部分写作的要求。

托福写作
TOEFL Writing

托福考试的写作也有两个部分，第二部分的"独立写作"与雅思写作的作文二非常相似，而第一部分的"综合写作"比较特殊。

 一、托福考试的综合写作
TOEFL Integrated Writing

托福考试的综合写作不仅考查写作，还兼顾听力与阅读。综合写作任务一般先给出一段阅读材料，再播放一段听力材料，两者话题密切关联，要求考生进行信息整合，实事求是地展示两种渠道提供的观点。

综合写作任务的阅读材料和听力材料之间的关系通常呈现为三种类型。第一，针锋相对型。阅读材料和听力材料的观点相互驳斥，考生需要理解并记录各自的总论点、分论点如何对立，并总结成文。第二，问题解决型。阅读材料给出一个亟待解决的难题，听力材料提供解决途径。第三，质疑方案型。阅读材料提出解决难题的对策，听力材料则对每一项对策提出质疑。

接下来将就综合写作任务的写作方法和语言使用提出建议。

1. 整合信息
How to Integrate Information

无论遇到何种类型的综合写作任务，考生都需要在充分理解阅读材料和听力材料的基础上，迅速提取关键信息、整理逻辑链条、如实总结两方面的观点，并避免流露出任何个人观点或判断。迄今为止，在几乎所有的综合写作任务中，阅读材料与听力材料的观点都倾向于对立，而非相互支持与佐证。

综合写作任务的阅读材料和听力材料本身是高度结构化的：第一段开门见山，讲述全文（或全讲座）的主旨；之后常分为三个分论点，从不同角度细化主旨；每个分论点段落基本都是"总—分"结构，段落第一句话一般是本段落的中心句，也是考生需要重点理解的语句。实际上，这种"总—分"结构为考生准备托福独立写作任务提供了积极的参考价值。

但需要注意的是，独立写作任务需要以结论段结束，即采用"总—分—总"结构，而综合写作任务的阅读材料和听力材料没有结论段。此外，在针锋相对型和质疑方案型写作任务中，阅读材料和听力材料的分论点是一一对应的。换言之，听力材料的第一个分论点针对的是阅读材料的第一个分论点，以此类推，这在一定程度上会减轻考生的写作压力。

在理解阅读材料时，考生应当着重注意总论点、各段分论点以及必要的细节；在播放听力材料时，则需要边听边记笔记，将注意力放在驳斥或质疑阅读材料观点的各个分论点上，对细节给予更多关注。

例8

阅读材料：

For hundreds of years, a civilization thrived on Easter Island, which is one of the most remote islands in the Pacific Ocean. However, sometime before the 19th century, the society on the island suffered a total collapse. The mysteriousness of the civilization's demise has given rise to a few ideas about what happened to the island and its inhabitants.

A compelling argument has attributed the civilization's run to an infestation of large rats. It is believed that the boats which brought the island's original inhabitants also carried rats, which were able to rapidly reproduce over the following few centuries. Since these rats mainly fed on the seeds of the palm trees which grew on the island at that time, they eventually caused major deforestation to occur. This deforestation may have caused erosion and soil loss, which in turn made it difficult for the inhabitants of the island to grow food. This lack of food may have spelled the end of the civilization on Easter Island.

A second possible cause of the civilization's decline might have been internal warfare among the population. Archaeological excavations have turned up thousands of small, curved blades—called *mata'a* in the local language—all over Easter Island. The people of the island probably used these as weapons, and the sheer number of them that have been found suggests that large-scale warfare occurred for much of the 14th century. As a result, long-term population decline was inevitable.

A third view points to the effects of exposure to diseases brought by visitors from Europe and South America. When large-scale contact with outsiders became extremely frequent in the 19th century, it is unlikely that the local population had biological resistance to some of the diseases they carried. It is estimated that thousands of residents may have died as a result of this. This sad effect is consistent with the decline of native populations in North America that were similarly diminished by contact with outsiders several centuries earlier.

听力材料:

Easter Island was once home to thriving and vibrant society, so its collapse is somewhat, um, baffling. Unfortunately, none of the current explanations really resolve the question of why it declined so completely.

Let me open the discussion by challenging the theory about rats. You know, it is true that rats were found on the island and there is evidence that they consumed the seeds of palm trees. But even if the island suffered deforestation, the population there would still have had enough food to eat. Studies of human remains on the island suggest that the islanders were prodigious fishers...and that up to 60% of their diet came from the sea! Not only that, we have evidence that they used special rock gardens to create specific areas with rich soil, even when erosion was common. They used these gardens to grow crops like potatoes, which means that they had enough food to eat all during their history.

Next, many people point to the presence of the bladed *mata'a* as proof that the residents of Easter Island engaged in large-scale warfare which destroyed their society. But careful analysis of the size and shape of these blades suggests that they weren't weapons at all. They aren't very sharp, and very few of them are even pointed. This tells us that they were more likely used as tools for cutting rock and other hard surfaces. It is likely that they were used in the construction of homes and large statues that are often found on the island and not for combat.

And last, frequent contact with outsiders was very detrimental to the population of Easter Island, but it wasn't the cause of the civilization's collapse. When that contact began, there was estimated to be about 3,000 people living on the island, and, yes, many of them suffered from the effects of foreign diseases. However, recent excavations indicate that in the 17th century the population of the island was close to 20,000 thousand people. This means that whatever caused the population to decline began long before contact with outsiders began.

写作要求：

Summarize the points made in the lecture to explain how they oppose the specific points made in the reading passage.

—cited from the website of TOEFL Resources

2. 完成综合写作任务
How to Complete an Integrated Writing Task

在理解信息并完成整合之后，考生需要尽快打字成文。在实际答卷过程中，想要简洁又如实地完成写作任务，考生一般应写 250 词以上。

综合写作任务的成文也是高度结构化的，甚至是模板化的。全文分四个或五个段落，采取"总—分（—总）"结构：第一段是引言，先分别介绍两篇材料的主题，再是各自的主旨；第二段至第四段分别总结阅读材料和听力材料的三个分论点，着重阐述各个分论点的互斥关系或后者质疑前者的关系。

综合写作任务通常不要求写结论段。但若考生水平较高，又有剩余时间，亦可完成简单的结论段，即再次重申两个材料之间的对立关系，但切勿直接搬用引言段原话，而要做转述（paraphrase）。

以下是引言段示例：

例9

The article/passage/text and the lecture/recording/presentation are both about...The article proposes/argues/suggests that...However, this hypothesis/point/argument/analysis/claim/perspective/suggestion/opinion is challenged/undermined/problematized/opposed by the professor/presenter/speaker, who, instead, holds/believes/argues that...

引言段之后的三个主体段落的结构高度一致。考生需要将一一对应的论点进行整合呈现，梳理其逻辑关系。主体段落写作须避免照抄阅读材料原句，需要考生自己组织语言进行写作。例 10 示范了主体段的常用结构：

例 10

The first solution/argument proposed in the article is that...Specifically, the author indicates that...Nonetheless/However/Nevertheless, the presenter strongly opposes this argument, holding that...Additionally, he/she mentions that...

3. 综合写作的语言
Language in Integrated Writing

通常情况下，综合写作全文使用一般现在时，例如 "The writer believes that..." 或 "...while the lecture contradicts this view."。此外，需要注意转述动词（reporting verbs）的选择。转述动词能够表达观点立场，显示不同语气。表 9.1 是阿德莱德大学总结的转述动词表，可供参考。

表 9.1　转述动词表

Function	Weaker Position	Neutral Position	Stronger Position
addition		add	
advice		advise	
agreement	admit, concede	accept, acknowledge, agree, concur, confirm, recognize	applaud, congratulate, extol, praise, support
argument and persuasion	apologize	assure, encourage, interpret, justify, reason	alert, argue, boast, contend, convince, emphasize, exhort, forbid, insist, prove, promise, persuade, threaten, warn
believing	guess, hope, imagine	believe, claim, declare, express, feel, hold, know, maintain, subscribe to, think	assert, guarantee, insist, uphold
conclusion		conclude, discover, find, infer, realize	
disagreement and questioning	doubt, question	challenge, debate, disagree, question, request, wonder	accuse, attack, complain, contradict, criticize, deny, discard, disclaim, discount, dismiss, dispute, disregard, negate, object to, oppose, refute, reject
discussion	comment	discuss, explore	reason
emphasis			accentuate, emphasize, highlight, stress, underscore, warn

（续表）

Function	Weaker Position	Neutral Position	Stronger Position
evaluation and examination		analyze, appraise, assess, compare, consider, contrast, critique, warn, evaluate, examine, investigate, understand, articulate, clarify, explain	blame, complain, ignore, scrutinize, warn
explanation		articulate, clarify, explain	
presentation	confuse	comment, define, describe, estimate, forget, identify, illustrate, imply, inform, instruct, list, mention, note, observe, outline, point out, present, remark, remind, report, restate, reveal, show, state, study, tell, use	announce, promise
suggestion	allege, intimate, speculate	advise, advocate, hypothesize, posit, postulate, propose, suggest, theorize	assert, recommend, urge

二、托福考试中的独立写作
TOEFL Independent Writing

托福考试的独立写作要求考生针对题目表达观点，在 30 分钟时间内写一篇 300 词以上的英语作文。题目通常涉及教育、衣食住行、运动、人生哲学等主题，要求考生解释某现象，或询问考生支持还是反对某观点，或作出什么选择。

托福的独立写作任务和雅思的作文二在结构上非常类似，也是四段式或五段式议论文，呈"总—分—总"结构。因此，本章第二节介绍的雅思作文二的写作方法同样适用于托福的独立写作任务。下面将介绍一些有助于提高独立写作水平的技巧。

1. 独立写作的策略
Strategies for Independent Writing

独立写作的策略主要有以下几点：

第一，考前练习限时写作（practice timed writing before the test）。托福考试的机考系统严格计时，时间一到即自动关闭。因此考生平时练习时需要在限时环境下完成构思、成文和检查，以免在考场上慌乱。每次限时练习结束后，考生可以仔细阅读所写文章，对照范文和评分标准找出不足，以便修改并作总结。

第二，写前进行头脑风暴（brainstorm before you start writing）。与雅思的作文二一样，托福的独立写作任务经常要求考生在两个相反论点之间作出选择，因此使用头脑风暴收集大量的观点是十分有必要的。写前的规划也必不可少，拿到题目后不要急于动笔，花 1~3 分钟厘清思路、思考论点和论据，并列出简单提纲。

第三，学习基本句型（learn some basic sentence patterns that you can use comfortably）。托福考官会考查考生造句的能力，因此作文中不能只有简单句，还需要更为丰富多样的句型，这意味着考生只有平时学会积累句型并加以练习，才能在考试中熟练使用。

第四，要有自己的观点（have your own opinion）。托福的独立写作任务要求考生能够就具有争议性、发散性的话题表达自己的立场与观点，这一要求与雅思作文二高度趋同。考生应首先就话题进行总体思考，定下基调，如"同意""不同意""部分同意"，再紧扣总观点进行发散，建立分论点，并且分论点之间在逻辑上应当做到并列。需要注意的是，托福作文并不考察考生的观点是否正面、正确、积极。换言之，立意无对错，写作备考的重点需要放在如何有逻辑、有组织地清晰且准确地表达观点，并论证观点。

第五，质量比数量重要（think quality, not quantity）。文章并非越长越好，能用简短的篇幅清晰地表述观点更重要。如果文章精练且观点清晰，则更容易打动考官。相反，过长篇幅会导致时间不够或是行文重复啰唆。在备考过程中，考生可以利用好每一道真题或模拟题，训练自己快速列提纲的能力，这样才能在考场上迅速发散思维并厘清思路，形成逻辑较为严密的内容框架。

2. 独立写作的论证
Argument in Independent Writing

托福的独立写作考试并不重点考查作文的立意内容、中心思想，任何一个题目都可以既论证正面论点，也可以论证反面论点。换言之，选取论点内容本身并不作为评分依据。考生可以根据题目列出两种持相反论点的提纲。

对于写作能力处于初级水平的考生来说，采用"一边倒"的论证较为安全，不会因为缺少正反论证、让步等难度较大的段落造成整体观点不够鲜明。而写作能力较好的考生，可以考虑较为全面地进行正反论证，加入让步段落和驳论段落，但需要注意以下几点：

- 论点应前后一致，避免因中途改变主意，造成开头段、主体段、结尾段的论点自相矛盾。
- 分论点应能有效地支持总论点，且分论点内部需要展开一定程度的说理，避免蜻蜓点水、一带而过。

- 让步段落需要有节制，不宜过分肯定反方观点，避免模糊全文总立场。
- 即使题目棘手，也需要明确观点，尽量不提出"因人而异""不一定"等模糊的观点。例 11 是一个提出了模糊观点的反例：

例 11

Topic: It is better for children to grow up in the countryside than in a big city. Do you agree or disagree?

Some people believe that it is better for children to grow up in the countryside than in a big city. However, other people think that a big city gives more opportunities and it is good for the long run. Personally, for several reasons I think that it is better for children's health to grow up in the country.

First of all, it is very important for a child to grow up in a healthy environment. Children need fresh air, not polluted by the huge number of cars and factories of the modern city. In the country they can spend more time exercising and walking with their friends. Scientists say that now children spend the same amount of time watching TV as they do at school. Probably, the possibility to join their friends to play will change this proportion. Another important aspect of this is that parents will have more time to spend with their children as a result of eliminating traffic jams and decreasing driving time as a whole.

From the other side, children have some advantages living in a big city. For example, they have more opportunities to choose from what they want to do. They can choose to attend ballet classes, art classes, gymnastics, etc. In the long run, it is good for them. They will be better prepared for a life in the "real world" and they will have more chances to make a good career and succeed. Moreover, a big city usually has many entertainment centers with movie theatres and play areas. When I was a child, I liked to go to the movie theatre with my parents to watch a premiere.

One more reason to choose a big city for a child is that a city provides better living conditions and services such as medical, dental, etc. My friend lived in the country for a while and one time he and his family had to drive a couple of hours to the nearest medical centre when his child got a heavy cough.

To summarise, I agree with those people who want to raise their family in a city. The plenty of opportunities offered by a city help children to find what they really like and be the best at it. Moreover, despite the air pollution, children get better medical service that is good for their health.

—cited from the website of IELTS Mentor

解读 这篇范文看似是一篇高质量的作文，但其引言和结论部分表达了截然相反的观点，说明作者在写前并未作好规划，导致严重的逻辑矛盾。

下面结合 11 中的题目来说明应该如何列提纲，如表 9.2 所示：

表 9.2　托福独立写作任务的示例提纲

观点	一边倒	带让步	带驳论
正面	儿童应当在乡村成长。 1. 乡村亲近自然的机会多。 2. 乡村儿童之间的社交互动更多。 3. 乡村安静便于集中注意力。	儿童应当在乡村成长。 1. 乡村亲近自然的机会多。 2. 乡村儿童之间的社交互动更多。 3. 诚然，城市有一些好处，如公共设施齐全、教育资源集中等，但从长远的性格养成发展来看，乡村更适合儿童成长。	儿童应当在乡村成长。 1. 乡村亲近自然的机会多。 2. 乡村儿童之间的社交互动更多。 3. 有人认为乡村的基础设施不如城市齐全，不适合儿童成长。但随着社会进步和科技发展，许多乡村的基础设施建设已经非常完善，如校车、体育馆、公园等。因此乡村更适合儿童成长。
反面	儿童应当在城市成长。 1. 城市更完善的基础设施让育儿更便利。 2. 城市集中了较好的教育资源。 3. 城市集中了较好的医疗资源。	儿童应当在城市成长。 1. 城市更完善的基础设施让育儿更便利。 2. 城市集中了较好的教育资源。 3. 诚然，在乡村成长的儿童有更多接触自然的机会，但城市提供的好处更多。	儿童应当在城市成长。 1. 城市更完善的基础设施让育儿更便利。 2. 城市集中了较好的教育资源。 3. 有人认为城市的环境不如乡村好，接触自然的机会少，但现在城市接触自然的机会在逐渐增多，尤其是管理完善的植物园、动物园、小农场等，能让儿童接触到世界各地的动植物，亲近大自然。

由表 9.2 可以看出，不论是正面还是反面的观点，它们都能被分成三种类型（一边倒、带让步和带驳论），考生可以根据自身英语写作水平和背景知识储备来列出提纲。以一边倒的正面论证（"儿童应当在乡村成长"）为例，可列出如下英文提纲：

- Main argument: Children should grow up in the countryside.

    Point 1: Children have greater access to nature in the countryside.

    Point 2: Children have more opportunities to interact with peers in the countryside.

    Point 3: Children are less distracted in the countryside.

    Conclusion: The countryside is more suitable for raising children.

再以带让步的反面论证（"儿童应当在城市成长"）为例，可列出如下英文提纲：

- Main argument: Children should grow up in an urban area.

  Point 1: It is more convenient to raise children in an urban area because of its more developed infrastructure.

  Point 2: The urban area provides high-quality educational resources.

  Point 3: While children in the country have greater access to nature, it cannot outweigh the benefits afforded by the city.

  Conclusion: An urban area is more suitable for raising children.

在备考时，考生可以把表 9.2 作为参考框架分析独立写作任务的题目，试着列出所有类型的提纲。尝试几次之后，考生就能摸索出适合自己的思维方式，迅速破题并进入写作阶段。例 12 是以带驳论的正面论证（"儿童应当在乡村成长"）为例给出的范文：

例 12

All parents around the world are concerned over the environment in which their children grow up. Some prefer the countryside, while others give precedence to cities. I believe the countryside would be an ideal place to raise children for its greater opportunities to engage with nature and for more interactions between children.

First of all, the countryside provides more abundant opportunities for children to engage with nature. There has been research showing a myriad of benefits of being exposed to and surrounded by nature, including reduced stress, enhanced cognitive development, and sharpened children's awareness of environmental protection. Compared to urban areas, parents and their children can easily grow gardens in the yard, take a long walk in a field or woods on a daily basis, and go camping or hiking over the weekend without having to wait until summer vacation. The more frequent children are involved in these nature-related activities, the more likely that they become less anxious or stressed, and become more aware of environmental issues.

Another benefit of growing up in the countryside is to enjoy higher quantity and quality peer interactions. While the children in the cities are more often buried in after-school programs or staying indoors to complete their assignments, their counterparts in the countryside usually have more unstructured time to hang out together, playing games, doing sports, chatting, and even running errands together. Through numerous interactions with peers, children would have a better understanding of peers' and their own characteristics and more importantly, how to work with people of different personalities. This skill is essential because tasks and projects in the future workplace heavily rely on cooperation and collaboration.

Nonetheless, some people have argued that the countryside can be inferior to urban areas in terms of infrastructure. While I agree that most cities have a more developed public transportation system and many more places of interests, it is dubious how these advantages can necessarily be sustained in modern society. Many small towns and villages in the countryside in China, for instance, have developed public sport centers, and the schools in the countryside have been equipped with school buses. In other words, the once seemingly insurmountable gap has been narrowing. Moreover, an increasing number of museums have developed VR systems, where the visitors can observe the items and attend lectures and tours virtually. This means children in the countryside can also have very similar experiences, even without setting foot in the actual institute.

In conclusion, although raising children in cities have some merits, I believe the countryside is a more favorable environment for children. Children in the country would have easier access to nature and to peers, which would provide long-lasting benefits for young children throughout their future lives.

解读 这篇范文是一篇带驳论的议论文，论证了乡村为什么比城市更适合儿童成长。第二段和第三段从"乡村亲近自然的机会多"和"乡村儿童之间的社交互动更多"两个角度作正面分析。第四段先提出相反观点"有人认为乡村的基础设施不如城市"，接着作出有节制的让步——"城市的公共交通系统更加发达，并有更多游乐场所"，但很快对此进行驳斥——"这些优势在现代社会并不能持续"，并就这一观点展开进一步论证。最后结论段总结上文观点，重申作者立场。

如果考生在考场上时间不够，亦可只写两个主题段落，之后迅速进入结论段写作，以确保文章有头有尾，论点前后呼应，并留下 1~3 分钟做检查。

第四节　关于国际考试中英语写作的其他建议
Miscellaneous Advice on International Essay Tests

1. 使用技术手段
Using Technology

写作是一个熟能生巧的过程，考生平时需要多练习，但并不是每次练习都有老师检查并给予反馈，因此可以尝试使用线上自动批改作文工具。尽管机器评阅的效果无法与真实的老师媲美，但仍不失为一个初步测评文章的好方法。另外，拼写检查器（spell checker）是一个强大的工具，它可以提供即时反馈，让考生能够及时更正拼写错误，避免浪费时间。

2. 练习拼写和打字
Practicing Spelling and Typing

线上辅助工具的缺点也很明显：考生会过度依赖技术来检查拼写。当面对真实的考试情境时，无论是卷面考试还是机器考试，没有了自动拼写检查器，考生会不习惯。为了克服这个问题，考生可以交替使用电脑辅助写作和纸上写作，并在备考时注意保持良好的拼写习惯。另外，部分考生一直习惯卷面考试，英文打字速度较慢，因此需要在备考时训练提高打字速度。

3. 选择英式英语还是美式英语？
British English or American English?

众所周知，雅思主要是英国的英语考试，而托福是美国的英语考试，但这并不意味着在考试中考生只能使用某个国家的通用英语。其实使用任何一种拼写形式都是可行的，但需要保持前后一致，例如在文章中先使用了 favor（美式）这样的拼写，就不要在后文中使用 neighbour（英式）这样的拼写。

4. 人为因素
Human Factor

雅思和托福考试的考官都经过正式的挑选和考核，并需要遵守严格的规定。绝大多数情况下，考试分数能够反映文章的质量和考生的真实水平，但也需注意，考官毕竟是真实的人，无法做到完全的客观。如果查询到的成绩明显低于（或高于）预期，那么可能是遇到的考官太过严格（或太过宽容）。如果的确对分数存疑，考生有权利申诉并要求重新评分。

5. 表达想法
Expressing Ideas

国际英语考试的写作任务具有一定难度，需要考生运用恰当的语法、正确的拼写、丰富的词汇、严谨的结构等，但最重要的还是要明确写作目的。写作的目的在于沟通，考生必须能够以清晰和合乎逻辑的方式表达想法和观点。如果仅有漂亮的词汇和复杂的句型，却无法恰当地表达想法，并让考官理解，那这算不上是成功的写作。因此，考生在写作时需要注意这三方面：确定读者、理解写作目的和与考官进行沟通（通过书面形式）。

附 录 一

中国学习者在英语写作中的常见错误
Common Errors in Chinese Learners' English Writing[1]

中国学习者在英语写作过程中会犯一些语言错误，其中有些错误非常普遍，究其原因，主要有两方面：一是对英语的语法、句法和词汇的掌握不到位；二是受汉语句子结构和表达习惯的影响，英文表达中出现母语负迁移的现象。

附录一针对中国学习者在英语写作中的常见错误进行归纳和分析，以帮助读者提高对错误的认知，并有效避免类似错误的发生。

1. 逗号粘连句
Comma Splices

逗号粘连句是英语写作中常见的错误，它是指用逗号连接两个（或多个）可以独立成句的主谓结构。中国学习者犯这种错误通常是受汉语逗号使用习惯的影响，因为在汉语中多个主谓结构之间可以用逗号连接。以下是错误示例：

例 1

- I go to school, my sister stays at home.
- The bus stopped suddenly, I found myself in an old lady's lap.
- The tomato is very popular today, it was once thought to be poisonous.
- Lizards become sluggish at night, they need the sun's warmth to maintain an active body temperature.

逗号粘连句的改正方式主要有三种：

---

1 附录一的部分例句参考了以下书目（或有修改）：《新编英语语法教程学生用书》《张道真大学英语语法》《实用英语作文》《高级英语写作教程思辨能力进阶》、*College Writing Skills with Readings*、*The Little Gold Grammar Book* 和 *The Little Red Writing Book*。

第一，用句号代替错误使用的逗号。例如，用句号可将例 1 中的四个逗号粘连句改成以下形式：

例 2

- I go to school. My sister stays at home.
- The bus stopped suddenly. I found myself in an old lady's lap.
- The tomato is very popular today. It was once thought to be poisonous.
- Lizards become sluggish at night. They need the sun's warmth to maintain an active body temperature.

第二，用符合逻辑关系的连词连接两个（或多个）主谓结构。例如，用连词可将例 1 中的四个逗号粘连句改成以下形式：

例 3

- I go to school **and** my sister stays at home.
- The bus stopped suddenly **and** I found myself in an old lady's lap.
- The tomato is very popular today, **but** it was once thought to be poisonous.
- Lizards become sluggish at night **because** they need the sun's warmth to maintain an active body temperature.

第三，用分号连接两个（或多个）主谓结构。例如，用分号可将例 1 中的四个逗号粘连句改成以下形式：

例 4

- I go to school; my sister stays at home.
- The bus stopped suddenly; I found myself in an old lady's lap.
- The tomato is very popular today; it was once thought to be poisonous.
- Lizards become sluggish at night; they need the sun's warmth to maintain an active body temperature.

以上三种方式都可以改正逗号粘连句在语法上的错误，但在写作实践中，这三种修改方式的适用情况仍有所区别。简单来说，第一种适用于两个主谓结构之间关联性较弱的情况；第二种适用于两个主谓结构之间逻辑关系比较清晰明确的情况；第三种更多地使用在句式相似、联系紧密的两个主谓结构之间。

请看以下这三个逗号粘连句：

例 5

- I got stuck in rush hour traffic, it took me an extra hour to get home.
- Lily was busy preparing the presentation, she didn't come to my birthday party.
- My brother likes tea, I prefer coffee.

以下是改正后的句子，请注意每个句子的改正方式：

例 6

- I got stuck in rush hour traffic. It took me an extra hour to get home. (用句号把两个关联性较弱的主谓结构分开，各自独立成句)
- Lily was busy preparing the presentation, **so** she didn't come to my birthday party. (用连词连接有明确逻辑关系的两个主谓结构)
- My brother likes tea; I prefer coffee. (用分号连接两个句式相似且联系紧密的主谓结构)

2. 不完整句
Sentence Fragments

不完整句是指在一个以句号结尾的"语句"中，句子的主谓成分不完整，因而不是一个语法完整句。它经常以短语、从属句或者无谓语句的形式出现。以下是错误示例，斜体部分为不完整句：

例 7

- *According to the opinions above.* I totally agree that charity begins at home.
- Some people do not have enough money to raise children. *So they choose to put more energy into work.*
- *When it comes to the relationship between global economy and national culture.* Many people believe the two are incompatible.
- I have a lot to do today. *Such as attending an online work meeting, getting my car repaired, and doing the laundry.*
- *The students often absent from classes.*
- We huddled together on the sofa to watch the movie. *Not expecting anything special of it.*

例 7 中的不完整句可以改成以下形式：

例 8

- According to the opinions above, I totally agree that charity begins at home.
- Some people do not have enough money to raise children so they choose to put more energy into work.
- When it comes to the relationship between global economy and national culture, many people believe the two are incompatible.
- I have a lot to do today, such as attending an online work meeting, getting my car repaired, and doing the laundry.
- The students are often absent from classes.
- We huddled together on the sofa to watch the movie and didn't expect anything special of it.

3. 副词 / 介词短语连接句子
Misuse of Adverbs or Prepositional Phrases as Conjunctions

由于对英语词性的忽略，英语写作中经常会出现用副词连接两个主谓完整句的情况，这样的句子也是粘连句的一种。常被误作连词的副词有：then、however、therefore、accordingly、consequently、conversely、only 等。另外，还有一些介词短语也常被误用来连接完整句，比如：at the same time、as a result、on the contrary 等。

误用副词 / 介词短语连接完整句时，如果它们之前或（和）之后同时使用了逗号，那么句子为逗号粘连句（comma splice）；如果在句子中间没有使用任何标点符号，则为另一种粘连句，叫融合句（fused sentence）。请注意甄别，以避免此类错误的发生。以下是错误示例：

例 9

- We thought the figures were correct **however** we have now discovered some errors.
- It rained **therefore** the football match was postponed.
- He was told to speak briefly, **accordingly,** he cut short his remarks.
- American consumers prefer white eggs, **conversely,** British buyers like brown eggs.
- **Only** these conditions are fulfilled can the application proceed to the next stage.

- The company went bankrupt, **consequently** he lost his job.
- I was afraid of her, **at the same time** I really liked her.
- It wasn't a good thing, **on the contrary** it was a huge mistake.

这类病句的改正方式主要有三种：一是把两个完整句用句号分为两个独立句，通常需要用逗号把第二句中的副词 / 介词短语和后面的主句分隔开；二是在副词 / 介词短语之前加一个连词；三是把副词 / 介词短语之前的逗号改成分号，如果是融合句，则在副词 / 介词短语之前添加一个分号。

例 9 中的病句可以改成以下形式：

例 10

- We thought the figures were correct. **However,** we have now discovered some errors.
- It rained **and therefore** the football match was postponed.
- He was told to speak briefly; **accordingly,** he cut short his remarks.
- American consumers prefer white eggs; **conversely,** British buyers like brown eggs.
- **Only if** these conditions are fulfilled can the application proceed to the next stage.
- The company went bankrupt, **and consequently** he lost his job.
- I was afraid of her, **but** at the same time I really liked her.
- It wasn't a good thing. **On the contrary,** it was a huge mistake.

4. 易错句型
Sentence Patterns Worth More Attention

（1）there be 句型

there be 句型在中国学习者的英语作文中使用频率很高，同时出错率也很高。该句型中的谓语是 there be 本身，there be 后面的名词为句子主语，所以这里的名词后面不能再加谓语动词，否则就是双谓语的病句。以下是错误示例，斜体部分是双谓语：

例 11

- *There are* many changes *have taken place* since then.
- *There are* some people *think* that honesty is fading in society.
- I think *there are* three important things *should be done*.

- *There are* so many things *disappointed* us.
- *There are* many students *think* e-leaning is convenient and efficient.
- *There are* a lot of people *want* to study in college.
- *There must be* somebody *is waiting* for you.

这类病句的改正方式主要有两种：一是去掉 there be；二是将主语后面的动词变成分词或者定语从句中的谓语动词，即变成修饰主语的定语成分。在大多数情况下，建议直接去掉 there be，以使句子更简洁明了。例 11 中的病句可以改成以下形式：

例 12

- Many changes have taken place since then.
- Some people think that honesty is fading in society.
- I think there are three important things that should be done.
- So many things disappointed us.
- Many students think e-leaning is convenient and efficient.
- A lot of people want to study in college.
- There must be somebody waiting for you.

（2）分词作状语置于句首

在英语写作中，为了避免文章句式单一，很多中国学习者会将分词作状语的结构置于句首。这的确是一种增加句式多样性的好方法，但在使用时须注意句子主语和分词的逻辑主语是否一致，以避免出现英语句法错误。以下是错误示例，斜线部分是句首分词和句子主语：

例 13

- *Asking* about his address, *the boy* didn't respond.
- *Seeing* from the hill, *the city* looks magnificent.
- *Facing* such problem, *my suggestion* is that developing countries should give priority to school education.
- *Considering* these reasons, *it* is easy to understand why DINK is increasing.
- *Living* in the era of information explosion, *it* is evident that social networking has permeated into every aspect of our social life.
- *Having said* all that, *what* is the panacea for the tricky problem?
- *Having taken* a series of strict measures, *there* still exists an immense amount of Internet abuse and rampant fake news.

这类病句的修改需要具体问题具体分析，即判断句子主语和句首分词之间的逻辑关系——句子主语是否为分词的逻辑主语，句子主语是分词动作的发出者还是承受者（由此决定用现在分词还是过去分词）。修改的要点就是使句首分词的逻辑主语和句子主语保持一致。

这类病句的改正方式主要有三种：一是根据句首分词和句子主语的逻辑关系选择分词的正确形式，使用现在分词或过去分词；二是句首分词保持不变，改变句子主语，使其成为分词的逻辑主语；三是改变句型。例 13 中的病句可以改成以下形式：

例 14

- **Asked** about his address, **the boy** didn't respond.
- **Seen** from the hill, **the city** looks magnificent.
- **Facing** such a problem, **developing countries** should give priority to school education.
- **Considering** these reasons, **we can easily** understand why DINK is increasing.
- **In the era of information explosion**, it is evident that social networking has permeated into every aspect of our social life.
- **All that being said**, what is the panacea for the tricky problem?
- **Although a series of strict measures have been taken**, there still exists an immense amount of Internet abuse and rampant fake news.

5. 人称不一致
Discordance in Personal Pronouns

在英语写作中，当涉及泛指人称时，中国学习者常会犯人称不一致的错误。这类错误的发生与汉语的表达习惯有关，需要注意区分。

英语和汉语一样，都可以使用第一、第二、第三人称复数和第二、第三人称单数来泛指一类人。在汉语中，当泛指一类人时，人们常会在不经意间转换不同的人称；在英语写作中，一个语篇内应尽量保持泛指人称的统一，包括人称的统一、人称和物主代词的统一、反身代词的统一和数的统一。

英语写作中常用来泛指"人们"的代词有 we、you、they、one，常用的名词有 people、men 等，还可根据不同场景用 students、children 等。这些用来泛指的名词都属于第三人称复数这一类别，在同一语篇内应避免同时使用第一人称复数，从而破坏人称的一致性。以下选段是错误示例，请注意叙述人称的选择：

例 15

We are all born into this world as equals, but for various reasons, not **all people** are treated as equals. This inequality begins when **you** reach the age of six, for that is when **you** will enter elementary school. In school, **we** are no longer "Mommy's darlings". **We** now have to prove **ourselves** to the other children and also to **our** teacher. If **we** seem different from the other children, **we** are treated differently.

> **解读** 这段中的第一句以第一人称开头，紧接其后却用了第三人称；第二句中开始变成第二人称，随后的三个句子中又改成了第一人称，这样就破坏了语篇里人称代词的一致性。正确的处理方式是尽量用从头到尾同一个人称。

例 15 可以改成以下形式：

例 16

We are all born into this world as equals, but for various reasons, not **all of us** (~~all people~~) are treated as equals. This inequality begins when **we** (~~you~~) reach the age of six, for that is when **we** ~~you~~ will enter elementary school. In school, **we** are no longer "Mommy's darlings". **We** now have to prove **ourselves** to the other children and also to **our** teacher. If **we** seem different from the other children, **we** are treated differently.

再来看一些人称代词不一致的句子，斜体部分为人称代词：

例 17

- *People* must be patient if *we* want to succeed.
- *Students* must be conscientious in *our* study if *we* value *our* opportunities of education.
- *You* never know whether *we*'re going to qualify for this test or not. *You* see the rules are changed every day.
- *One* must remember to remain very still when *we* attend a concert.
- If *one* doesn't want to get lost in the mountains, *you* must have a guide.

改正之后变为以下形式：

例 18

- **We** must be patient if **we** want to succeed.
- **Students** must be conscientious in **their** study if **they** value **their** opportunities

of education.

- **You** never know whether **you**'re going to qualify for this test or not. **You** see the rules are changed every day.
- **You** must remember to remain very still when **you** attend a concert.
- If **one** doesn't want to get lost in the mountains, **he** must have a guide.

6. 用词错误
Wrong Diction

在英语写作中，如何使用用恰当的词汇来精准地表达思想或观点是一个宏大的命题。这里的"用词错误"专指由于缺乏对英语词汇的正确认知，中国学习者将汉语词汇直译成英语词汇，从而造成歧义或表达错误。

下文仅讨论三种常见的因汉语思维导致的英语用词错误情况，借此给予提醒和启示。

（1）固化的汉语翻译导致搭配错误

不少中国人学习英语的方式是以英汉单词一一对应为基础的。这种习惯主要体现在两个方面：一是在遇到一个英语单词时，他们通常不是用英语的思维来理解其在特定语境中的意义，而是用脑海中与之相对应的一个汉语词汇来机械地翻译；二是他们在写英语作文时，通常是脑海里先浮现汉语词汇，再找到与之机械对应的英语词汇来进行翻译。这样一来，用词错误就难免了。例如，接受教育（accept education）、有文化（have culture）、解决问题（solve a question）均为错误表达，正确表达应为：接受教育（receive education）、有文化（well-educated/literate）、解决问题（solve a problem）。

再如"影响"这个词，大多数学习者看到之后联想的第一个英语单词就是influence。这二者有时的确是一一对应的关系，但实际上"影响"所指代的语境非常复杂，绝不是一个influence就可以全部涵盖的。试翻译以下句子：

例19

- 不要谈恋爱啊，会影响学习。
- 你爸在开车，不要影响他。
- 老戴耳机会影响听力。
- 很多航班取消，数以千计的乘客受到影响。
- 发展中国家将会受到直接影响。
- 梵高对现代绘画有重大影响。

这些句子用英语可以这样表达：

例 20

- Don't fall in love because it would **interfere with** your study.
- Father is driving. Don't **distract** him. / Don't **distract** your father while he is driving.
- Frequent use of earphones will **damage** your hearing.
- Many flights were cancelled and thousands of passengers **were affected**.
- The real **impact** will be felt in the developing world.
- Van Gogh **had a major influence on** the development of modern painting.

由此可知，不要被某个英语词汇的主要汉语翻译所限制，而要考虑词汇本身的意思和其所处的语境。

（2）固化的汉语翻译导致词汇理解错误

以 doubt 和 suspect 这一组词为例。它们作为动词时均有"怀疑"的意思，但并不是近义词，而是表达相反意义的一组词。简单来说，doubt 表示"不相信"，而 suspect 为"相信"，它们被翻译成"怀疑"的基础在于"没有确凿的证据"，而不在于"是否相信"。请看以下示例：

例 21

- I **doubt** that he is a thief.
  我不觉得他是贼（别人说他是贼，但我怀疑这个判断，觉得他不是个贼）。
- I **suspect** that he is a thief.
  我觉得他是个贼（虽然我没有证据证实这个想法）。

（3）忽视词语特性造成的表达错误

以"存在"这个词为例。在汉语中，"存在"后面常接"问题""隐患"这一类词，而句子的主语是有这些问题或隐患的主体，在结构上表现为：出现问题的主体 + 存在 + 问题。当英语中使用 exist 表示"存在"的意思时，照搬这样的结构容易出错，因为 exist 是不及物动词，不能接宾语。以下是错误示例：

例 22

- Agriculture also exists problems.
- Various aspects, such as teaching arrangement, teachers, methodology, and textbooks exist problems.

正确表达上面句意的句子结构是：问题 + exist + 介词短语 / 状语（表示问题出现的地点），如例 23 所示：

例 23

- Problems also **exist** in agriculture.
- Problems **exist** in various aspects, such as teaching arrangement, teachers, methodology, and textbooks.

7. 动词不定式符号 to 和介词 to 的混淆和误用
The Confusion of "to" as a Preposition and as an Infinitive Marker

许多中国学习者在英语写作中常会混淆动词不定式符号 to 和介词 to 的用法。以下是错误示例：

例 24

- Many local people object **to** build the new airport.
- She devotes herself **to** help the children in the village.
- He was a person accustomed **to** sleep eight hours a night.

在例 24 中，介词 to 被误认为动词不定式符号，正确的用法应为：

例 25

- Many local people object **to** the building of the new airport.
- She devotes herself **to** helping the children in the village.
- He was a person accustomed **to** having eight hours' sleep a night.

事实上，英语中介词 to 的使用非常广泛，主要有以下六类：

（1）动词 + 介词 to。例如：

例 26

- For ten months he **adhered to** a strict no-fat low-salt diet.
- I must **confess to** knowing nothing about computers.
- He reluctantly **yielded to** their demands.

（2）动词 + 名词 / 代词 + 介词 to。例如：

例 27

- He **ascribed his failure to** bad luck.

- She **dedicates herself to** her work.
- He **resigned himself to** his fate.

（3）动词过去分词 + 介词 to。例如：

例 28

- The number of employees **was reduced to** 25.
- He couldn't **be reconciled to** the prospect of losing her.
- He's **given to** going for long walks on his own.

（4）动词 + 副词小品词 + 介词 to。例如：

例 29

- I hope to **get round to** answering your letter next week.
- She had to **face up to** the fact that she would never walk again
- I'm **looking forward to** seeing you again.

（5）形容词 + 介词 to。例如：

例 30

- Our farmland is **adjacent to** the river.
- He is **averse to** any change.
- He was **deaf to** my requests for help.

（6）以介词 to 结尾的复合介词。例如：

例 31

- **In addition to** these arrangements, extra ambulances will be on duty until midnight.
- He bought the warehouse **with an eye to** converting it into a hotel.
- The company's position **with regard to** overtime is made clear in their contracts.

8. 单词连写和分开写的混淆与误用
Confusion of Compound Words and Separate Forms

英语里有一些词汇在分开和组合时的意义是不一样的，这让很多中国学习者在英语写作中产生困扰并犯错误。以下是错误示例：

例 32

- It **maybe** necessary to resort to extreme measures.
- We go there **may be** once or twice a month.

以上两个句子应改为：

例 33

- It **may be** necessary to resort to extreme measures. (may be 是动词短语，情态动词 may 后面接 be 动词的原形，意为"也许是……")
- We go there **maybe** once or twice a month. (maybe 是副词，意为"也许")

类似的因连写和分开写导致词义不同、易被混淆的词汇还有：

（1）anyone 和 any one。anyone 是名词，指"任何人"；any one 是"形容词 + 名词"的组合，指"任何单个的人、物或事"，可以与 of 连用。例如：

例 34

- Does anyone else want to come?
- Any one of these green vegetables is good for you.

（2）anytime 和 any time。anytime 是副词，指"一段不确切的时间"；any time 是"形容词 + 名词"的组合，指"一段时间（量）"。例如：

例 35

- Call me anytime.
- This weekend, I won't have any time to twitter.

（3）everyday 和 every day。everyday 是形容词，意为"普通的""平常的"或"每天发生的"；every day 是"形容词 + 名词"的组合，意为"（在）每天"。例如：

例 36

- Complaints seen to be an everyday occurrence.
- We should eat fresh fruit every day.

（4）everyone 和 every one。everyone 是名词，意为"每人""人人""所有人"；every one 是"形容词 + 名词"的组合，意为"每个"，既可以用来指人，也可以用来指物，后面可跟介词 of。例如：

例 37

- Everyone knows who did it!
- Every one of the runners who crossed the finish line was exhausted but jubilant.

（5）sometime 和 some time。sometime 是副词，指"某个时候"；some time 是"形容词 + 名词"的组合，指"一段时间"。例如：

例 38

- We must get together sometime.
- We went fishing early in the morning, but it was some time before we landed our first trout.

9. 不符合语法的无主句
Incorrect Sentences Lacking a Subject

汉语中存在大量的无主句，在一些英语谚语或者祈使句当中，也会出现无主句。但是中国学习者在英语写作中，常会把汉语表达习惯中的无主句生搬硬套到英语中，导致出现语法、句法错误。以下是错误示例：

例 39

- Firstly, is the difference between Chinese and English sentence structure.
- Next, revert to the topic, how can we possibly resolve this problem?
- Lastly revise it, paying attention to every single word.

例 39 中的三个病句可改成以下形式：

例 40

- Firstly, there is a major difference between Chinese and English sentence structure.
- Next, let's revert to the topic. How can we possibly resolve this problem?
- Lastly, we need to revise the translation version, paying attention to every single word.

再来看一些常见的汉语无主句及其翻译：

例41

- 下雨了！（It is raining!）
- 留得青山在，不怕没柴烧。（Where there is life, there is hope.）
- 吃一堑，长一智。（A fall into the pit, a gain in your wit.）
- 昨晚抓住了三个小偷。（Three thieves were caught last night.）
- 从她那儿能找到解决问题的办法。（We can turn to her for a solution.）
- 明年将出版更多的儿童读物。（More books for children will be published next year.）

从例41可以看出，当汉语的无主句变成英语时，需要根据不同的情况作不同的处理：根据语意添加英语主语、添加关联词、找对应的英语谚语、把汉语的宾语变成英语被动语态中的主语等。

10. 赘述
Redundancy

赘述是指在不必要的情况下重复某个词汇或某个观点，此时就需要删减。为了使英语写作更加简洁，能用一个词表达清楚的，就不用短语；能用一个短语表达清楚的，就不用从句；能用一个句子表达清楚的，就不用两个甚至多个。此外，句子不应包含不必要的词语，段落不应包含不必要的句子，文章不应包含不必要的段落。

在用词层面，如果一个词已经包含了和它连用的修饰成分的意思，那么就有必要删除不必要的重复部分，表1枚举了一些例子：

表1 赘述用词和简洁用词

Redundant	Better
attractive in appearance	attractive
big in size	big
blue in color / blue colored	blue
charming in character	charming
combined together	combined
completely full	full
consensus of opinion	consensus
continue to remain	continue *or* remain
curious in nature	curious
descend down	descend
deliberately chosen	chosen

（续表）

Redundant	Better
exceptionally outstanding	exceptional
few in number	few
final outcome	outcome
inexperienced beginner	beginner
may perhaps	may *or* perhaps
modern world of today	modern world
mutual agreement	agreement
new initiatives	initiatives
new innovation	innovation
past experience	experience
past history	history
positive benefits	benefits
reflect back	reflect
repeat (over) again	repeat
return back	return
sadly tragic	tragic
serious crisis	crisis
sink down	sink
tall in height	tall
true facts / hard facts	facts
undergraduate student	undergraduate
unexpected emergency	emergency
unique and one-of-a-kind	unique *or* one-of-a-kind
unsubstantiated rumors	rumors
young juvenile	juvenile

—cited from *The Little Red Writing Book*

11. 矫揉造作的用词
Pretentious Words

在英语写作中，有些中国学习者会走入一个误区——认为用词越难、越罕见、越晦涩，写作水平就越高。其实，英语写作真正应该遵循的原则是从简原则，即在不影响意思表达的前提下，用词越简单、越清楚，写作效果越好。矫揉造作的用词会使文章读起来拗口、空洞，甚至表意不清。以下是错误示例：

例 42

- It was a marvelous gamble to procure some slumber.

- We relished the delectable noon-hour repast.
- The officer apprehended the imbibed operator of the vehicle.
- The female had an affectionate spot in her heart for domesticated canines.

更简洁、更自然的表达可以是：

例 43

- It was an excellent chance to get some sleep.
- We enjoyed the delicious lunch.
- The officer arrested the drunk driver.
- The woman had a warm spot in her heart for dogs.

表 2 列举了更多矫揉造作的用词和简洁的用词：

表 2　矫揉造作用词和简法用词

Inflated Words	Simpler Words
ameliorate	improve
amplitude	fullness *or* abundance
apprise	tell
augment	increase
delineate	describe *or* explain
disseminate	send out
enumerate	list
moribund	dying *or* wasting away
habituated	accustomed *or* familiar
locality	place
obfuscate	obscure
obviate	avoid
substantiate	prove

—cited from *The Little Red Writing Book*

12. 修饰语错位
Misplaced Modifiers

在英语写作中，还需要留意修饰成分的位置，尽量避免因位置不当而造成歧义。以下是错误示例：

例 44

- Kelley could not lift the chair *with a broken arm*. (Did the chair have a broken arm or did Kelley?)
- *After the wedding*, George told his friend at his stag party that he would start behaving like a responsible adult. (When did George say so?)

为了避免歧义，修饰语需要尽量靠近被修饰部分，例 44 可改成以下形式：

例 45

- **With a broken arm**, Kelley could not lift the chair.
- George told his friend at his stag party that he would start behaving like a responsible adult **after the wedding**.

再来看以下三组示例，句子意思因为修饰语位置的变化而发生改变。

例 46

- He nearly brushed his teeth for twenty minutes every night. (他每天马马虎虎地刷牙刷 20 分钟。)
- He brushed his teeth for nearly twenty minutes every night. (他每天刷牙差不多要刷 20 分钟。)

例 47

- The speaker discussed the problem of cheating at the college. (演讲者讨论了大学里的作弊问题。)
- At the college, the speaker discussed the problem of cheating. (演讲者在大学里讨论了作弊的问题。)

例 48

- Unique local creations are available in Xi'an, such as terra-cotta figures and the three colored glazed pottery of the Tang Dynasty. (到西安你可以买唐朝的兵马俑和三彩像等当地特色手工产品。)
- Unique local creations are available in Xi'an, such as the three colored glazed pottery of the Tang Dynasty and terra-cotta figures. (到西安你可以买兵马俑、唐三彩等当地特色手工产品。)

附录二

常用英语标点符号及其用法
A Concise Guide to Punctuation in English Writing[1]

表 1　常见英语标点符号一览表

英语名称	英语标点符号	汉语名称	汉语标点符号
full stop / period	.	句号	。
interrogation mark / question mark	?	问号	?
exclamation mark	!	感叹号	!
comma	,	逗号	,
semicolon	;	分号	;
dash	——	破折号	——
colon	:	冒号	:
quotation marks	" " 或 ' '	引号	" " 或 ' '
dots/ellipsis	...	省略号	……
apostrophe	'	撇号	无
hyphen	-	连字符	无
brackets/parentheses	( )	（圆）括号	（ ）
slash/oblique	/	斜线号	/

　　从表 1 可以看出，英语和汉语的标点符号并非一一对应：英语的标点符号里没有汉语的顿号和书名号，汉语的标点符号里没有英语的撇号和连字符。汉语使用顿号的情况在英语中通常用逗号替代。汉语的书名号在英语中可用斜体或引号替代：英语书名、期刊名、报纸、杂志等通常用斜体表示，而文章、歌曲、诗歌等短篇作品的名称通常用引号表示。

1　附录二中的部分例句参考了以下书目（或有修改）:《张道真大学英语语法》《牛津高阶英汉双解词典》第 6 版的附录 4、*College Writing Skills with Readings* 和 *The Little Gold Grammar Book*。

1. 句号
Full Stop (BrE) / Period (AmE)

（1）常用于陈述句和祈使句结尾（used at the end of a statement or probably an imperative sentence）。例如：

例 1

- El Niño is the name given to the mysterious and often unpredictable change in the climate of the world.
- Be careful of what you are doing.

（2）有时用于缩写（sometimes used in abbreviations）。例如：

例 2

- Jun.
- e.g.
- a.m.

2. 问号
Interrogation Mark / Question Mark

（1）用于疑问句结尾（used at the end of a question）。例如：

例 3

- Are you from China?
- Where have you been?
- Would you like coffee or tea?
- This is your office, isn't it?

（2）与日期连用时表示存疑（express doubt when used with a date）。例如：

例 4

- Johan Marston (?1575–1634)

3. 感叹号
Exclamation Mark

（1）用于感叹句结尾（used at the end of an exclamation）。例如：

例 5

- What heavy snow it is!
- How well he plays the violin!

（2）在祈使句结尾处加强语气（express strong emotion when used at the end of an imperative sentence）。例如：

例 6

- Look out!
- Don't speak rudely!

（3）在陈述句结尾处添加感情色彩（show strong emotion when used at the end of a statement）。例如：

例 7

- You nearly got hit by that bicycle!

4. 逗号

Comma

（1）用于分隔一句话中的平行成分（separate words in a list）。例如：

例 8

- The street vendor sold watches, necklaces ,and earrings. (分隔宾语)
- Joe peered into the hot, still-smoking engine. (分隔定语)
- Time is a versatile performer. It flies, marches on, heals all wounds, runs out and will tell. (分隔谓语动词)
- The exercise instructor told us to inhale, exhale, and relax. (分隔宾语补足语)
- A group of young men were standing there, talking, laughing, and teasing each other. (分隔状语)

（2）分隔主句和由 and、as、but、for、or 等连词连接的从句（separate a main clause and a subordinate clause linked by a conjunction such as *and, as, but, for, or*)。例如：

例 9

- The length of your education is less important than its breadth, and the length of your life is less important than its depth.

- He saw her, as they were both getting off the bus at the same time.
- We had been looking forward to our holiday all year, but unfortunately it rained every day.
- It must be very late now, for all the shops have closed.
- The workers were cheerful, or at least they appeared to be cheerful.

（3）把置于句首或句中的分词、独立主格、介词短语、动词不定式、主语补足语、状语从句等与句子其他成分隔开（separate a participial, or an absolute construction, or an adverbial phrase, or a subject complement, or an adverbial clause that is at the beginning or in the middle of the sentence, from the rest of the sentence）。例如：

例 10

- She walked slowly, stopping frequently to rest. (分隔主句和分词)
- The day being fine, we decided to go swimming. (分隔主句与置于句首的独立主格)
- Just in time, Sherry applied the brakes and avoided a car accident. (分隔主句与置于句首的介词短语)
- To make a long story short, they smoothed out their misunderstanding and became good friends again. (分隔主句与置于句首的动词不定式)
- The hallway, dingy and dark, was illuminated by a bare bulb hanging from a wire. (分隔置于句中的主语补足语与句子其他成分)
- Although he is rich, he is not happy. (分隔主句与置于句首的状语从句)

（4）置于非限定性定语从句之前或之后，使其与主句隔开（used before or after a non-restrictive attributive clause to separate it from the rest of the sentence）。例如：

例 11

- Marty's computer, which his wife got him as a birthday gift, occupies all his spare time.
- The boy didn't pass the exam, which disappointed his parents very much.

（5）把同位语或插入语与句子其他成分隔开（separate an appositive or a parenthesis from the rest of the sentence）。例如：

例 12

- We have two foreign teachers, a Canadian and an American. (分隔同位语)
- This, I think, was mainly due to our lack of experience. (分隔插入语)

（6）用在附加疑问句之前，使其与句子其他部分隔开（separate a tag question from the rest of the sentence）。例如：

例 13

- It's quite expensive, isn't it?
- You live in Shenzhen, right?

（7）其他用法（some other usages）

① 表示某些词已省略（主要用于并列句）（show the omission of some words）。例如：

例 14

- My room is on the second floor, and hers, on the third.

② 表示停顿（indicate pauses in the sentence）。例如：

例 15

- The mistake can be, and should be, corrected.

③ 注明日期和地址（used in addresses or in dates）。例如：

例 16

- 1888 Zhongxin Avenue, Nanshan District, Shenzhen
- The conference is scheduled for the 3rd of July, 2021.

5. 分号
Semicolon

（1）用于连接两个或多个意思联系比较紧密的句子（link two or more main clauses, especially when the two clauses are closely related to each other）。例如：

例 17

- Lonnie heard a noise and looked out the window; the only thing he saw was his reflection.

- Modesty helps one to go forward; conceit makes one lag behind.
- People make history; unusual people make history interesting.
- Your car is new; mine is six years old.

（2）连接的并列成分中已含有逗号时（replace a comma to separate parts of a sentence that already contains commas）。例如：

例 18

- Maya's children are named Melantha, which means "black flower"; Yonina, which means "dove"; and Cynthia, which means "moon goddess".
- My parents' favorite albums are *Rubber Soul*, by the Beatles; *Songs in the Key of Life*, by Stevie Wonder; and *Bridge over Troubled Water*, by Simon and Garfunkel.

6. 破折号
Dash

（1）最常置于解释性的单词、短语或分句前面（mainly used before an explaining word, phrase, or clause）。例如：

例 19

- There are only two things certain in this life—death and taxes.
- I was so exhausted that I fell asleep within seconds—standing up.
- It's an environmental issue—that's not a small matter.

（2）用于解释性的插入语前后（与括号作用相当）（before and after an explaining parenthesis）。例如：

例 20

- He had many good qualities—sincerity, honesty and thoughtfulness—yet he had few friends.
- During my vacation—I must have been insane—I decided I would ski.

（3）表示意思的突然转折（indicate a sudden twist in meaning）。例如：

例 21

- The pardon from the manager finally arrived—too late.

（4）表示迟疑犹豫（show hesitation）。例如：

例 22

- "I—I—I rather think—maybe—Amy has taken it."

（5）总括前面列举的若干事物，或是对前面内容的总结（indicate that what follows is a summary or conclusion of what has gone before）。例如：

例 23

- New houses, larger schools, more sheep, more pigs and chickens, more horses and donkeys—everywhere we saw signs of prosperity.
- Men were shouting, women were screaming, children were crying—it was chaos.

7. 冒号
Colon

（1）常用在完整的陈述句后面，引出将列举的事项（used at the end of a complete statement to introduce a list）。例如：

例 24

- There are two articles in English: the definite article and the indefinite articles.
- The store will close at noon on the following dates: November 26, December 24, and December 31.

（2）引出将引用的话语，尤其是当引用部分较长时（introduce a long quotation）。例如：

例 25

- In his book *Life Lines*, Forrest Church maintains that people should cry more: "Life is difficult. Some people pretend that it is not, that we should be able to breeze through. Yet hardly a week passes in which most of us don't have something worth crying about."

（3）引出解释（introduce an explanation）。例如：

例 26

- Here's a temporary solution to a dripping faucet: tie a string to it, and let the drops slide down the string to the sink.
- The good news and bad news about village life are the same: You become intimately involved with the lives of other people.

8. 引号
Quotation Mark

（1）表示直接引语（enclose words and punctuation in direct speech）。例如：

例 27

- "I'm giving up smoking tomorrow," said Jason.
- The nurse said, "Some babies cannot tolerate cow's milk."

（2）表示文章、歌曲、诗歌等短篇作品的名称（set off titles of short works, such as articles, songs, poems, etc.）。例如：

例 28

- the essay "On Self-Respect"
- the article "The Problem of Acid Rain"
- the chapter "The Lion"
- the story "Hands"
- the poem "When I Have Fears"
- the song "Starry Night"

（3）表示强调或区分（show emphasis or distinction）。例如：

例 29

- In grade school, we were taught a little jingle about the spelling rule "i before e".
- What is the difference between "it's" and "its"?

当引语中又包含引语时，通常使用单引号（a quotation within a quotation is indicated by single quotation marks）。例如：

例 30

- The teacher asked, "Who said 'Give me liberty or give me death'?"

9. 省略号
Ellipsis

（1）表示已省略类似的罗列（show the omission of a list）。例如：

例 31

- The dinner yesterday was very rich. Peter's mom prepared fried chicken, pizza, muffins, beer, fruit juice...

（2）表示迟疑而没有说出的话（show unspoken words）。例如：

例 32

- "But, she is...?" he asked, hoping it wasn't a rude question.

（3）表示思考而做的停顿（indicate a pause for thinking）。例如：

例 33

- I am considering whether to accept his proposal...Yes, I will.

（4）表示意犹未尽后的省略（indicate that words have been omitted, especially from a quotation or at the end of a conversation）。例如：

例 34

- I described what happened. After a long while, he said softly: "I see..."

（5）表示转折前的停顿（indicate a pause before a twist of meaning）。例如：

例 35

- "Thank goodness! Finally, I've come back...When I wasn't at home, what were you doing?"

10. 撇号
Apostrophe

（1）构成名词所属格（show ownership or possession）。例如：

例 36

- Mark's umbrella
- the children's toys

（2）表示省略一个或几个字母（show where one or more letters are omitted）。例如：

例 37

- "Yes, ma'am," Robert said.

（3）构成字母或数字的复数形式（form the plural of letter or numbers）。例如：

例 38

- You mustn't forget to dot your i's and cross your t's.
- How many A's have you got?
- during the 1990's

（4）构成动词短语的缩略形式（show the omission of one or more letters in a contraction）。例如：

例 39

- I've got something to tell you.
- I'd like to have a try.

11. 连字符
Hyphen

（1）用来构成合成词（used with two or more words that act as a single unit）。例如：

例 40

- mother-to-be
- a never-ending war
- a pet-friendly store
- up-to-standard products
- word-for-word translation

（2）用在书写或印刷换行时（换行时连字符要用在音节与音节之间）（divide a word at the end of a line of writing or typing; when you need to divide a word at the end of a line, divide it between syllables）。例如：

例 41

- Selena's first year at college was a time filled with numerous new pressures and responsibilities.

12. 圆括号
Parentheses

圆括号用来分隔句中的附加信息或解释性说明（set off extra or incidental information from the rest of a sentence）。例如：

例 42

- In 1913, the tax on an annual income of four thousand dollars (a comfortable wage at that time) was one penny.
- In the series, Murder, She Wrote, Jessica Fletcher solved murders for twelve seasons (1984–1996).

13. 斜线号
Slash/Oblique

斜线号用来分隔可供选择的词或短语（separate alternative words or phrases）。例如：

例 43

- have a pudding and/or cheese
- single/married/widowed/divorced
- Please forward cheque / bank note / post order to Head Office.

参考文献

References

陈冬花. 2005. 实用英语写作指导. 上海：上海交通大学出版社.

陈立平. 2020. 全新英语应用文写作. 西安：西安交通大学出版社.

崔珣丽. 2016. 高级英语写作教程思辨能力进阶. 北京：清华大学出版社.

崔长青. 2010. 英语写作技巧. 北京：中国书籍出版社.

傅似逸. 2015. 英语写作：应用文写作. 北京：北京大学出版社.

教育部高等学校大学外语教学指导委员会. 2020. 大学英语教学指南（2020 版）. 北京：
　　高等教育出版社.

李莉文. 2015. 大学思辨英语教程：说明文写作. 北京：外语教学与研究出版社.

刘梅华. 2014. 英语议论文读写教程. 北京：清华大学出版社.

刘锡庆. 1992. 外国写作教学理论辑评. 呼和浩特：内蒙古教育出版社.

陆谷孙. 2004. 牛津高阶英汉双解词典. 北京：商务印书馆.

马德高. 2013. 张道真大学英语语法. 合肥：安徽人民出版社.

秦穗. 1999. 实用英语作文. 长沙：湖南人民出版社.

荣维东. 2016. 交际语境写作. 北京：语文出版社.

慎小嶷. 2015. 十天突破雅思写作. 北京：机械工业出版社.

石坚，帅培天. 2010. 英语写作：句子·段落·篇章. 北京：外语教学与研究出版社.

涂靖. 2017. 大学英语写作教程. 上海：上海交通大学出版社.

汪开虎. 2018. 星火英语. 上海：上海交通大学出版社.

汪开虎. 2021. 星火英语全真试题 + 标准模拟. 上海：上海交通大学出版社.

王素华，叶玲立. 2012. 英语应用文写作指南. 武汉：武汉大学出版社.

杨鲁新，王素娥. 2015. 大学思辨英语教程：记叙文写作. 北京：外语教学与研究出版社.

殷小琴. 2012. 学术英语写作教程. 杭州：浙江大学出版社.

张翠萍. 2011. 大学英语互动写作教程. 北京：北京师范大学出版社.

张道真. 2015. 张道真大学英语语法. 合肥：安徽人民出版社.

张凯宏. 2013. 高分新托福写作 120. 北京：科学出版社.

章振邦. 1995. 新编英语语法教程学生用书. 上海：上海外语教育出版社.

Bruce, I. (2010). *Academic writing and genre: A systematic analysis.* London: Continuum.

Cambridge ESOL. (2007). *Cambridge English IELTS 6 with answers.* Cambridge: Cambridge University Press.

Flower, L., & Hayes, J. R. (1981). A cognitive process theory of writing. *College Composition and Communication, 32,* 365–387.

Fulkerson, R. (1996). *Teaching the argument in writing.* Urbana: National Council of Teachers of English.

Gill, C. M. (2014). *Essential writing skills for college & beyond.* Ohio: Writer's Digest Books.

Hacker, D., & Sommers, N. (2015). *A writer's reference* (8th ed.). New York: Bedford/ St. Martin's.

Hyland, K. (2004). *Genre and second language writing.* Ann Arbor: University of Michigan Press.

Jakeman, V., & McDowell, C. (2011). *New insight into IELTS: Student's book with answers.* Cambridge: Cambridge University Press.

Johnson, K., & Johnson, H. (2001). *Encyclopedic dictionary of applied linguistics: A handbook for language teaching.* Beijing: Foreign Language Teaching and Research Press.

Langan, J. (2014). *College writing skills with readings* (6th ed.). Beijing: Foreign Language Teaching and Research Press.

Lam, R. (2015). Understanding EFL students' development of self-regulated learning in a process-oriented writing course. *TESOL Journal, 6*(3), 527–553.

Manchón, R. (2012). *L2 writing development: Multiple perspectives.* Boston: Walter De Gruyter.

Oshima, A., & Hogue, A. (2006). *Writing academic English* (4th ed.). New York: Pearson Educaion Press.

Putlack, M. A., & Poirier, S. (2009). *How to master skills for the TOEFL iBT Writing Advanced.* Beijing: Qunyan Press.

Ramage, J. D., Bean, J. C., & Johnson, J. (2015). *The Allyn & Bacon guide to writing* (7th ed.). Boston: Pearson Education.

Royal, B. (2010). *The little gold grammar book.* Calgary: Maven Publishing.

Royal, B. (2016). *The little red writing book.* Calgary: Maven Publishing.

Santi, V. B. (2002). *A reader for developing writers.* New York: McGraw-Hill.

Savage, A., & Maye, P. (2005). *Effective academic writing 2: The short essay.* Oxford: Oxford University Press.

White, E. B. (2004). *Charlotte's web.* Shanghai: Shanghai Translation Publishing House.

Williams, A. (2011). *Writing for IELTS.* London: HarperCollins.

Wyrick, J. (2008). *Steps to writing well* (10th ed.). Beijing: Peking University Press.

Zimmerman, B. N. (1997). Becoming a self-regulated writer: A social cognitive perspective. *Contemporary Educational Psychology, 22,* 73–101.